The Affordable City

In the series
Conflicts in Urban and Regional Development,
edited by John R. Logan and Todd Swanstrom

The Affordable City

Toward a Third Sector Housing Policy

EDITED BY JOHN EMMEUS DAVIS

Temple University Press
Philadelphia

Temple University Press, Philadelphia 19122

Published 1994
Printed in the United States of America

The paper used in this publication meets the minimum requirements of American National Standard for Information Sciences—Permanence of Paper for Printed Library Materials, ANSI Z39.48-1984 ♾

Library of Congress Cataloging-in-Publication Data
The Affordable city : toward a third sector housing policy / edited by John Emmeus Davis.
p. cm. — (Conflicts in urban and regional development)
Includes bibliographical references and index.
ISBN 1-56639-109-1 (cl : alk. paper)
1. Public housing—United States. 2. Housing policy—United States. I. Davis, John Emmeus, 1949–
II. Series.
HD7288.78.U5A34 1994
363.5′8′0973—dc20 93-705

Contents

Acknowledgments

Many people helped to enhance the quality of this collection—critiquing our drafts, checking our facts, and challenging our basic assumptions. Some of them are mentioned by name in notes accompanying the text. Some are not. All deserve our sincere thanks.

Other help on this project came not so much from critical suggestions for revision as from critical support for the time and space to make it happen. My colleagues in Burlington's Community and Economic Development Office—Michael Monte, Richard Moffi, and Tom Dillon, in particular—graciously shouldered added responsibilities for an entire year while I was away playing professor at MIT. My companions at home, Bonnie and Dia, generously endured my weekly departures by attic and air while I labored to bring this book to completion. These simple, precious gifts of time are gratefully acknowledged.

I must also express my gratitude—and profound respect—for the hundreds of neighborhood leaders and municipal officials who persevered in seeking better ways of housing low- and moderate-income people despite a dozen years of diminishing dollars and diminishing concern at the national level for the plight of U.S. cities. The determination, devotion, and sheer inventiveness of these local activists have drawn third sector housing gradually into the mainstream of urban policy. Without them, this book would not have been possible.

J.E.D.
Burlington, Vermont

INTRODUCTION
Toward a Third Sector Housing Policy

JOHN EMMEUS DAVIS

There was a time, not too long ago, when U.S. cities that were overwhelmed by mounting shortages of affordable housing and worsening conditions of dilapidation, overcrowding, and homelessness could look to Washington for new funding and new ideas to alleviate their problems. The 1980s brought that era to an end. For more than a decade, municipal governments grappled with housing problems of a size and severity seldom seen in the United States since the Great Depression, while the federal department entrusted with the task of addressing those problems was systematically stripped of its former funding by a conservative Republican presidency and a submissive Democratic Congress.

As federal funding for the production, rehabilitation, and operation of affordable housing was being cut to a trickle, so too was the federal flow of new ideas. Administrators, analysts, consultants, and contractors who had played key roles in developing new housing, new programs, and new policies for urban neighborhoods departed the U.S. Department of Housing and Urban Development in droves.[1] By the decade's end, no one outside Washington could seriously believe that tomorrow's solutions to the housing problems of U.S. cities were likely to spring from the nation's capital.

Municipal officials learned to look elsewhere. Indeed, they learned to look largely to themselves. Few people at the local level had any illusions about the ability of cities and towns to replace the billions of dollars removed from the federal housing budget during the 1980s, but neither did they have the luxury of pretending (as their Washington counterparts did) that the pressing problems of U.S. cities did not exist or would soon be washed away by a rising tide of deregulated market activity. Municipalities were forced, by necessity and by default, to develop new sources of funding for affordable housing, along with new strategies for producing and preserving such housing.

Local innovation was concentrated, in the beginning, on the *production* side of the housing ledger. Municipal governments in Boston, San Francisco, Santa Monica, and San Diego adopted linkage programs, demanding new housing units or in-lieu-of-production cash contributions from the developers of downtown commercial space. Dozens of cities followed the lead of municipalities in New Jersey and California in enacting inclusionary zoning, requiring the developers of residential projects to set aside a specified percentage of affordable units for low- and moderate-income residents. Seattle, Denver, Hartford, Miami, and twenty-seven other cities established housing trust funds, dedicating monies from a variety of local sources to the production of affordable housing. Some cities made use of the federal Community Reinvestment Act or enacted linked deposit ordinances to pressure local banks into making more funds available for housing construction and rehabilitation in lower-income neighborhoods. Other municipalities put their faith in the talisman of "incentive zoning," believing that density bonuses, streamlining, and other regulatory relief might entice for-profit developers into producing the kind of housing that lower-income families could afford.

All of these measures have been widely noted and closely watched by planners, academics, and policymakers. A rapidly developing literature of articles, reports, books, and briefs is documenting the successes and failures of these municipal experiments in housing production. Meanwhile, far less attention has been paid to the other side of the housing ledger. Few commentators on the changing municipal role in housing have noticed that many of these locally generated innovations for *producing* affordable housing have been accompanied by equally creative strategies for *preserving* affordable housing after it is built. They have overlooked a major shift in municipal policy: a new emphasis on perpetuating the affordability of privately owned housing produced or assisted by the public.[2]

This newfound concern for preservation does not yet match the widespread commitment to production. Not every city that adopted new ways of financing and producing affordable housing during the 1980s has been as quick to embrace new ways of owning and controlling such housing once its initial affordability has been secured. There are still cities that do not impose affordability protections on housing produced through municipally sponsored programs like commercial linkage, inclusionary zoning, housing trust funds, density bonuses, and the like. Other cities impose affordability protections only for a short duration.

Such disregard for the long-term fate of publicly assisted, privately owned housing is becoming less common, however, as more municipal officials and community activists have begun to question the timeworn practice of investing scarce dollars in residential projects in which those subsidies may soon be lost. Especially where municipal government has taken the political initiative—and the political risk—of using its powers and resources in creative ways to address local housing problems, many people have questioned the wisdom of working so hard to produce affordable housing if the affordability of those units may soon be lost.

Skepticism about past municipal practice has provided fertile ground for the heretical view that affordability should be preserved as long as possible for housing brought by the dollars or powers of the public within the reach of persons of modest means. This simple, sensible idea is the seed of a new municipal policy. It is changing the way affordable housing is promoted by the public sector. It is changing the way affordable housing is produced by the private sector. It is even changing the way such housing is owned, rented, and resold, as municipal officials and community activists seek new models for making the affordability of publicly assisted, privately owned housing last longer than ever before—perhaps even "forever."

THIRD SECTOR HOUSING

When it comes to the affordability of private housing, the idea of "forever" seems wildly out of place. The average costs of market-rate rentals and market-priced sales have increased far faster in most American cities than average incomes over the last two decades. The "affordability gap" between the income needed to purchase or rent a home and the income earned by the average household has grown wider, a disparity that even the recession of 1990–1992 did not come close to eliminating.[3]

Despite such market realities—indeed, in large measure *because* of them—a policy goal of perpetuating the hard-won affordability of publicly assisted, privately owned housing has gradually gained wider acceptance among municipal officials and community activists alike. So too have various models of privately owned, price-restricted housing designed to achieve this goal: deed-restricted, owner-occupied houses; community land trusts; limited equity condominiums; limited equity (or zero equity) cooperatives; mutual housing associations; nonprofit rental housing; and multiple variations of each.

These new models of housing tenure represent a clear alternative to the more familiar models of both the market and the state: a *nonmarket* alternative to the for-profit rentals and market-priced homeownership of the private sector; a *private* alternative to the publicly owned projects of metropolitan housing authorities or the military. Together with a wide array of nonprofit organizations dedicated to making such models a reality, while expanding the supply of price-restricted housing, these private, nonmarket models of tenure are part of a larger institutional web of activities, organizations, and relationships variously known as *nongovernmental organizations*, the *independent sector*, or the *nonprofit sector*. Severyn Bruyn (1987: 5–6) has dubbed this sector the *social economy*, a new order that is "not a variation of state capitalism or state socialism but a different system . . . evolving in the interstices of modern economies." Its more generic title is the *third sector*, described by Osborne and Gaebler (1992: 44) as follows:

> This sector, it seems to us, is made up of organizations that are privately owned and controlled, but that exist to meet public or social needs, not to accumulate private wealth. By this definition, large nonprofit firms that exist primarily to accumulate wealth would not qualify. But for-profit institutions that exist to meet social or public needs (development banks, for instance) would qualify. For lack of a better term, we call this group of institutions the "third sector."

Over the last two decades, third sector organizations dedicated to meeting the social need for affordable housing have proliferated in the United States. While some operate regionally or nationally, the vast majority are community-based organizations operating in a single neighborhood, area, or town with a governing board recruited from that particular locale. Believed to number nearly 2,000 by the start of the 1990s, these nonprofit, community-based organizations were producing between 29,000 and 45,000 newly constructed or newly rehabilitated housing units every year.[4]

Most of this housing is being produced for people of limited means. A national survey conducted by the National Congress for Community Economic Development in 1991 found that 95 percent of all the rental housing being developed by community-based development organizations and 88 percent of all owner-occupied housing is "targeted to provide decent, affordable shelter for people with incomes below 80 percent of the area median" (NCCED, 1991: 3).

Initial affordability is only one of the attributes of the housing being produced by these community-based nonprofits. A more distinctive (and significant) feature is the *continuing* affordability of much of it. As Rachel Bratt (1989a: 198–199) has observed:

> Although not all community-based developers are committed to maintaining affordable housing, preferring instead to allow cooperative or homeowner units to appreciate as would any privately owned unit, these instances seem to be far fewer than the long-term use restrictions imposed by most contemporary nonprofits. . . . [The] commitment of most community-based housing developers is more similar to the long-range commitment of public housing authorities and contrasts with the relatively short-lived involvement of private, for-profit developers of subsidized housing.

It is the perpetuation of affordability, more than its initial creation, that makes the housing produced by these nonprofit developers fundamentally different from the housing produced by their for-profit counterparts. It is the perpetuation of affordability that removes the products of nonprofit production from the marketplace, turning *nonprofit* housing into *third sector* housing. Not every nonprofit, as Bratt notes, is fully committed to long-term affordability; not every project produced by nonprofits contains housing that is made a permanent part of the private, nonmarket sector situated, in Bruyn's words, "beyond the market and the state." On the other hand, just as more municipalities have realized that hard-earned subsidies and hard-won affordability should be preserved, so too have numerous nonprofits. Much (perhaps most) of the nonprofit housing being produced today is not only *of* the third sector, but securely *in* it.

What does it mean for housing to be securely within this private, nonmarket domain? Such housing has three defining characteristics:

- It is *privately owned.* Title to residential real estate is held by an individual, a family, or a private corporation. The property is owned by neither an instrumentality of the state nor a municipal corporation (i.e., a public housing authority).
- It is *socially oriented.* The property's primary function is to meet the social needs of current—and future—occupants, not to accumulate wealth for the property's owners. While the need for safe, decent, and

affordable housing is paramount here, the property's "social orientation" often includes a collaborative component as well; that is, individual households are linked together in a residential network of pooled risk, mutual aid, and/or operational support.

- It is *price-restricted*. A contractual limit is placed on the future price at which the property's units may be rented or resold, preserving their affordability for a targeted class of low-income or moderate-income residents. Prices are established by a predetermined formula, not by the market. Moreover, these price restrictions do not lapse when the housing changes hands; nor do they expire after a short duration to allow owners to cash in on the housing's appreciated value. By design and intent, the housing is to *remain* affordable far into the future.

This last characteristic requires more comment. Perpetual affordability is, for many of their staunchest proponents, the raison d'être of private, nonmarket models of housing. Ideally, whatever affordability has been achieved at the outset will be perpetuated (and perhaps enhanced) over time. This ideal can prove fairly elusive, however, in the face of shifting organizational, social, or economic realities. Thus, while there is a striving for affordability that lasts "forever," many proponents of price-restricted housing have been willing to settle for something much closer to "long-term": affordability lasting longer than the twenty-year expiration date on many federally subsidized projects; affordability lasting as long as the "useful life" of the housing.

Various names have been attached to such private, nonmarket housing: *nonspeculative housing*, *decommodified housing*, *perpetually affordable housing*, or, when applied solely to homeownership arrangements, *limited equity housing*. A slightly more accessible (though somewhat less accurate) name for the same idea was coined by Commissioner John Papandrea and his colleagues at the Connecticut Department of Housing in the late 1980s. Declaring that "state-assisted housing should be permanently removed from the speculative market," they began directing more resources toward limited equity housing cooperatives, community land trusts, mutual housing associations, and other nonprofit models and organizations committed to preserving "the long-term affordability of housing generated by public funds." They called their policy—and the nonmarket models supported by it—*forever housing*.[5]

Most housing professionals in the United States and Canada tend to prefer *social housing* for describing residential units that are privately owned, socially oriented, and price-restricted. *Third sector housing* is a solid substitute, however—a term that describes the same sort of private, nonmarket tenure as "social housing," while avoiding some of the latter's definitional and political difficulties.[6] Both terms refer to forms of residential ownership that are different from those traditionally employed by either the market or the state; both denote a nongovernmental domain within which the preeminence of social needs over private accumulation is institutionalized—and perpetuated.

What does a municipality do differently once a commitment has been made to support and promote such housing? What does it mean, practically and programmatically, for a municipality to adopt a third sector housing policy? The simplest answer is that such a policy directs an increasing proportion of a municipality's scarce resources toward various models of privately owned, socially oriented, price-restricted housing. The goal here is to expand, year by year, the number of units brought into the realm of these private, nonmarket models of tenure.

A third sector housing policy tends to promote, as well, an increasing municipal reliance on nonprofit, community-based organizations to produce and preserve affordable housing. This represents, as Stegman and Holden (1987), Clay (1990), Mayer (1991), Goetz (1992), and many others have noted, a new kind of housing delivery system. Nonprofit developers are made priority recipients of a municipality's financial and technical largess and are assigned leading roles in implementing that municipality's housing policy.

This second component of a third sector housing policy is inseparable from the first in cases in which a nonmarket model for *owning* affordable housing—and for maintaining affordability—is combined with a nonprofit organization committed to *developing* affordable housing on a continuous basis. The community land trust and the mutual housing association, for example, are two of several models that combine new forms of tenure with an organizational mission of ongoing production.

Social ownership and nonprofit production do not always go together, however. Some nonprofit organizations are effective and sophisticated developers of affordable housing but are not convinced the housing they produce should be removed from the market in order to preserve its affordability—especially when that housing is owner occupied. Conversely, some models of social housing are quite effective at preserving affordability but are not oriented toward expanding their own domains.

Furthermore, not every municipality that has made a commitment to the long-term affordability of publicly assisted housing has chosen to implement that policy through a nonprofit housing delivery system. An effective linkage or inclusionary zoning ordinance, for example, will often extract many more units of price-restricted housing from for-profit developers than a city's nonprofit developers can deliver during the same period of time. To the extent that such municipally mandated restrictions on rents and resales are made to last, and that the affordability of the extracted units is maintained for many years, this housing is made as securely a part of the third sector as the price-restricted units produced by (many) nonprofit organizations.

There is good reason, therefore, to draw some distinction between *nonmarket forms of housing tenure* that preserve affordability and a *nonprofit mode of housing production* that relies primarily upon community-based organizations for its impetus and implementation. A true third sector housing policy will always include the first; it will often include the second.[7]

MUNICIPAL RATIONALE FOR THIRD SECTOR HOUSING

The circumstances under which a municipality comes to support these nonmarket models and nonprofit organizations are as diverse as the politics and personalities that distinguish one city from another. A third sector housing policy is sometimes the result of careful municipal planning; sometimes a response to grassroots pressure; sometimes a by-product of new personnel, new funding, or a new administration. Often, the policy—and its rationale—evolve over time as various aspects of this new approach are stumbled over, tried out, and fitted together piece by piece. Thus a municipal decision to "recycle" scarce subsidies for affordable housing may lead to long-term restrictions on the rents and resale prices of assisted units; this may lead, in turn, to municipal support for nonprofit organizations willing to develop such housing or to enforce such restrictions on the city's behalf. Conversely, a municipal decision to target funds to a successful nonprofit that happens to be developing price-restricted housing may demonstrate the wisdom of "locking in" *all* public subsidies for housing and lead to a broader municipal commitment to long-term affordability.

When considering the most common and compelling reasons why cities have begun adopting third sector housing policies, therefore, it is well to remember that the rationale behind this new approach is often more messy, serendipitous, and after-the-fact than any orderly recitation might suggest.

This caveat aside, I believe it is possible to sort out at least eight different reasons for the growing municipal support of private, nonmarket models of tenure and nonprofit modes of production: the failure of past programs, the scarcity of present resources, limits to growth, the risk of negative externalities, the retreat of private enterprise, the limits of public enterprise, the allure of homeownership, and the limits of residential autonomy.

Failure of Past Programs

The checkered past of much federally assisted or municipally regulated housing, whether publicly or privately owned, has led municipal officials to search for new ways of producing and preserving affordable housing. Public ownership has been widely perceived as a failure, despite the facts that most of the nation's 3,060 public housing authorities are well operated and all guarantee perpetual affordability for the units under their control.[8] By contrast, private ownership that is publicly subsidized, though it has enjoyed far more popularity and political support, has finally been recognized as an accident waiting to happen. All of the rent-stabilized units created through federal programs like Section 236, Section 221(d)(3), Section 8, and Section 515 have continuing affordability under multiyear contracts, but every contract contains an escape clause allowing the private, for-profit owners to opt out at a future date—five to twenty years down the road. Perpetual affordability was never a priority of these federal programs, never a part of the project design. As a result, between .5 million and 1.4 million units of federally assisted, privately owned housing may be threatened with loss during the 1990s unless municipal officials, nonprofit developers, and tenant advocates find enough public money to repurchase, rehabilitate, and refinance numerous projects the public has already paid for once.[9]

Rent control is another public program frequently proposed as a means of preserving residential affordability. Rent control is intended to restrict rent increases in privately owned housing, keeping rents affordable over time. Outside of New Jersey and California, however, the number of American cities employing rent control has never been large, except during World War II. Where rent control has been adopted, moreover, its opponents have nearly always managed to limit its coverage and reduce its effectiveness, either from the start or with later amendments. In some cities, rent control programs with a long history have been repealed altogether. Public controls over the profitability of privately owned housing, when imposed through the police power, have proven easy to attack and difficult to sustain.[10]

Municipal support for third sector housing is a marked departure from these earlier attempts to create a stable supply of affordable housing. Unlike *public housing*, any units constructed or rehabilitated under such a policy are held in private hands. Unlike *federally assisted private housing*, affordability protections are designed to last. Unlike *rent control*, long-term price controls are secured through private contracts, not through a municipality's police power (although this line becomes somewhat blurred in the case of linkage and inclusionary housing programs that *force* a developer to accept a contractual limitation on future rents or resale prices). Each of these features tends to make municipal support for third sector housing more politically palatable than most public programs of the past.

Scarcity of Present Resources

While there has never been enough federal money for low-income housing, American cities experienced drastic cutbacks in what little they had during the 1980s—at a time when their need for these funds was soaring. One federal housing program after another was sharply curtailed or simply eliminated. At the local level, the scarcity of resources resulting from these federal cutbacks forced even conservative politicians and city officials to face the fact they could no longer afford to invest scarce public dollars in neighborhood projects that did not "lock" these subsidies in place. Cities had to do more with less, while keeping what little they had from being siphoned off in short-term gains for a fortunate few.

It was not only the *amount* of money that modified local attitudes about long-term affordability but the *source* of the money that remained. In trying to cope with problems made worse by the federal retreat, municipalities began to extract new resources for affordable housing from local taxpayers, developers, landlords, and banks. Having expended so much of their own political capital on developing resources that were local in origin and limited in amount, municipal officials have been increasingly loathe to squander them on projects with benefits either narrow or transient. As quick as municipalities may have sometimes been to squander federal funds on projects with short-term affordability, they have been much slower to squander their own.[11]

Limits to Growth

There are cities where creating a permanent stock of affordable housing has become an acceptable policy not because of a scarcity of available funds but because of a scarcity of buildable sites. The construction of housing on *empty* sites is constrained by the locality's shortage of lands that are vacant or by the community's protection of lands that are open, wet, or wild. The construction of housing on *occupied* sites is constrained by the developer's cost of demolishing buildings or by the community's protection of buildings with historic, cultural, or sentimental value.

Limits to growth render ineffective any municipal strategy that is dependent upon a constantly replenished stock of newly constructed, low-cost housing to meet the locality's affordable housing needs. Streamlining the permit process, for example, or waiving impact fees so that developers will build more housing for lower-income residents, or writing down the cost of purchasing a home with public subsidies that are later recaptured (sometimes with a share of the home's appreciation) are all strategies that typically allow first-time homebuyers to resell their publicly assisted "starter homes" for whatever the market will bear. Such strategies assume that any affordable housing later lost to the market on resale will soon be replaced by new construction. When replacement becomes impractical, however, preservation becomes prudent. Perpetuating the affordability of housing that already exists becomes both reasonable and acceptable when producing more housing is impeded by a shortage of sites, by a preponderance of sentiment against further growth, or by a hoarded treasure of open lands or older buildings a community holds dear.[12]

Risk of Negative Externalities

Another reason why municipal governments have turned to models of housing that preserve long-term affordability is a growing concern about the unintended consequences of public investment. This is not so much a perception that past programs have failed as a recognition that some of these programs have succeeded too well—but with secondary effects that damaged or disrupted fragile neighborhoods. Deteriorated housing has been improved, public facilities have been upgraded, and disinvested neighborhoods have been "rediscovered" by private lenders. These improvements, however, have often brought higher rents for low-income tenants, higher taxes for homeowners on fixed incomes, the elimination of multiunit housing, and the eventual displacement of disadvantaged classes or races from newly gentrified neighborhoods.

This has prompted a search, in some cities, for alternative strategies of municipal investment and improvement. By targeting their dollars to projects and places with a high proportion of housing units that are perpetually restricted in price and permanently controlled by neighborhood residents, municipal officials hope that public investment can occur without fueling speculation, without promoting the conversion, demolition, or abandonment of affordable housing, and without causing the displacement of vulnerable residents. Their hope, in short, is that investing in third sector housing may be a way to avoid some of the negative externalities that have plagued many municipal initiatives of the past.

Retreat of Private Enterprise

In many areas of the country, the 1980s witnessed a wholesale retreat by for-profit developers and investors away from the production of affordable housing, particularly affordable rental housing. Several factors lay behind this shift. For-profit developers were drawn into the more lucrative business of producing luxury housing for upper-income buyers in speculative markets where real estate values were soaring. Public controls over the use and development of land frequently excluded affordable, multiunit projects from suburban communities. Federal programs that had subsidized the production of low-income rental housing through the use of project-based rental assistance were phased out in favor of tenant-based assistance. Since developers—and their financial backers—could no longer be assured that federal subsidies would *remain* with a project for a predictable period of time, they were no longer willing to build housing for "risky" tenants in "risky" neighborhoods.

The most significant factor in spurring the retreat of private investors, however, was the Tax Reform Act of 1986. The changes wrought by this act were devastating to investment in low-income housing. It lengthened the depreciable life of rental housing from 15 years to 27.5 years; it raised the rate of taxation on capital gains; it increased the minimum taxes and restrictions on passive losses; and it eliminated the favorable tax status of industrial development bonds, which many state and local housing finance agencies had used to provide below-market financing for rental housing. Attempting to offset these disincentives to affordable housing investment, Congress added a tax credit for investors in housing projects serving low-income tenants. This tax credit, however, proved technically burdensome and generally unworkable without additional public subsidies, which became less plentiful during the late 1980s, not more.[13]

The disappearance of profit-oriented investors from the affordable housing field created something of a vacuum. If housing was still going to be constructed and rehabilitated in lower-income neighborhoods, municipal officials were going to have to find new investors and new partners to fill this void. They discovered, in some cities, a nonprofit infrastructure of community-based organizations ready and willing to play this role. In other cities, municipal officials had to create or nurture this infrastructure themselves. Sometimes by default and sometimes by design, nonprofit developers were soon receiving in one city after another the lion's share of whatever money a municipality still had available for affordable housing.

Limits on Public Enterprise

That public housing has historically had difficulty winning and sustaining popular support has already been mentioned, as has the opposition that has regularly been mounted against public controls over private rents. Little more needs to be said on either count. It is important to point out, however, that these political constraints on municipal "interference" in the private real estate market may be matched by political, financial, or legal constraints that limit a municipality's ability to develop, own, or manage housing units with long-term controls over their affordability. A particular municipality may have neither the capacity within its staff nor the authority within its charter to play such an activist role in producing and preserving affordable housing.

Municipal support for price-restricted models of social housing—and for the nonprofit developers of such housing—allow a city to operate within these constraints even while exceeding them. These models and organizations, which are situated within the private sector but allied with the public sector, can extend the reach of municipal government, attracting funds, pursuing projects, and taking risks a municipality may not. Equally important, because these nongovernmental organizations have members and constituencies of their own, they can engage in the kind of grassroots organizing and outreach that municipal officials must avoid, thus expanding the base of political support for a particular administration or a particular policy.[14]

Public-private partnerships between municipal housing agencies and nonprofit housing developers, in short, can serve as something of a strategic end run around ideological, financial, or political limits that can render a city all but helpless in addressing complex problems like affordable housing. Activist administrations forced to operate passively within such constraints have discovered in their partnerships with third sector organizations the means to do more while playing by the rules of a local status quo that would have them do less.

Allure of Homeownership

Third sector housing encompasses many models of privately owned, socially oriented, price-restricted housing, including several that come close to traditional owner-occupied housing. Generally known as *limited equity housing* or *limited equity homeownership*, these models have held great appeal for municipal officials who had hoped to help selected tenants to become independent homeowners but who discovered that public funds were inadequate to close the widening gap between tenancy and homeownership.

Reluctant to abandon their original plans because of either an ideological commitment to homeownership or a political commitment to constituents, these officials have become increasingly receptive to new forms of private, nonmarket housing that bring homeownership within the reach of lower-income tenants.[15] They have come to realize that what is needed—and what is possible with meager municipal resources—is the introduction of *new* rungs into the local tenure ladder, new forms of limited equity housing that allow people of modest means to climb out of housing situations that are presently precarious and toward those that are more secure.[16]

Limits of Residential Autonomy

Finally, municipal support for third sector models and organizations is rooted in the belated realization by some housing officials that neither homeownership nor tenancy, as traditionally conceived in the United States, may be appropriate for every household, even if initial barriers to access are eliminated. Whether prospective homeowner or permanent tenant, every household is expected to bear individually the costs and risks of gaining and retaining residency in a separate unit. Yet many people do not possess the income, skills, physical health, or mental capacity to find their way individually to safe, decent, affordable housing—or to keep such housing once it is theirs. Many other people cannot bear individually the burdens and risks of owning a home or negotiating the terms and conditions of a lease.

Housing professionals inside and outside of government have been slow to acknowledge that many people are ill-equipped for the independent living that market housing demands and need various kinds of support to be successfully housed.[17] They have been even slower to recognize how inappropriate and inaccessible much of the existing supply of housing has become in the face of the changing demographics of the American household, especially the surging growth in single-person households and single-parent families. These "atypical" households are not easily accommodated by tenures and types of housing typical to most housing markets in the United States.[18]

As housing professionals have begun to recognize these social realities, they have begun to acknowledge the importance of the kind of collaboration and mutual aid that characterizes most forms of social housing: the burdens and risks of housing are shared, scarce financial resources and scant personal clout are pooled, and separate households are linked together in common cause. Although the benefits of such residential collaboration are not confined to persons with special needs, persons whose lives are physically or financially precarious clearly have the most to gain from forms of tenure that do not force everyone to "go it alone."[19]

Residential autonomy is unattainable, unsustainable, or unacceptable for a growing number of people. Most forms of social housing acknowledge that fact and attempt to do something about it. Most forms of market housing do not.

THIRD SECTOR HOUSING IN STATE AND FEDERAL POLICY

By the 1990s, public support for third sector models and organizations had become a significant ingredient in the general mix of municipal housing programs in a number of American cities. In a few, it had become the touchstone for nearly every policy and every program affecting the construction or rehabilitation of affordable housing.

Above the municipal level, a similar shift in public policy has begun to occur, although belatedly and more slowly. Twenty-eight states established housing trust funds in the last decade. Many of them, like the trust funds created by municipal governments, require assisted housing to remain affordable for multiple years as a condition of public support. Several states have gone even further in their commitment to the continuing affordability of publicly assisted, privately owned housing—and to the nonmarket models and nonprofit organizations that make such housing a reality. Connecticut's "forever housing policy" has already been mentioned. Despite a change in administration in 1990 and several years of fiscal belt-tightening, Connecticut's programs for cooperatives, community land trusts, and other nonprofits guaranteeing the future affordability of state-assisted housing have survived. Vermont has made perpetual affordability a threshhold criterion for most state assistance for affordable housing since 1987. Other states, such as Massachusetts and Minnesota, have made extraordinary financial commitments to limited equity housing cooperatives and to nonprofit developers of price-restricted rental housing.[20]

At the federal level, meanwhile, much less interest has been shown in third sector housing until recently. National support for these nonmarket models and nonprofit organizations has been confined largely to a few leftover programs from the past. Abundant funding for the nonprofit provision of elderly-occupied rental housing was once available under HUD's 202 program. Modest funding for the development of housing cooperatives was once available under a variety of federal programs.[21] By the late 1980s, most of these programs were gone, however, and those that remained were starved for funds.

Outside of the United States, third sector housing has fared far better. Indeed, a number of Western countries have long made federal support for social housing and nonprofit production a prominent part of their national housing programs. Sweden, Denmark, and Canada have gone the farthest in this regard, although France and West Germany have also given substantial assistance to various forms of tenant-owned cooperative housing with long-term controls over rents and resales. In Sweden, where Social Democrats have been in power almost continuously since 1932 (except for 1976–1982), government planning and funding have combined to steer new housing construction away from the private, for-profit sector and toward a combination of publicly owned rentals and private, price-restricted cooperatives.[22] In Denmark, where public housing is almost nonexistent, governmental support for affordable housing has centered on grants, low-interest loans, and other construction subsidies for nonprofit and cooperative associations. Fully half of all housing units constructed in Denmark between 1945 and 1970, note Gilderbloom and Appelbaum (1988), were constructed by these third sector organizations.[23]

Canada, too, has given major support to third sector housing. During the 1950s and 1960s, governmental funding for low-income housing was centered on a public housing program similar to that of the United States. In 1973, however, as the U.S. was busily replacing its public housing program with subsidies and incentives for private, for-profit developers, Canada decided to pursue a different course. The national government began directing an increasing share of its housing funds into the hands of zero equity housing cooperatives and nonprofit developers of price-restricted rental housing. By the early 1980s, almost all federal subsidies for new housing were being directed into this third sector, and about 25,000 new units were being produced each year. Although the annual production of social housing had dropped to 18,000 new units by 1988, after successive cutbacks by a Conservative government elected in 1984, this was still an extraordinary level of housing activity; it represented "about the same number," observe Dreier and Hulchanski (1990: 121), "as HUD subsidized that year for a country with ten times Canada's population."

There is little likelihood that the United States will soon be following Canada's lead, even under the first Democratic administration in a dozen years. Nevertheless, there are signs that third sector housing may finally be finding a niche in U.S. policy. A new receptiveness to the kinds of housing long supported by Canada and by other Western democracies is especially evident in the Cranston-Gonzales National Affordable Housing Act (NAHA) enacted in 1990. Title II of NAHA mandates long-term affordability as a condition of funding for both rental and owner-occupied housing. This section of NAHA, known as the HOME program, requires assisted *rental* housing to "remain affordable, according to binding commitments satisfactory to the Secretary, for the remaining useful life of the property" and assisted *owner-occupied* housing to carry resale restrictions that "ensure that the housing will remain affordable to a reasonable range of low income homebuyers." Furthermore, HOME supports the expansion of a nonprofit housing delivery system through a 15 percent set-aside of available funds for "community housing development organizations" (CHDOs). Since HOME holds out the promise (if it is ever fully funded by Congress) of billions of dollars for affordable housing, even jurisdictions that have yet to embrace long-term affordability, nonmarket models, and nonprofit organizations may be tempted to do so.

On the other hand, NAHA has been derisively described as "one law, two programs, no policy" (Rapp, 1991: 73). One of these programs, HOME, *is* a hopeful sign of growing public support for new models of long-term affordability and new modes of community-based development. Clouding this sunny assessment, however, are subsequent revisions undertaken by HUD and Congress that obscure NAHA's original commitment to perpetuate the affordability of HOME-assisted units.[24] A colder shadow is cast by NAHA's second new housing program, known as HOPE (Homeownership Opportunities for People Everywhere). Aggressively promoted by former HUD Secretary Jack Kemp, HOPE was designed to reduce further the government's role in providing affordable housing by moving publicly owned and publicly assisted housing back into the marketplace. Thus, while HOME has the potential for expanding the supply of price-restricted housing, HOPE has the purpose of shrinking the supply that already exists.

At the national level, Congress will be wrangling over the relative merits of these contradictory approaches to affordable housing for many years, despite Kemp's departure from HUD. To an unusual degree, however, the outcome of this national debate over HOME and HOPE will be shaped by what happens at the local level. Indeed, NAHA presents local proponents of third sector housing with two opportunities. The first is to take full advantage of the preferential treatment NAHA offers nonprofits to produce and preserve a significant quantity of affordable housing. As Barry Zigas, former president of the National Low-Income Housing Coalition, has pointed out, "If the nonprofit housing sector cannot prove it is at least equal to the modest tasks in the statute, it's unlikely they'll ever be offered a larger role" (1991: 8).

The second opportunity presented by NAHA is for municipalities to use whatever funds are made available for both HOME and HOPE to expand the local supply of privately owned, socially oriented, price-restricted housing. Municipal governments are given the option, under the rules for HOME and for HOPE, of extending the minimum periods of affordability for housing assisted through these programs (though such extensions are difficult, at present, for HOPE). They have the option, as well, of exceeding the minimum amounts set aside for Community Housing Development Organizations. They may invest funds from both these federal programs, in other words, in nonmarket housing and in the nonprofit sponsors of such housing.

Such a third sector housing policy may eventually prove the best way—perhaps the only way—for cities to resolve the programmatic contradiction that Washington's warring political factions have dumped in their laps. If successful, local housing officials and their nonprofit partners may end up fashioning not only a municipal policy for the 1990s, but a national policy as well. As David Rapp has observed: "The more innovative among them will probably find a way to do what Congress couldn't: put HOME and HOPE together into a coherent housing program. Given the federal government's inability to provide clear direction, local officials will have to be the true architects of U.S. housing policy in the 1990s" (Rapp, 1991: 73).

THE AFFORDABLE CITY: CONTENT AND CONTEXT

Despite the interest now being shown by state and federal authorities, third sector housing remains essentially a local phenomenon. It is in the neighborhoods of America's cities that the nonmarket models and nonprofit organizations that are the mainstays of this innovative policy have had their earliest success. It is in the chambers of city government that this idea of perpetuating the publicly subsidized affordability of privately owned housing has had its first hearing. It is at the local level, too, that such price-restricted housing has faced—and will continue to face—its stiffest test, as tenants and homebuyers of modest means are asked to wager their fortunes on this new approach to affordable housing being better than the old.

Since third sector housing is an innovation that has percolated up from the bottom more than it has trickled down from the top, this book is about the affordable *city*. Its subject is municipal policy and various programs, models, and organizations functioning primarily at the neighborhood level. Its purpose is to address, descriptively and analytically, such basic questions as: Why are some municipal governments reorienting their support for affordable housing toward privately owned, socially oriented, price-restricted housing and toward its nonprofit, community-based sponsors? What models are being used to implement this policy? What resources are needed to make this policy a success? What barriers stand in the way?

The book's overall purpose is rhetorical and strategic, as well. Arguments for third sector housing are presented with a view toward persuading public officials, city planners, and community activists of the wisdom and worth of this innovative approach to affordable housing. Arguments against third sector housing are treated as problems to be solved: predictable obstacles in the political landscape in which this policy must make its way; correctable flaws in the models, organizations, and partnerships that make the policy a reality. Practitioners who would adopt such a policy need to know not only how to answer the objections of their opponents but how to enhance the effectiveness of their programs. Consequently, arguments on behalf of third sector housing yield quickly in the coming chapters to critical assessments of obstacles and flaws and to practical strategies for removing both.

Although the practice of third sector housing is clearly the focus of *The Affordable City*, any discussion of this innovative policy and of the models and organizations supported by it cannot be separated from a number of larger theoretical and political debates. The most interesting pertain to the privatization of publicly assisted housing and the surprising emergence in the United States of the "progressive city." A third sector housing policy also raises important questions about public innovation in a time of economic restructuring. These issues provide a general context for the more specific content of *The Affordable City*.

Privatization

The ascendancy of conservative ideologies during the 1970s and 1980s, especially in Britain and the United States, produced national housing policies with the dual aim of transferring responsibility for housing provision from the public sector to the private sector and removing regulatory constraints imposed by the public on private enterprise. The principal assumptions behind these policies were: (1) the public sector is the principal cause of housing shortages; (2) the private sector can deliver affordable housing at a lower cost and with greater efficiency than the public sector, particularly if government can be gotten out of the way; and (3) the poor can be "empowered" by purchasing the public-assisted housing in which they currently reside as tenants. By becoming homeowners, the poor can gain not only greater control over their lives, but greater wealth from their homes, reaping the same rewards from appreciating property values as any other homeowner.

Privatization in Britain during the 1980s focused mainly on the sale of council housing to current residents. More than a million units of publicly owned housing have been sold in this way (Forrest, 1991; Forrest and Murie, 1988; Kleinman, 1990). In the United States, the privatization of federal housing policy by the Reagan administration focused more on impoverishing the public sector than on transferring public assets into private hands. One housing program after another was either sharply curtailed or terminated altogether.[25] This funding picture improved only slightly under the Bush administration, although privatization was pushed in new directions by HUD Secretary Jack Kemp, a vocal advocate for both the deregulation of housing construction and the private ownership of public housing. The first initiative was embodied most clearly in Kemp's Advisory Commission on Regulatory Barriers to Affordable Housing (1991); the second in eighteen HUD demonstration projects turning over the management (and eventual ownership) of some two thousand units of public housing to their residents. This "Public Housing Homeownership Demonstration," proposed by Kemp when he was still a member of Congress, became the model for Title IV of the 1990 National Affordable Housing Act—the HOPE program.

Internationally, the trend toward privatization has spurred intense debate over whether deregulation combined with private ownership actually results in significant cost savings and greater efficiency.[26] In the United States, the debate has centered on the extent to which Reagan's policy of impoverishing public sector housing efforts engendered the high-level scandals at HUD, caused the rise in homelessness, and contributed to the widening "affordability gap" of the 1980s.[27] The debate surrounding the policies of Bush and Kemp focused on the dubiousness of the claims of cost efficiency from deregulation and privatization, the inadvisability of selling off public housing, and the likelihood of current programs like HOPE and the Low Income Housing Tax Credit program repeating the costly mistakes of the past by allowing publicly assisted housing to return to the market after a relatively short period of affordability.[28]

A third sector housing policy adds a new dimension to these disputes over privatization. To the extent that such a policy enlists public resources and public powers in support of models of tenure and modes of provision that are clearly within the private sector—and to the extent that such support is couched in terms of maximizing the efficiency of the public dollar—third sector housing is consistent with conservative preferences for private property and private enterprise. In addition, many of these models bring homeownership within reach of the same lower-income tenants that Jack Kemp wanted so much to "empower." The nonprofit developers of affordable housing, moreover, often share many of the same complaints about publicly imposed regulatory barriers to private housing production commonly voiced by their for-profit counterparts.

On the other hand, the advocates and beneficiaries of a third sector housing policy are among the loudest critics of any proposal to privatize housing provision by impoverishing public sector housing programs. After all, the "thousand points of light" being kindled by these grassroots groups are among the first to be extinguished when government withdraws from the housing field.[29] Their argument is not only that government should continue investing in affordable housing but that it should do so more wisely, investing in nonmarket models and nonprofit organizations that promise the highest, and longest, return.

The more distinctive contribution that a third sector housing policy makes to the privatization debate, however, lies less in augmenting the chorus of opposition to federal budget cuts than in marking out a middle path between public enterprise and private enterprise, between housing that is retained as a permanently affordable resource under the ownership of government and housing that is returned to the market as an ultimately unaffordable commodity. The models and organizations of this third path redefine the basic terms of the debate.[30] Housing that is affordable "perpetually" is no longer synonymous with housing that is "public"; housing that is "private" is no longer synonymous with housing that is priced and conveyed through the "market." Although as biased as any conservative toward private sector solutions to local housing problems, advocates of a third sector housing policy endorse models of private, nonmarket housing that "decommodify" residential property just as thoroughly as public ownership—and for just as long. Private ownership and perpetual affordability go hand in hand, creating new possibilities for achieving the private initiative and personal empowerment that Kemp desired without the resource depletion his critics deplored.[31]

The Progressive City

During the 1980s, there emerged in a number of U.S. cities municipal regimes that consciously steered in an opposite direction from the probusiness, progrowth, antigovernment course being laid out in Washington. Pierre Clavel was among the first to study this unexpected urban phenomenon, dubbed by him "the progressive city":

> At a time when urban government in general retreated before and came to accommodation with private interests and factions, these cities established substantive governments. Rather than claim to satisfy all factions, they made explicit choices in favor of broad classes of people. Most important, at a time when national politics had moved to the right, leaders in these cities favored poor and working people, and represented the interests of their cities' residents against suburban, absentee, and property-owning factions. (Clavel, 1986: 1–2)

Clavel described progressive politics in five American cities: Hartford, Cleveland, Berkeley, Santa Monica, and Burlington. Others might have been added to the list, especially the administrations of Ray Flynn in Boston and Harold Washington in Chicago. Some of these regimes lasted only a few years; some remained in power for most of the 1980s and beyond. All made attempts to enact fundamental changes in economic and political relationships in their cities, including alterations in property rights carried out through measures like rent control, restrictions on condominium conversions, and municipal support for private, nonmarket housing.

This is not to say that a third sector housing policy has been a key feature of *every* progressive city. Few regimes, for example, have placed as high a priority on supporting nonmarket models of housing and nonprofit organizations as those in Burlington and Boston. Conversely, not every city that has adopted one or more elements of a third sector housing policy can be described as "progressive." Indeed, it would have been hard to find a more conservative political climate than San Diego's during the 1980s; yet by the decade's end, San Diego had created one of the largest housing trust funds in the United States and had begun targeting significant resources toward projects, organizations, and forms of ownership that preserve affordability over time.

Nevertheless, while the match between a local commitment to progressive politics and a local commitment to third sector housing may not be exact, there has been a high correlation. Their origins and constituencies are similar. Both tend to be rooted in the same popular opposition to downtown "growth coalitions," the same popular reaction to downtown disregard for inner-city neighborhoods and disadvantaged populations, the same grassroots challenge to the legitimacy of concentrated, absentee-controlled property and power.[32] Support for progressive regimes and support for third sector housing have so frequently and tightly been intertwined that the study of one may shed considerable light on the study of the other. A better understanding of the "affordable city," in other words, may produce a better understanding of the "progressive city." And vice versa.

Public Innovation

There is some danger in concentrating too exclusively on the "progressive city," however, for such a focus suggests that only a handful of cities have the discretion, the conditions, and the resources to respond in innovative ways to problems created by a retreating central government and a restructuring national (and international) economy. The rest are condemned to local passivity in the face of political and economic forces beyond their control or, at best, to limited action within the rigid constraints of a growth-oriented agenda set by mobilized elites (see Peterson, 1981).

Logan and Swanstrom (1990), among others, have challenged this notion of inevitable and insurmountable "city limits" to what a municipality can do to protect its citizens, promote social welfare, and redistribute the benefits and burdens of growth during a time of transition in the world economy. They acknowledge the dominant influence of changing economic relations on urban development and urban policy, but they argue that a "great deal more discretion exists to shape economic and urban restructuring than is commonly believed" (p. 6).

Many cities during the last decade—and not just those with "progressive" regimes—have, in fact, found ample opportunity for activist, innovative, and effective responses to many of the social problems created by restructuring and retrenchment at the national level. This is not to say they have entirely solved these problems nor that they have managed to replace the billions of dollars removed from urban areas during the 1980s by a changing economy, a shifting demography, and a reworking of federal priorities to favor rich over poor, suburb over city, and military wants over domestic needs.[33] Nevertheless, they have done what they could with the little they had and, in many cases, made significant progress toward addressing the problems that are theirs.

Affordable housing is a case in point. In no other area has there been more public innovation during the last decade, at least below the federal level. As Mary Nenno (1991: 470–471) has observed:

> The story of low-income housing in the 1980s is largely one of state and local governments undertaking a broad array of categorical programs and interventions to address the needs of a changing low-income population in dynamic housing markets impacted by economic change. . . . While the experimentation continued as the 1980s ended, a new maturity could be observed at both the state and local levels.

She goes on to document dozens of initiatives aimed at financing, constructing, and rehabilitating affordable housing—initiatives she deems "a challenge to federal involvement, which has not undergone a similar evolutionary change in assistance policies" (p. 491).

Municipal support for third sector housing is an important tributary of this contemporary flood of public innovation. I would argue, in fact, that when it comes to affordable housing, nothing is happening at any level of government that is *more* innovative than the experimentation currently occurring in cities throughout the United States in support of new models of nonmarket housing and new modes of nonprofit development.

Some have seen in such public support for third sector organizations—whether in housing, health care, economic development, or other service areas—an entirely new approach to government.[34] David Osborne (1988), for one, has discovered in these partnerships between the public sector and the third sector a "new paradigm" for American public policy, a significant departure from both traditional liberalism and Reagan conservatism. Where liberals tended to "throw money" at problems, and conservatives of Reagan's ilk responded by taking money away, the "new paradigm" says that public resources are relatively scarce and must be carefully invested. Where liberals expanded government and conservatives labored to cut it back, the "new paradigm" says that government's role in meeting social needs must be "reinvented" to allow closer cooperation with other sectors. As Osborne (1988: 327) has put it: "The fundamental goal is no longer to create—or eliminate—government programs; it is to use government to change the nature of the marketplace. To boil it down to a slogan, if the thesis was government as solution and the antithesis was government as problem, the synthesis is government as partner."

Despite the fact that municipal support for third sector housing fits Osborne's "new paradigm" rather closely,[35] this innovative policy has received little attention outside the ranks of those who labor day to day to make it a reality. Such neglect has not stopped the spread of privately owned, socially oriented, price-restricted housing, nor has it discouraged hundreds of nonprofit, community-based organizations from developing such housing. Furthermore, it has not prevented dozens of municipal governments from devoting an increasing proportion of their tightening budgets for affordable housing to nonmarket models and nonprofit organizations dedicated to perpetuating the hard-won affordability of publicly assisted, privately owned housing.

On the other hand, because national attention and national resources have been directed elsewhere, this third sector housing movement has remained relatively small in the United States. Being out of the spotlight has slowed the process of evaluation, refinement, and legitimation that transforms an innovation into an institution. It has delayed the day when the preservation of affordability is as common a priority of public policy as the construction of new housing or the rehabilitation of old.

Washington may be poised at last, after many years of ignoring the problems and needs of U.S. cities, to begin debating the elements of a new urban policy. Third sector housing should be included in that debate. This innovative approach to affordable housing has been rehearsing quietly in the wings for over a decade, awaiting a wider audience and a larger role. The time has come to give the nonmarket models, the nonprofit organizations, and the public-private partnerships of a third sector housing policy the attention they deserve. This book is a modest beginning.

NOTES

1. Between fiscal years 1981 and 1989, new commitments of federal housing assistance dropped from $30 billion a year to $7.5 billion—a cut of 75 percent. During that same period, HUD experienced a 40 percent reduction in new budget authority and a 38 percent reduction in its Washington office staff (Nenno, 1989). Staff shortages, which plagued HUD throughout the decade, grew even worse during the final years of the Bush administration. HUD's Office of the Inspector General, in its December 1992 semiannual report on the agency's activities, revealed that HUD had been regularly understating the number of workers needed to administer complicated housing programs and warned that unless HUD soon got more well-trained employees, "another HUD scandal is a distinct possibility."

2. There are exceptions to this general neglect. See, for example, Achtenberg (1989), Achtenberg and Marcuse (1983), Bratt (1989a), Dreier (1989), Hartman and Stone (1986), Institute for Policy Studies (1989), Mallach (1984), Mayer (1991), Stegman and Holden (1987), and M. E. Stone (1993).

3. For an excellent review of affordability trends over the last two decades, covering both owner-occupied and renter-occupied housing, see Apgar (1990).

4. The lower nonprofit production estimate is taken from NCCED (1991); the higher estimate is Vidal's (1989).

5. Both quotes in this paragraph are from a widely distributed brochure published by the Connecticut Department of Housing, circa 1987, describing the department's Forever Housing Programs. More information on Connecticut's "forever housing" policy can be found in Kunz (1991).

6. *Social housing* is often defined more broadly than I am defining it here to include publicly owned housing and, sometimes, federally assisted private housing. Indeed, in England public housing and social housing are virtually synonymous (see, for example, Lowe and Hughes, 1991). This definitional association with public ownership contributes to the term's political problems, at least in the United States. Using "social housing" to describe private, nonmarket models of tenure gives conservative opponents an easy opening to distort its meaning and to conjure up specters of "social welfare housing" and "socialist housing." It should be admitted, however, that *third sector housing* has disadvantages of its own. It carries the risk of implying either (1) that *all* housing produced by nonprofit developers is automatically part of the price-restricted domain of the third sector or (2) that *only*

housing produced by nonprofit developers is securely within this domain. Both implications are wrong.

7. Because this book focuses on what municipal governments are currently doing to promote third sector housing, we emphasize only two components of a third sector housing policy: social ownership and nonprofit production. There is, in fact, a third component—a third prerequisite—that public policy at all levels of government has barely begun to address: social finance. Michael Stone (1993) speaks to the importance of this often-overlooked component of a third sector housing policy when he writes: "Only if social financing replaces dependence on profit-motivated investors will the growing number of community-based and regional nonprofit housers be able to achieve true social ownership."

8. In the case of public housing, popular perception has rarely reflected social reality. See, for example, Bratt (1986, 1989a), Stegman (1990), and Atlas and Dreier (1992).

9. The "expiring use" problem created by these federal housing programs of the past is discussed in more detail by Achtenberg (1989), Clay and Wallace (1990), and Pedone (1991).

10. The criticism of rent control from the Left has less to do with the questionable use of the police power than with the questionable effectiveness of rent control in guaranteeing long-term affordability. As Capek and Gilderbloom (1992: 261) suggest, in their study of Santa Monica's rent control battles, social housing may do better in this regard: "While rent control is useful for organizing tenants politically and for eliminating the most blatant abuses, it is vulnerable to numerous attacks from landlords; thus, the immediate gain seems short term. On the other hand, limited equity cooperatives, while not so 'sexy' an issue as rent control, provide a solution that will eventually result in even lower housing payments than under rent control."

11. At the local level, federal funds are often perceived as "free" money with so many strings already attached that it makes little sense for a municipality to add any more. ("If the feds don't care about long-term affordability, why should we?") Local money, on the other hand, is seen as costly, precious, and fair game for any conditions that might prevent its loss.

12. What I am suggesting is that public support for social housing is most likely to flourish when the "growth coalition" that dominates most municipal politics is out of power, out of favor, or held in check.

13. Additional information on the 1986 Tax Reform Act can be found in Gilderbloom and Appelbaum (1988: 80–82), Roistacker (1990), and Stegman (1991).

14. Goetz (1992: 434) has called special attention to the political resources that housing nonprofits like community development corporations (CDCs) often bring with them: "Because of their community base, CDCs represent a potential constituency for local officials. Providing support to nonprofit CDCs is not simply a

technical decision about how to implement housing policy but also a political decision that provides officials the opportunity to respond to neighborhood-based constituencies."

15. As Stegman and Holden (1987: 5) have noted, municipally sponsored affordable housing programs tend to have "more of a homeownership emphasis than their federal counterparts have had." This emphasis, combined with the shorter term of much local assistance, is "stimulating experimentation in ways to assure the continuing availability of locally subsidized housing to low-income people over the longer term."

16. It should be noted, however, that this same bias toward homeownership can cause municipal officials to ignore social housing models toward the *rental* end of the tenure ladder. It can also induce them to abandon price restrictions at the first opportunity. After turning a few tenants into homeowners, there is an ideological itch to make them "real" homeowners as soon as possible by removing any restrictions on their home's value or use.

17. Policymakers at all levels of government have been especially slow to relinquish the popular belief in the desirability and sustainability of homeownership for all. Even when programs premised on this belief have failed—Section 235 being a prime example—the tendency has been to blame the victim instead of the tenure. As Meehan (1979: 157) has noted: "Owning the family home is an aspiration almost as firmly entrenched in the pantheon of American values as free enterprise and the independent family. Indeed, when homeownership is tried and fails to produce expected results . . . the impulse is to query the training, motives, or competence of the persons involved rather than question the value of the institution."

18. For more information about household diversification and its likely effect on the "demand profile," see Sternlieb and Hughes (1991) and Hughes (1991). For a discussion of the implications of these "new households" for housing *design* and housing *type*, see Franck and Ahrentzen (1991), although very little is said in their book about housing *tenure*.

19. The limits of residential autonomy and the benefits of residential collaboration are being slowly recognized not only by those who seek housing for the poor but by middle-class consumers seeking housing for themselves. This is part of the impulse behind the growing interest in cohousing and other forms of collaborative housing in the United States, as well as the interest in cooperative housing shown by many persons whose income allows them considerable choice in housing. See Fromm (1991) and McCamant and Durrett (1989).

20. For more on Vermont and Massachusetts, see Harmon (1992), Libby (1990), and Bratt (1989b).

21. Housing cooperatives have been supported under Sections 213, 221(d)(3), 236, and 202 of various national housing acts. Section 213 allowed co-ops to take advantage of Federal Housing Administration (FHA) mortgage insurance. Section 221(d) (3) provided 100 percent financing at below market interest rates (BMIR)

for zero equity and limited equity cooperatives established for low- and moderate-income families. (Rental units and market rate cooperatives were also constructed under this program—in numbers far exceeding the units controlled by BMIR zero equity or limited equity cooperatives.) Cooperatives providing housing exclusively for the elderly were established under Section 202.

22. By 1975, private rentals accounted for only 38 percent of Sweden's stock of multifamily housing—down from 80 percent in 1945; almost a fourth of the multi-family housing stock was owned by cooperatives (Gilderbloom and Appelbaum, 1988: 165–180).

23. Although their relative share of new housing starts dropped to 30 percent during the 1970s and to 17 percent by the early 1980s, nonprofit and cooperative housing associations continue to provide affordable, price-restricted housing for a significant portion of the Danish population.

24. Despite NAHA's strong statutory language supporting long-term affordability, HUD promulgated rules in 1991 defining "remaining useful life of the property" to be five to twenty years, depending on the amount of HOME funds invested in a project. Responding to public comments criticizing its short-sighted interpretation of "remaining useful life," HUD declared that these terms are minimums; participating jurisdictions can adopt longer affordability controls if they choose to do so. Congress then did some backtracking of its own, softening its original endorsement of long-term affordability. The Housing and Community Development Act of 1992 amended NAHA to allow cities and states the choice of either restricting the resale prices of owner-occupied units or recapturing HOME funds from these assisted units.

25. Some examples: Between 1981 and 1988, total Section 8 expenditures declined by 82 percent; Section 8 expenditures for new construction declined by 97 percent; federal expenditures for public housing declined 85 percent; federal loans for elderly and handicapped housing declined by 85 percent; Housing Development Action Grants for the construction of rental housing were eliminated, along with federal appropriations for low-income homeownership (Gilderbloom and Appelbaum, 1988: 77–78). Two other elements in Reagan's privatization policy were the federal shift toward tenant-based rental assistance beginning in 1983 and the creation of the Low Income Housing Tax Credit program in 1986.

26. See, for example, Forrest (1991), Lundqvist (1988), Swann (1988), Tosics (1987), and Van Vliet (1990).

27. See, for example, Dreier (1989), Gilderbloom and Appelbaum (1988), Hopper and Hamberg (1986), and Ringheim (1990).

28. See, for example, Silver (1990), Gilderbloom and Appelbaum (1988: Chapter 6), Hartman (1991), Steinglass (1989), Hartman (1992), Stegman (1991), Rohe and Stegman (1992), and Vale (1992).

29. Osborne and Gaebler (1992: 45) make this point rather well: "Ronald Reagan often argued that by cutting public sector spending, we could liberate volun-

tary efforts from the oppressive arm of government. Where we followed his lead—particularly in low-income housing—we often had the opposite effect, crippling community-based organizations."

30. This is not to argue that publicly owned units should be privatized but merely that privatization, if warranted, can be accomplished in ways other than turning public housing into market housing. In the United States, in particular, selling off public housing to impoverished tenants who have grown even poorer during the last decade is probably unwarranted, unfeasible, and unwise. HUD now estimates that more than 80 percent of the nonelderly public housing population lives below the poverty line. About three-quarters of public housing families receive no income from employment (Vale, 1992 and 1993).

31. This difficult feat of political balance is made possible because social housing has the ability not only to introduce "private" incentives and responsibilities into (former) public housing but to add "public" opportunities and obligations to private housing. A more detailed discussion of the property relations and interests that distinguish the owner-occupants of social housing from other homeowners can be found in Davis (1991).

32. For other discussions of the "progressive city," see Magnusson (1989), Rosdil (1991), Shearer (1989), and C. Stone (1987).

33. The extent to which these changes have separated—and distanced—the economies and societies of city and suburb is well documented by Goldsmith and Blakely (1992).

34. Despite the emphasis that Osborne (1988) and Osborne and Gaebler (1992) place on the newness of this partnership between government agencies and nonprofit organizations, it should be pointed out that such partnerships have a long history in American society. See, for example, Hall (1987) and Salamon (1989, 1987a, 1987b).

35. The most common impetus for such a third sector housing policy is the desire to invest the scarce resources of municipal government more effectively, "recycling" subsidies for maximum effect. The vehicle by which this is achieved is a network of nonprofit organizations working in partnership with governmental agencies to develop and manage affordable housing. The models of price-restricted tenure being sponsored by these nonprofits alter quite substantially the rules under which housing is rented and resold without entirely replacing the market for land, labor, materials, and capital through which housing is produced. These aspects of third sector housing are all compatible with the "new paradigm" discussed by Osborne.

REFERENCES

Achtenberg, Emily. "Subsidized Housing at Risk: The Social Costs of Private Ownership." In S. Rosenberry and C. Hartman (eds.), *Housing Issues of the 1990s*, pp. 227–267. New York: Praeger, 1989.

Achtenberg, Emily, and Peter Marcuse. "Towards the Decommodification of Housing." In Chester Hartman (ed.), *America's Housing Crisis: What Is to Be Done?* pp. 202–231. Boston: Routledge & Kegan Paul, 1983.

Advisory Commission on Regulatory Barriers to Affordable Housing. *Not in My Backyard: Removing Barriers to Affordable Housing*. Washington, D.C.: HUD, 1991.

Apgar, William C. "The Nation's Housing: A Review of Past Trends and Future Prospects for Housing in America." In Denise DiPasquale and Langley Keyes (eds.), *Building Foundations: Housing and Federal Policy*, pp. 25–59. Philadelphia: University of Pennsylvania Press, 1990.

Appelbaum, Richard, and Peter Dreier. "Recent Developments in Rental Housing in the United States." In W. van Vliet and J. van Weesep (eds.), *Government and Housing*, pp. 97–114. Newbury Park, Calif.: Sage Publications, 1990.

Atlas, John, and Peter Dreier. "From 'Projects' to Communities: How to Redeem Public Housing." *American Prospect*, no. 10 (Summer, 1992): 74–85.

Bratt, Rachel. "Public Housing: The Controversy and Contribution." In Rachel G. Bratt, Chester Hartman, and Ann Meyerson (eds.), *Critical Perspectives on Housing*, pp. 335–361. Philadelphia: Temple University Press, 1986.

———. *Rebuilding a Low-Income Housing Policy*. Philadelphia: Temple University Press, 1989a.

———. Community-based Housing in Massachusetts: Lessons and Limits of the State's Support System." In S. Rosenberry and C. Hartman (eds.), *Housing Issues of the 1990s*, pp. 277–311. New York: Praeger, 1989b.

Bruyn, Severyn T. "Beyond the Market and the State." In Severyn T. Bruyn and James Meehan (eds.), *Beyond the Market and the State: New Directions in Community Development*, pp. 3–27. Philadelphia: Temple University Press, 1987.

Capek, Stella M., and John I. Gilderbloom. *Community versus Commodity: Tenants and the American City*. Albany, N.Y.: State University of New York Press, 1992.

Clavel, Pierre. *The Progressive City*. New Brunswick, N.J.: Rutgers University Press, 1986.

Clay, Phillip. *Mainstreaming the Community Builders*. Cambridge, Mass.: Department of Urban Studies and Planning, MIT, 1990.

Clay, Phillip, and James Wallace. "Preservation of the Existing Stock of Assisted Private Housing." In Denise DiPasquale and Langley Keyes (eds.), *Building Foundations: Housing and Federal Policy*, pp. 313–331. Philadelphia: University of Pennsylvania Press, 1990.

Davis, John Emmeus. *Contested Ground: Collective Action and the Urban Neighborhood*. Ithaca, N.Y.: Cornell University Press, 1991.

Dreier, Peter. "Affordable Housing without Profit or Scandal." *Shelterforce* 11, no. 6 (1989): 12–15.

Dreier, Peter, and David Hulchanski. "Affordable Housing: Lessons from Canada." *American Prospect*, Issue 1 (Spring 1990): 119–125.

Forrest, Ray. "The Privatization of Collective Consumption." In M. Gottdiener and Chris Pickvance (eds.), *Urban Life in Transition*, pp. 169–195. Newbury Park, Calif.: Sage Publications, 1991.

Forrest, Ray, and A. Murie. *Selling the Welfare State: The Privatisation of Public Housing*. London: Routledge & Kegan Paul, 1988.

Franck, Karen A., and Sherry Ahrentzen (eds.). *New Households, New Housing*. New York: Van Nostrand Reinhold, 1991.

Fromm, Dorit. *Collaborative Communities*. New York: Van Nostrand Reinhold, 1991.

Gilderbloom, John I., and Richard P. Appelbaum. *Rethinking Rental Housing*. Philadelphia: Temple University Press, 1988.

Goetz, Edward. "Local Government Support for Nonprofit Housing: A Survey of U.S. Cities." *Urban Affairs Quarterly* 27, no. 3 (1992): 420–435.

Goldsmith, William W., and Edward J. Blakely. *Separate Societies: Poverty and Inequality in U.S. Cities*. Philadelphia: Temple University Press, 1992.

Hall, Peter D. "A Historical Overview of the Nonprofit Sector." In W. W. Powell (ed.), *The Nonprofit Sector*, pp. 3–26. New Haven: Yale University Press, 1987.

Harmon, R. Natasha. *Affordable Housing: The Vermont Model (Perpetual Affordability through Community-Based Non-Profits)*. Amherst, Mass.: Center for Rural Massachusetts, University of Massachusetts, 1992.

Hartman, Chester. "Comment on Anthony Downs's 'The Advisory Commission on Regulatory Barriers to Affordable Housing: Its Behavior and Accomplishments.'" *Housing Policy Debate* 2, no. 4 (1991): 1161–1168.

———. "Debating the Low Income Housing Tax Credits: Feeding the Sparrows by Feeding the Horses." *Shelterforce* 14, no. 1 (1992): 12, 15.

Hartman, Chester, and Michael E. Stone. "A Socialist Housing Alternative for the United States." In Rachel G. Bratt, Chester Hartman, and Ann Meyerson (eds.), *Critical Perspectives on Housing*, pp. 484–513. Philadelphia: Temple University Press, 1986.

Hopper, Kim, and Jill Hamberg. "The Making of America's Homeless: From Skid Row to the New Poor, 1945–1984." In Rachel G. Bratt, Chester Hartman, and Ann Meyerson (eds.), *Critical Perspectives on Housing*, pp. 12–48. Philadelphia: Temple University Press, 1986.

Hughes, James. "Clashing Demographics: Homeownership and Affordability Dilemmas." *Housing Policy Debate* 2, no. 4 (1991): 1217–1250.

Institute for Policy Studies (IPS). *The Right to Housing: A Blueprint for Housing the Nation*. Washington, D.C., 1989.

Kleinman, Mark. "The Future Provision of Social Housing in Britain." In Willem van Vliet and Jan van Weesep (eds.), *Government and Housing*, pp. 84–96. Newbury Park, Calif.: Sage Publications, 1990.

Kunz, Jonathan D. "Forever Housing: State Support for Community Based, Permanently Affordable Housing in Connecticut." M.C.P. thesis, Department of Urban Studies and Planning, MIT, June 1991.

Libby, James. "Vermont's Housing and Conservation Trust Fund: A Unique Approach." *Clearinghouse Review*, February 1990.

Logan, John R., and Todd Swanstrom. "Urban Restructuring: A Critical View." In *Beyond the City Limits: Urban Policy and Economic Restructuring in Comparative Perspective*, pp. 3–24. Philadelphia: Temple University Press, 1990.

Lowe, Stuart, and David Hughes (eds.). *A New Century of Social Housing*. Leicester, Eng.: Leicester University Press, 1991.

Lundqvist, L. J. "Privatization: Towards a Concept for Comparative Analysis." *Journal of Public Policy* 8 (1988): 1–19.

Magnusson, W. "Radical Municipalities in North America." Paper presented at the American Political Science Association Annual Meeting, Atlanta, 1989.

Mallach, Alan. "Creating and Maintaining Lower-Income Occupancy in Inclusionary Housing Programs." In his *Inclusionary Housing Programs*, pp. 133–165. New Brunswick, N.J.: Rutgers Center for Urban Policy Research, 1984.

Mayer, Neil. "Preserving the Low-Income Housing Stock: What Nonprofit Organizations Can Do Today and Tomorrow." *Housing Policy Debate* 2, no. 2 (1991): 499–533.

McCamant, Kathryn, and Charles Durrett. *Cohousing: A Contemporary Approach to Housing Ourselves*. Berkeley, Calif.: Habitat Press, 1989.

Meehan, Eugene J. *The Quality of Federal Policymaking: Programmed Failure in Public Housing*. Columbia: University of Missouri Press, 1979.

National Congress for Community Economic Development (NCCED). *Changing the Odds: The Achievements of Community-based Development Corporations*. Washington, D.C., December 1991.

Nenno, Mary. "H/CD after Reagan: A New Cycle of Policies and Partners." *Journal of Housing* (March/April 1989): 75–82.

———. "State and Local Government: New Initiatives in Low-Income Housing Provision." *Housing Policy Debate* 2, no. 2 (1991): 467–497.

Osborne, David. *Laboratories of Democracy*. Boston: Harvard Business School Press, 1988.

Osborne, David, and Ted Gaebler. *Reinventing Government: How the Entrepreneurial Spirit is Transforming the Public Sector*. Reading, Mass.: Addison-Wesley, 1992.

Pedone, Carla. "Estimating Mortgage Prepayments and Defaults in Older Federally Assisted Rental Housing and the Possible Costs of Preventing Them." *Housing Policy Debate* 2, no. 2 (1991): 245–288.

Peterson, Paul E. *City Limits*. Chicago: University of Chicago Press, 1981.

Rapp, David. "The Latest Word on Housing: One Law, Two Programs, No Policy." *Governing* (February 1991): 73.

Ringheim, Karin. *At Risk of Homelessness: The Roles of Income and Rent*. New York: Praeger, 1990.

Rohe, William, and Michael Stegman. "Public Housing Homeownership: Will It Work and for Whom?" *APA Journal* 58, no. 2 (1992): 144–157.

Roistacher, Elizabeth A. "Housing Finance and Housing Policy in the United States: Legacies of the Reagan Era." In Willem van Vliet and Jan van Weesep (eds.), *Government and Housing*, pp. 158–172. Newbury Park, Calif.: Sage Publications, 1990.

Rosdil, Donald. "The Context of Radical Populism in U.S. Cities." *Journal of Urban Affairs* 13, no. 1 (1991): 77–96.

Salamon, Lester. "The Scope and Theory of Government-Nonprofit Relations." In W. W. Powell (ed.), *The Nonprofit Sector*, pp. 99–117. New Haven: Yale University Press, 1987a.

———. "Of Market Failure, Voluntary Failure, and Third-Party Government: Toward a Theory of Government–Non-profit Relations." *Journal of Voluntary Action Research* 16, no. 1–2 (1987b): 29–49.

———. "The Changing Partnership between the Voluntary Sector and the Welfare Sector." In V. Hodgkinson, R. Lyman, and Associates, *The Future of the Nonprofit Sector*, pp. 41–60. San Francisco: Jossey-Bass, 1989.

Shearer, Derek. "In Search of Equal Partnerships: Prospects for Progressive Urban Policy in the 1990s." In G. Squires (ed.), *Unequal Partnerships*. New Brunswick, N.J.: Rutgers University Press, 1989.

Silver, Hilary. "Privatization, Self-Help, and Public Housing Ownership in the United States." In Willem van Vliet and Jan van Weesep (eds.), *Government and Housing*, pp. 123–140. Newbury Park, Calif.: Sage Publications, 1990.

Stegman, Michael. "The Role of Public Housing in a Revitalized National Housing Policy." In Denise DiPasquale and Langley Keyes (eds.), *Building Foundations: Housing and Federal Policy*, pp. 333–364. Philadelphia: University of Pennsylvania Press, 1990.

———. "The Excessive Costs of Creative Finance: Growing Inefficiencies in the Production of Low-income Housing." *Housing Policy Debate* 2, no. 2, (1991): 357–373.

Stegman, Michael, and J. David Holden. *Nonfederal Housing Programs*. Washington, D.C.: Urban Land Institute, 1987.

Steinglass, David. "When Jack Kemp Says Empowerment, What Does He Mean?" *Shelterforce* 12, no. 2 (1989): 6–7, 16.

Sternlieb, George, and James Hughes. "Private Market Provision of Low Income Housing: Historical Perspective and Future Prospects." *Housing Policy Debate* 2, no. 2 (1991): 123–156.

Stone, C. "Summing Up Urban Regimes, Development Policy, and Political Arrangements." In C. Stone and H. Sanders (eds.), *The Politics of Urban Development*. Lawrence: University Press of Kansas, 1987.

Stone, Michael E. *Shelter Poverty: New Ideas on Housing Affordability*. Philadelphia: Temple University Press, 1993.

Sultemeier, Debbie. "Buying In or Selling Out: The Future of Public Housing." *Shelterforce* 10, no. 1 (1987): 12–14.

Swann, Dennis. *The Retreat of the State: Deregulation and Privatization in the UK and US*. Ann Arbor: University of Michigan Press, 1988.

Tosics, I. "Privatization in Housing Policy." *International Journal of Urban and Regional Research* 11, no. 1 (1987): 61–78.

Vale, Lawrence J. "Jack Kemp's Pet Delusion." *Washington Post*, August 3, 1992.

———. *Occupancy Issues in Distressed Public Housing*. Washington, D.C.: U.S. Government Printing Office, 1993.

Van Vliet, Willem. "The Privatization and Decentralization of Housing." In Willem van Vliet and Jan van Weesep (eds.), *Government and Housing*, pp. 9–24. Newbury Park, Calif.: Sage Publications, 1990.

Vidal, A. C. *Community Economic Development Assessment: A National Study of Urban Community Development Corporations*. New York: Community Development Research Center, New School for Social Research, 1989.

Zigas, Barry. "The National Affordable Housing Act: Whole New Ball Game." *Shelterforce* 13, no. 4 (1991): 6–8.

PART ONE

Components and Dilemmas of a Third Sector Housing Policy

1

Social Housing: U.S. Prospect, Canadian Reality

PETER DREIER AND J. DAVID HULCHANSKI

The past decade has witnessed a remarkable emergence of community-based housing organizations in cities, suburbs, and rural areas across the United States. The nonprofit sector, though still a marginal part of the housing industry, is growing, and it has found increasing support from foundations, private industry, and government at all levels.

By contrast, Canada has nurtured a large and thriving nonprofit sector (called *social housing*) for several decades. In Canada, social housing is a widely used (though imprecise) term encompassing many forms of private, nonmarket housing developed through various governmental subsidy programs. An examination of Canada's social housing system can offer some policy lessons for the United States.

COMPARISONS OF THE UNITED STATES AND CANADA

The housing systems of the United States and Canada are similar in many ways. Most housing is constructed by private builders and financed by private lenders. Almost two-thirds of the households in both countries own their own homes, which are mostly detached, single-family houses. During the 1980s, housing prices skyrocketed in the largest urban areas, particularly in Vancouver and Toronto. Middle-class Canadians, like their counterparts to the south, complain that the dream of homeownership is increasingly illusive.

But for poor and working-class residents, housing conditions are considerably better in Canada than in the United States. Canada has no slums to match the physical and social deterioration in U.S. inner cities. Nor are Canada's cities overwhelmed with citizens sleeping in shelters, on the streets, and in subway stations. Of course Canada has homeless people, and many lower-income households have extreme difficulty affording adequate housing, but the magnitude of the problem is dramatically different than in the United States. When large-scale public housing projects were discontinued in both countries in the early 1970s, the policy response was very different. Canada went one way (expanding the social housing sector), while the United States went another (promoting market-oriented solutions).

What accounts for these differences? Put simply, Canada's governments —federal, provincial, and local—have made a commitment to assist people who are not served by the private housing marketplace. They have recognized that the market can do certain things and not others, not even with massive subsidies. Indeed, an official report by the Canada Mortgage and Housing Corporation (CMHC) acknowledges that "the private market, even if operating efficiently, [is] incapable of providing adequate housing at an affordable cost for every Canadian." It is hard to imagine the U.S. Department of Housing and Urban Development (CMHC's counterpart) making such a statement.

Like the United States and Great Britain, Canada has recently experienced a conservative national regime that sought to reduce the role of government and cut government-sponsored social programs. In the United States and Great Britain, the conservative agenda was to privatize existing subsidized housing and substitute rent supplement (voucher) programs for government-sponsored housing developments. Unlike the Reagan and Thatcher regimes, however, Canada's Conservative government (led by Prime Minister Brian Mulroney), which took office in 1984, did not seek to privatize existing social housing, although it slashed budgets for new social housing construction. Canada's less draconian response to fiscal restraint was due to the relative strength of progressive political forces and overall public support for social housing programs. The major political difference between the two countries is that Canada has a three-party system and a strong labor movement with a unified national voice, the Canadian Labour Congress, and a political arm, the New Democratic Party (NDP). Since its founding in the 1930s, the NDP, a progressive social democratic party, has always had at least some seats in the national Parliament. In recent decades, it has received 10 to 20 percent of the national vote. Four of the ten provinces have had NDP governments. In the early 1990s, three provinces representing about 55 percent of the country's population—Ontario, British Columbia, and Saskatchewan—elected NDP governments. As a result, Canadian progressives have a stronger voice in the public debate than their U.S. counterparts. To cite one example, Canada's health care program was first advocated by the NDP. The party has also been a strong advocate of social housing.

REASSESSMENT OF PUBLIC HOUSING

Canada's population of 25 million is approximately one-tenth that of the United States. Canada now subsidizes a slightly greater fraction of its total housing supply than does the United States.[1] There are some 550,000 subsidized public and nonprofit rental housing units (including cooperatives). Fairly traditional public housing projects, mainly built during the 1960s and early 1970s, provide about half (205,000 units) of Canada's subsidized rental housing. Social housing agencies (apartment projects owned by nonprofit organizations as well as resident-owned cooperatives) developed over the past sixteen years have produced the other half. Of these, nonequity cooperative housing accounts for 75,000 units. Overall, social housing represents 5.5 percent of Canada's housing stock (see Table 1-1).

The United States has 4.3 million subsidized units, about 4.5 percent of all housing. However, more than half of these units are owned by private, for-profit landlords and none have long-term affordability requirements; they are not social housing in the Canadian sense.

What is known as *public housing* in Canada and the United States consists of federally subsidized housing owned and managed by public housing authorities. All public housing units are targeted for the poor. Direct government provision of housing was initiated with great reluctance in both Canada and the United States as housing of last resort only for those incapable of meeting their needs in the private market. The program—as well as the housing units themselves—was designed to avoid competing with, let alone replacing, private market provision of housing.

The United States has about 1.3 million public housing units. Built primarily from the late 1940s through the 1970s, they account for 1.4 percent of the nation's housing stock. The number of public housing units is decreasing due to neglect and demolition.

Table 1-1. Government Support of Rental Housing in Canada and the United States

Market Rental Housing

Private Rental: Privately owned and managed for general population. Often includes various federal tax advantages and mortgage insurance, but no other direct subsidies targeted to lower-income households. Both Canada and the United States have this form of rental housing.

Private Rental with Project-based Subsidies: Privately developed, owned, and managed housing subsidized by the federal government (and some state governments) with rent supplements and below-market mortgages targeted to the *development,* rather than the occupants. Owners required to rent units to lower-income households for 20 or 40 years, depending on the program (Sec. 8, Sec. 221(d)(3), and Sec. 236). The United States has about 1.9 million units in this inventory; a small portion are owned by nonprofit organizations. Canada has no similar program.

Private Rental with Tenant-based Subsidies: Privately developed, owned, and managed housing subsidized by the federal government (and some state governments) through rent supplements targeted to the *occupants,* who must meet income guidelines. The subsidy pays the difference between a portion of occupants' income and the market rent. Both Canada and the United States have this program.

Nonmarket Rental Housing

Public Housing: Government-built housing developments managed by a public housing authority with means test criteria and targeted 100% for the poor. Canada has about 205,000 units built during the 1950s and 1960s. The United States has about 1.3 million units built primarily from the late 1940s through the 1970s.

Private Nonprofit: Housing developed, owned, and managed by not-for-profit organizations, sometimes community based, for low- and moderate-income households. Canada has about 170,000 private nonprofit units built between 1965 and the present, all with long-term affordability provisions. The United States has only the Section 202 program (for elderly residents) and the new Community Housing Partnership program, neither of which involves long-term affordability restrictions.

Public Nonprofit: Small-scale housing projects developed, owned, and managed by local government, sometimes with tenants and community members on the boards of directors. Canada has about 100,000 public nonprofit housing units built between 1975 and the present. There is no similar government program in the United States.

Nonequity Cooperatives: A hybrid of ownership and rental housing usually developed by nonprofit, community-based "resource groups" (developers), directly subsidized by government, owned and managed by residents, housing a mix of low- and moderate-income households, with members neither making an investment in the project nor taking out any gains when they leave. Canada has about 75,000 nonequity cooperative housing units, most of them built since the late 1970s. There is no similar government program in the United States.

Canada's immediate postwar governments hoped to keep all housing in the private sector. But as the needs of lower-income households became more acute, a small public housing program was introduced in 1949—a decade later than in the United States. By U.S. standards, Canada's public housing is extremely well managed. While Canada has a few high-rise public housing developments with heavy drug use and related crime, it has nothing to match the ugly, crime-ridden "vertical ghettoes"—such as the now defunct Pruitt-Igoe in St. Louis, Boston's Columbia Point (now privatized and called Harbor Point), or Chicago's Cabrini Green—that U.S. citizens often associate with public housing.

Canadian public housing projects have not acquired a bad image because they tend to be better designed and are generally on a smaller scale. There are relatively few very large public housing projects. Close to 80 percent of Canada's projects contain fewer than fifty units. Only 11 percent have one hundred or more units. These are very large developments accounting for roughly half the total number of units. Early advocates of public housing in Canada managed to ensure that a mean-spirited "warehousing" of poor people at the lowest possible cost would not replace the broader social objective of providing decent accommodation.

Canada's public housing stock is relatively young (the vast majority, 87 percent, of projects are less than twenty years old), and most projects are in good condition. Only 4 percent of the units were built between 1949 and 1964, and many were under construction when the program was terminated in the early 1970s. Half the units exclusively house senior citizens; the other half house families, mainly single mothers and their children. Almost two-thirds of public housing residents are female, a reflection of the preponderance of female-headed households among single-parent families and the greater longevity of women (CMHC, 1990).

By the late 1960s there was widespread dissatisfaction in both countries with public housing and with the urban renewal projects it was usually linked to. Housing professionals and activists sought alternatives. In the United States in the mid-1960s, the federal government created a small program designed to encourage private developers to build low-rent housing by providing mortgage insurance and tax breaks. Further changes were introduced during the Nixon administration by the 1974 Housing Act, which created the Section 8 program that provides private developers and landlords with subsidies for housing the poor.[2]

SOCIAL HOUSING IN CANADA

Faced with its own concerns about public housing, Canada in 1969 initiated a national review of housing policy that led to the cancellation of the public housing program. For much the same reason that the United States moved away from traditional public housing, Canada switched to third sector housing in the 1970s. As in the United States, Canadian public housing was often part of a large urban renewal project composed of large-scale buildings occupied only by the very poor. Small-scale projects, developed and managed by local citizens, including the residents themselves, were viewed as preferable both for consumers and for the communities asked to accept them.

The election of a majority Liberal government in 1968, during a period when urban affairs and housing were high on the public agenda, led to the creation of the Federal Task Force on Housing and Urban Development. Task force members traveled the country collecting the views and advice of citizens and local officials. Its report (Canada, 1969) was highly critical of large-scale public housing projects and the bulldozer approach to urban renewal. Both these programs were ended, and the debate over improved programs continued for several years.

On the brink of adopting major new housing programs in 1972, the Liberal government failed to win a majority of seats in a national election and required support from the NDP in Parliament in order to continue as the governing party. In exchange for its temporary support (i.e., for preventing the fall of the Liberal government in a vote of no confidence), the NDP obtained Liberal backing for parts of its agenda, including a more comprehensive set of housing programs. The 1973 amendments to the National Housing Act introduced public, private, and cooperative versions of nonprofit housing as well as nonprofit housing programs for rural and native peoples. Together, these are now commonly referred to as *social housing*, meaning that they are socially assisted (receive direct governmental subsidies), that they house people with a broader social and income mix than the previous public housing program, and that they permanently remove privately owned housing from the marketplace ensuring its long-term affordability.

The 1973 act essentially launched Canada's nonprofit housing supply program. In addition to providing financial subsidy, the program assisted community groups, church organizations, labor unions, and municipal governments to become sophisticated housing developers. For the past decade, federal housing funds have been directed, almost exclusively, to this strengthened third sector.

While the Conservative Party, first elected in 1984, was never a strong supporter of social housing programs, it did not want to suffer the inevitable political consequences of ending them. Instead, it gradually cut funding and thus reduced the number of social housing units created each year. During the 1970s, social housing accounted for 9.1 percent of Canada's housing starts; during the 1980s, it accounted for 6.3 percent. The peak year in federal funding of social housing supply was 1980, when 31,400 units were funded. (This is about the same number as HUD subsidized that year in a country with ten times Canada's population). Annual production had fallen to 15,000 units by 1990, and to 8,200 units by 1992.

In the late 1980s, like the Reagan and Bush administrations in the United States, the Conservative Party made a decision to target subsidies to the most needy. They used "core housing need" indicators to establish regulations to determine who qualifies for access to social housing. The Conservative government's effort to target social housing has been part of the private development sector's attack on social housing. The view behind this attack is that all people should be in private sector housing and that, if there is to be social housing, only the "truly needy" should be admitted to it.[3] Because such targeting could have the result of turning social housing into a version of the previous public housing program, third sector builders and housing activists, as well as many provinces and most municipalities, opposed this shift.

Time will tell whether the new policy was the right choice. The new emphasis delivers more units to low-income households, but it jeopardizes the goals of social and economic integration. There is variation across the country as to how targeting is implemented, however. In Ontario, for example, the broader, socially mixed approach is still being implemented for social housing produced exclusively with provincial funds.

The Conservative Party used the 1992 budget to cancel the federal cooperative housing program, which had declined under the Conservatives from more than five thousand units per year to two thousand units. The elimination of this program is likely to be temporary, however, because both of the other major parties support it and will reinstate it if they capture the government after the next federal election.

Varieties of Social Housing

Canada now has almost twenty years' experience with nonprofit social housing—that is, housing sponsored and managed by nonprofit organizations outside market forces in order to guarantee long-term affordability. Social housing is part of what Canadians call the "third sector," housing which is outside of both the public sector and the private, for-profit sector.

In Canada, not only the national government funds social housing supply programs; over the past decade, about half of the ten provincial governments have created their own programs as well. In 1986, in order to encourage the provinces to become more active in housing, the federal government entered into agreements with each province whereby the province plays a more significant role in implementing federal programs in their jurisdiction. In exchange, the provinces began paying a share (about 25 percent) of the program costs (Banting, 1990).

Canada's social housing is sited in low- and mid-rise structures averaging about fifty units and located in all parts of metropolitan areas—central city as well as suburban. They are carefully integrated into existing neighborhoods in order to avoid the stigma frequently associated with low-income projects. Until recent changes in federal guidelines, they were also socially mixed, housing a range of people from very poor to middle class.

Social housing programs are designed so that most residents pay about 25 percent to 30 percent of their income for rent. Between 25 and 100 percent of residents in a social housing project pay rent based on their incomes. A formula determines what a household is able to pay; a federal subsidy covers the rest.

A key feature of all of Canada's social housing programs is that both the land and the housing units are permanently removed from the real estate market. Neither can be resold or privatized. All nonprofit housing organizations and housing cooperatives enter into binding agreements tied to their mortgage financing, which guarantee the not-for-profit nature of the housing. These contracts guarantee the perpetual affordability of any privately owned units that have been assisted by the public.

Canada's third sector housing includes three types of nonprofit housing development organizations. The *public nonprofits* are housing companies established by local government. The *private nonprofits* are established by church groups, unions, and community organizations. Municipalities that build housing under the federal nonprofit program generally establish separate housing organizations to manage the units. The board of directors is usually appointed by a municipal council and often includes members of the council. Tenants are sometimes appointed to the boards. Private nonprofits are private corporations operated on a not-for-profit basis under the regulations of the federal program. They vary widely, from ethnic or church groups that build only one project for senior citizens associated with their group to highly innovative, community-based organizations that build a number of housing projects and meet a diversity of housing needs.

The most interesting innovation is the nonprofit, nonequity housing cooperative. Unlike the public and private nonprofits, the co-ops have members that actually own and manage their own projects. Units cannot be sold or even passed on to a friend. When someone moves out, another family from the co-op's waiting list moves in. Because residents do not invest in them, they take no equity with them when they leave. Canada's housing co-ops are a democratically owned and managed version of subsidized housing. A majority (70 percent) of Canada's housing cooperatives are managed directly by the residents on a voluntary basis. About 30 percent of the cooperatives, usually the larger ones, retain full-time or part-time paid managers.

Since housing costs in cooperatives are based on actual operating expenses, cooperative members have an incentive to run their housing efficiently. A recent CMHC evaluation of the cooperative housing program found that this self-management feature paid off: operating costs in co-op housing are half what they are in public housing, and 15 percent to 60 percent lower than they are in nonprofit rental housing, depending on the type of project.

Canada's approach to social housing, therefore, provides a full range of options to suit local needs and special needs groups within the population, including (in the case of cooperatives) those who want self-managed housing.

There is an ongoing debate over who has jurisdiction over the nation's social housing (Banting, 1990; Carter and McAfee, 1990; Rose, 1980). As a result of a broader tax base and national pressures to help those in need, the federal government has played the major role in promoting social housing. The provincial governments sometimes initiate their own programs, depending on economic conditions and political pressures. Some municipal and provincial governments actively support social housing as well; others simply accept federal funding without much enthusiasm.

The NDP is a consistent and committed supporter of social housing. NDP provincial governments make affordable housing a general priority and expand social housing production. In Ontario, for example, 72,000 new nonprofit and co-op housing units were built between 1986 and the early 1990s, the period when the NDP supported a minority Liberal government. In addition, a major provincial initiative aimed at improving rooming houses in Toronto was launched in 1991. A pilot project, which includes funding for social services, is in the process of rehabilitating or building 550 rooming house units.

The Municipal Role

Canadian housing policy and programs have historically originated at the federal and provincial levels of government, not at the municipal level. Like the United States, Canadian municipalities rely primarily on property taxes for funding; consequently, an inadequate tax base has limited the range of municipal activities undertaken on behalf of affordable housing. Municipal governments would occasionally study local housing issues and use their regulatory authority to affect housing supply and maintenance through zoning, building, and safety codes. In general, however, they left the active role in the provision of housing to the private sector and (in the case of subsidized housing) to the provincial and federal levels. Even rent control is a provincial responsibility.

The municipal role began to change in the 1970s (Hulchanski et al., 1990; Carter and McAfee, 1990). Canada's larger cities grew rapidly, and citizens clamored for affordable housing. They elected reform-minded politicians who supported more direct government involvement in the supply of housing. With the rise of citizen participation in planning, more elected officials and active citizens focused on local housing conditions and sought local solutions.

Several cities provided land for social housing at below-market value, and others offered zoning bonuses to make social housing financing formulas work on expensive land. During the 1970s and 1980s, some cities became sites for large-scale urban redevelopment projects with direct municipal government involvement. In Montreal, Toronto, and Vancouver, to cite only the three largest cities, this proactive approach led to the municipal development of several large, socially mixed neighborhoods. Many municipalities established housing corporations to develop social housing, and established social housing policies, zoning incentives, and property tax exemptions to facilitate the supply of social housing. Toronto, for example, created a municipal nonprofit housing corporation in 1974, with a broad mandate that includes research, land acquisition, construction of social housing, purchase and renovation of existing housing, property management, housing policy, and program coordination for the city. It has built and currently manages about seven thousand rental and cooperative housing units and has a development program that produces five hundred to six hundred new units per year. The board of directors that manages this portfolio is drawn from the city council, tenants, and the community at large.

During the 1970s, many Canadian municipalities took an active role in social housing, more often facilitating projects than (like Toronto) actively developing them. By 1981, thirteen of the major metropolitan areas had municipal nonprofit housing corporations (Carter and McAfee, 1990). In some metropolitan areas, regional housing development corporations like the Greater Vancouver Housing Corporation and the Region of Peel Non-Profit Housing Corporation (in Toronto's suburbs) emerged, primarily to develop or manage nonprofit housing for families. By the 1980s, as Canada's housing crisis became even more acute, most municipalities had begun to play a significant role in facilitating social housing supply and rehabilitating and maintaining existing affordable rental housing.

Broad Support for Social Housing

The important lesson for the United States is that local and community-based organizations can create good housing and that such housing can remain a permanent community asset, never to be sold to speculators or converted to upscale units. Canada's provinces also have very strong tenants' rights laws, in both private and social housing, protecting residents from arbitrary evictions and unfair rent increases.

Canada has not solved its housing problems, but it has created the foundation for doing so. It has demonstrated that public funds can be most efficiently spent to create a permanent stock of affordable housing.

Canadian officials and housing advocates from across the political spectrum acknowledge that federal and provincial funds for social housing are spent wisely. They do not argue over whether to support social housing but over how much more should be spent and how better to meet special needs. There's been almost no tint of scandal, influence peddling, or political favoritism to detract from the government's support for the nonprofit sector—nothing comparable to the HUD scandal, for example. In fact, the Canadian federal watchdog, the auditor general, recently lauded CMHC's "high performance," its "clear policies," and its "strong sense of mission and purpose, continuity in management and staff, pronounced focus on clients, and open communication."

As a result, public opinion is overwhelmingly positive. In general, the middle class supports social housing programs for the poor and the near-poor. This has meant a continued willingness to put taxpayers' dollars into such housing.

Social housing has come into its own as a major component of Canada's housing industry. The private, for-profit sector builds market housing for people who can afford what the market has to offer; the federal and provincial governments offer a range of housing programs targeted for people with special needs, such as the native population, rural people, and the homeless; the third sector provides and manages the social housing stock.

The strong and growing system of nonprofit and cooperative housing organizations is the result of long and persistent grassroots activity. Organized on the local, provincial, and national levels, Canada's social housing industry is rooted in a progressive labor movement and progressive political parties, including the left-wing New Democratic Party, as well as church and university student organizations, which sponsored several early cooperatives.

The Canadian Housing and Renewal Association is the major trade association for the social housing network. In addition, both the cooperative housing groups and the nonprofit housing organizations have local, provincial, and national organizations. For example, in 1968 a national organization was established, the Cooperative Housing Foundation (now the Cooperative Housing Federation of Canada) as a joint effort by the Canadian Labour Congress, the Cooperative Union of Canada, and the Canadian Union of Students. National, provincial, and local tenants organizations provide political support for social housing programs. So, too, do women's rights organizations and antipoverty groups (such as the Canadian Council on Social Development). As a group, municipalities in Canada, through their national association (the Federation of Canadian Municipalities) are also very strong supporters of social housing.

Among the major parties, only the NDP is a dependable supporter of social housing. The other two parties have to be lobbied and pushed continually. Because of this pressure, however, whatever party is in power, CMHC generally supports the nonprofit housing sector. Canadian housing policy is thus relatively consistent and coherent, and that continuity has allowed both government planners and housing builders to learn the rules and develop the capacity to succeed.

"You don't get major mood swings in housing programs," explained Peter Smith, former president of the Canadian Housing and Renewal Association. "You do get subtle changes, but no big surprises."

Because of this continuity, the nonprofit housing groups are relatively stable. Staff members are paid decent salaries, and few see employment in the nonprofit sector as a way station to jobs with for-profit development firms.

THE NONPROFIT SECTOR IN THE UNITED STATES

In the United States, housing nonprofits have been around since the late 1800s and early 1900s, when settlement houses, labor unions, and wealthy philanthropists built apartment houses and cooperatives for working-class families (Birch and Gardner, 1981; Keating, Rasey, and Krumholz, 1990).

In the late 1960s and early 1970s, community activists across the country, particularly in inner cities and rural areas, formed community development corporations (CDCs) to fight the war against poverty and gain "community control." In many cases, their efforts were the only development activities taking place in these communities. Their two biggest patrons were the Ford Foundation and the federal government. Between 1972 and 1981, the federal government funded about one hundred CDCs to engage in business development, human services, and housing; community activists, churches, and social service agencies formed a few hundred more. A few small federal programs—the Community Service Agency's Title VII program, HUD's Neighborhood Self-Help Development Program and Neighborhood Development Demonstration program, and the Comprehensive Employment and Training Act (CETA) job-training program—helped pay part of the CDCs' operating costs. All of these programs were axed by the Reagan administration (Mayer, 1990).

Evaluations of these early nonprofit groups reported modest success in completing development projects. But many were organizationally and financially unprepared to undertake large-scale community economic revitalization. Some projects and some groups fell on hard times and folded. Although the for-profit and nonprofit development groups that participated in the federal government's housing programs during this period had roughly equal rates of success and failure, the CDCs' mistakes were more visible.

The groups that survived the 1970s faced a new decade with few federal resources and little collective understanding of their own history, accomplishments, and problems. Nevertheless, during the 1980s, as federal housing assistance dried up, the number of community-based nonprofit groups engaged in housing mushroomed. According to a recent survey by the National Congress for Community Economic Development, the number of these groups has increased tenfold to about two thousand in the past decade. These groups—with origins in community organizations, churches, unions, social service agencies, and tenant groups—have developed almost 320,000 units of housing and created (or retained) almost 90,000 permanent jobs. Thirty-nine percent of the CDCs in the survey had been in business for less than ten years (NCCED, 1991).

With the dismantling of federal housing programs during the 1980s under the Reagan administration, for-profit developers essentially withdrew from low-income housing development. To try to fill the vacuum, nonprofit entrepreneurs had to patch together resources from local and state governments, private foundations, businesses, and charities. Because nonprofit developers enjoy no national support system like the one in Canada, it is difficult to assess their overall impact on the affordable housing problem. Even so, a recent study by the New School for Social Research found that these nonprofit groups have succeeded against overwhelming odds in building and rehabilitating affordable housing in many inner city neighborhoods. Subsidy funds, the study discovered, went to build housing for people of modest means, not for fancy offices or extravagant consulting fees. Most groups began by fixing up a small building or two. Many are still at that early stage of evolution. But quite a few now have the sophistication to construct multimillion-dollar developments (Mayer, 1990; Vidal, 1992).

Roles of Foundations and Corporations

During the 1980s, private foundations and private business groups played key roles in supporting the nonprofit housing sector.

A study by the Council for Community-based Development found that in 1987, 196 corporations and foundations made grants totaling almost $68 million to support nonprofit development. By 1989, the numbers had grown to 307 funders and $90.1 million. That year, 55 of the nation's 100 largest foundations provided grants for community-based development (CCD, 1991).

Two entities—the Local Initiatives Support Corporation (LISC) and the Enterprise Foundation—have been major catalysts for corporate and foundation support to CDCs. LISC was created by the Ford Foundation in 1979 to channel corporate funds to nonprofits. Since then, it has helped more than 700 CDCs in thirty cities produce more than 29,000 units for low- and moderate-income residents (as well as more than 6 million square feet of commercial and industrial space). Developer James Rouse, famous for his new town of Columbia, Maryland, and for urban festival marketplaces in Baltimore, Boston, and New York, set up the Enterprise Foundation. Since 1982, it has provided financial and technical help to more than 190 CDCs in twenty-eight communities, adding more than 17,000 housing units.

In 1978, in response to the public outcry over the banking industry's redlining practices, Congress created the Neighborhood Reinvestment Corporation, chartered to set up local coalitions called neighborhood housing services (NHSs) of banks, local governments, and neighborhood residents to improve housing conditions in urban neighborhoods. Neighborhood Reinvestment Corporation groups have built or repaired nearly 100,000 housing units through 304 NHS chapters in 145 cities, many of which serve as nonprofit development organizations.

In the late 1980s, Boston's United Way began funding CDCs and was so successful that the United Way of America began to fund similar projects in Houston, Chicago, Rochester, York (Pennsylvania) and Pontiac (Michigan). The Lilly Endowment, a large Indianapolis-based foundation, recently established a program to foster cooperation between church groups and nonprofit community developers.

There are other national and regional networks of nonprofit housing organizations. The Georgia-based Habitat for Humanity has a network of local groups with roots in Protestant churches. The McAuley Institute provides technical support to local housing groups affiliated with the Catholic church. The Development Training Institute in Baltimore, Community Builders in Boston, Community Economics in Oakland, California, the Chicago Rehab Network, and the Institute for Community Economics in Springfield, Massachusetts, are five of a growing number of organizations that provide technical assistance to help nonprofit groups improve their management and development capacities.

Municipal Governments and Public-Private Partnerships

As in Canada, the housing crisis of the 1980s, exacerbated by federal cutbacks, put more pressure on municipal governments to address local housing problems. Prior to the 1980s, most large and middle-size cities in the United States ran public housing authorities and regulated housing through zoning and building codes; a few cities adopted laws to protect renters from skyrocketing rents and arbitrary evictions. In terms of developing low-income housing, however, cities generally served solely as conduits for federal funds. During the 1980s, cities took increasing initiative to help expand low-cost housing. In addition to targeting more of their shrinking federal Community Development Block Grant (CDBG) funds to housing, they also donated land; they eased zoning, building code, and fee requirements; they fast-tracked approvals; they provided tax abatements; and they created off-budget housing trust funds from special assessments.

As part of this more proactive approach to housing and community development, a growing number of local governments have provided support to the nonprofit housing sector. Rather than undertake development themselves, most cities have used community-based nonprofit groups as vehicles for housing development and rehabilitation (Nenno, 1986).

Boston is one of several cities that has played a major role in expanding the capacity of this sector. Under Mayor Raymond Flynn, Boston has targeted city funds (including "linkage," CDBG, and HOME funds) and the disposition of city-owned buildings and land directly to about thirty CDCs and other nonprofit developers. Together, they account for more than three-quarters of the subsidized housing created during Flynn's first two terms (1984–1992). In one precedent-setting example, Boston even delegated its authority to seize property by eminent domain to a community group (the Dudley Street Neighborhood Initiative) to assist the group in assembling property for development and neighborhood revitalization in Roxbury. Boston also adopted a "linked deposit" policy to allocate public funds to banks that participate in affordable housing programs with local nonprofit organizations (Dreier and Keating, 1990).

New York City has helped create an impressive array of nonprofit groups to rehabilitate city-owned properties into cooperatives and low-rent apartments. The massive Battery Park City commercial development generated $400 million in funds that the city targeted for affordable housing, most of it sponsored by nonprofits. Oakland, California, used several million dollars from its City Center Development Fund to leverage financing for more than one thousand low-income housing units. San Francisco, like Boston, adopted a linkage program, imposing a tax on commercial projects to fund low-income housing sponsored by nonprofit agencies. Burlington, Vermont, created a citywide community land trust to buy land and buildings, hold the land in trust, and sell the buildings to low- and moderate-income families under affordability controls that last forever.

In Cleveland, Boston, Chicago, San Francisco, Baltimore, Providence, Pittsburgh, New York, Minneapolis, and other cities, business leaders have joined with government officials, foundations, and neighborhood groups to form public-private-community partnerships. Typically, these partnerships serve as umbrella organizations to raise operating funds for CDCs, offer financing for housing projects, streamline approvals, and expand the capacity of nonprofits to undertake large-scale development (Suchman, 1990).

Since 1985, for example, the Boston Housing Partnership has helped neighborhood-based CDCs rehabilitate more than two thousand units of low-rent housing and has recently embarked on a program to help CDCs create limited equity cooperative housing. Businesses participate in CDC-developed housing by providing charitable support to CDCs, by making equity investments in projects (primarily through the federal low-income housing tax credit), and by making loans (on favorable terms) to housing development projects and homebuyers.

The explosion of nonprofit developers represents a real backyard revolution. For example:

- In New York City's decaying East Brooklyn neighborhood, residents raised more than $8 million from their local and national churches to create the Nehemiah Homes, named after the biblical prophet who rebuilt Jerusalem. More than 1,500 homes, sold to working-class families for under $50,000 each, have already been built on thirty-five blocks of vacant land donated by the city.
- In Boston, the bricklayers and laborers' unions set up a nonprofit housing group that in three years has already constructed more than two hundred Victorian-style brick townhouses on city-owned land in three neighborhoods. The unions pressured the bank that holds their pension fund to provide a loan at reduced rates. Families earning an average of $25,000 have purchased the homes for about half their market value under resale restrictions that prevent them from getting windfall profits.
- In Omaha, fifty-eight low-income families are now homeowners, thanks

to the Holy Name Housing Corporation, a church group that trains and employs neighborhood residents to rehabilitate abandoned buildings and sells them to the poor. The group, which has also built a thirty-six-unit apartment building for senior citizens, convinced several local insurance companies to provide low-interest loans to reduce the fix-up costs.

- In Chicago's West Garfield Park neighborhood, Bethel New Life has already completed four hundred homes for the poor and has another four hundred in the pipeline. These are the area's first new homes in more than twenty years. In addition to its housing efforts, the church-based group also runs job-training and recycling programs, operates a health center, provides home care services for the elderly, and employs more than three hundred local residents. Bethel New Life also organizes neighborhoods to get parks improved and streets repaired and to obtain other services.

Because affluent suburbs still resist low-income housing, most nonprofit housing developers are located in inner cities and rural areas. But there are exceptions. For example, in the wealthy community of Santa Barbara, California, where the average home in 1989 sold for more than $275,000, the nonprofit Community Housing Corporation has constructed 462 units—including single-family homes, limited equity cooperatives, and a rooming house hotel—for low-income families and elderly residents.

By now, most state governments have made some effort to support nonprofit housing developers. Some provide funds for technical assistance to help groups improve their capacity to build, own, and manage housing. Some set aside a portion of their housing development budgets specifically for nonprofit organizations. During the Dukakis administration, Massachusetts had perhaps the most expansive state program in the United States assisting nonprofit housing developers (Bishop, 1991; Nenno, 1986).

Dilemmas and Obstacles

Even with these allies in local and state government, business, and foundations, however, the nation's nonprofit housing sector faces at least five serious dilemmas and obstacles to moving from the margins to the mainstream.

First, the nonprofit sector is composed mainly of relatively small organizations whose size limits their ability to achieve economies of scale in terms of development, staffing, management, and overall community impact. Of the 1,160 groups responding to the NCCED survey, only 421 had produced one hundred or more housing units. This represented a significant increase from the 244 groups with that production level only two years earlier, but it reveals that most CDCs are still small-scale operations.

The small size of most CDCs is exacerbated by the complexities of their task, especially under adverse funding conditions. The patchwork of funding sources makes the development of affordable housing extremely complex. To create a twenty-five-unit housing development, for example, a CDC may need to obtain subsidies and grants from ten different sources—corporations, foundations, governments. The various funding programs have different, in fact, often conflicting, deadlines, timetables, and guidelines. As a result, CDC staffpersons often spend more time "grant-grubbing" than developing and managing housing. The legal and financial complexities also require CDCs to engage the services of many lawyers and consultants, adding to the cost and time for getting housing projects underway.

Second, it is difficult to recruit and retain skilled staffpersons within this sector. Most nonprofit housing development groups live from year to year and project to project because they do not have steady, predictable streams of operating funds. Many staffpersons joined the nonprofit world as part of a larger social change agenda, not to get rich. But the frustrations, relative low pay, and insecurity of working in the nonprofit sector leads to a high rate of staff burnout and turnover.

Because most CDCs have few staffpersons, the organizations have little room for upward mobility. And because the nation's nonprofit sector is relatively small and fragmented, it has no clear career path. Some go to work for groups like LISC or Enterprise or for technical assistance groups. In cities that support the nonprofit sector, such as Boston, Chicago, and Baltimore, there is often a "revolving door" between the CDCs and government agencies (which typically offer higher salaries and, in some cases, more job security).

Many CDC staffers came out of the protest and neighborhood movements of the past few decades. Some studied planning and real estate development in college or graduate school, but most learned the highly technical skills required to do development "on the job." Groups such as LISC, Enterprise, the Neighborhood Reinvestment Corporation, the Development Training Institute, and others offer one-day or week-long training programs for CDC staff. But the CDC "industry" has yet to develop a coherent professional training program.

Third, the small scale of individual CDC organizations, the scarcity and unpredictability of operating and development funds, along with the minimalist planning and development efforts of most municipal governments undermine the capacity of CDCs to revitalize entire neighborhoods. CDCs typically work on an incremental, project-by-project basis. In some cases, these efforts fit into a larger overall vision that guides the organization. Some CDCs engage in comprehensive neighborhood planning efforts on their own or in tandem with local government agencies. But even for groups with the resources and skills to undertake these planning efforts, the plans are often unrealized because the resources to implement them are not available. Thus, CDC projects are often isolated efforts within the larger canvas of neighborhood decay.

Fourth, CDCs act as owners and managers of rental and cooperative housing; some establish small business enterprises as well. This means that, despite their social reform mindset, CDCs are also landlords and employers, placing them in a potentially adversarial relationship with their tenants and employees.

The CDC-as-landlord dilemma is particularly troublesome because of the crime, drugs, single parenthood, and related issues that tend to plague the very poor communities in which most CDC projects are located. Some CDCs have developed mixed-income housing, but such projects are difficult to support because it is difficult to attract middle-class residents to troubled neighborhoods. Further, the funding sources for most subsidized housing projects (such as the federal Low Income Housing Tax Credit program) typically require the assisted housing to serve only (or predominantly) the very poor.

As more and more CDCs face the realities of becoming landlords and managers, they are recognizing that they have to deal with human issues as well as with bricks-and-mortar issues. Moreover, most CDCs realize that the problems facing tenants are larger than a well-managed building alone can solve. CDC-sponsored buildings—whether rental, co-op, or ownership—cannot succeed as islands of good management in a sea of neighborhood problems.

A growing number of CDCs have sought to develop job-training, counseling, recreational, child care, and even tenant-organizing and neighborhood crime watch programs to address the social and economic needs of residents. The Resident Resource Initiative of the Boston Housing Partnership, for example, provides funds for CDCs to hire organizers, social workers, and other advocates to assist residents. However, few CDCs have the resources to engage in these efforts. The tight operating budgets for low-income housing rarely provide for adequate security, much less this host of other concerns.

Fifth, and finally, the nonprofit sector is caught in an inherent tension regarding the role of CDCs as community-based housing organizations. For the most part, these groups define themselves as *developers*, focusing on the bricks-and-mortar issues of building housing. The day-to-day task of accomplishing this goal is overwhelming. But most of these groups also affirm their mission to revitalize and empower neighborhoods. That task requires mobilizing community residents, often around controversial issues and against powerful foes—banks, corporations, politicians, and others. Since most CDCs must rely for funding and support on the very institutions that community residents rebel against, they find themselves in a difficult position. They must challenge banks for engaging in redlining; politicians for ignoring the needs of low-income neighborhoods; private firms for discriminatory hiring practices, polluting neighborhood environments, or paying poverty-level wages; or charities (such as the United Way) whose spending priorities may favor the well-to-do (Hadrian, 1988).

With some notable exceptions, the corporations, foundations, governments, and other groups (such as LISC and Enterprise) that provide support to CDCs favor a development agenda over an organizing or mobilizing agenda. Few CDCs can afford to devote much time, resources, or thinking to advocacy.

Some groups, however, do engage in both development and organizing. For example, the Industrial Areas Foundation works with a network of community organizations—such as East Brooklyn Churches in New York City and BUILD in Baltimore—that are involved in Alinsky-style direct action organizing and also develop affordable housing as part of their neighborhood improvement efforts. In Lowell, Massachusetts, the Coalition for a Better Acre recognizes the complementarity of community development and community organizing.

These dilemmas and obstacles are ultimately rooted in the severe shortage of public and private funding for affordable housing. The bootstrap approach has serious limitations. Subsidy funds required to fill the gap between what poor and working-class families can afford and what housing costs to build and operate are scarce. The combined resources provided by all these public and private sources are woefully inadequate to meet the housing needs of most poor and working-class Americans.

Fragmentation and Voluntarism

The fragmented nature of the nonprofit sector has made it difficult to develop the kind of organizational coherence and political support that is found in Canada. Even in the relatively small world of the nonprofit housing sector, there is considerable competition between various national and regional networks over who can "speak for" the movement.

In most cities and states, CDCs and other nonprofit housing groups have no organized voice. There are a few exceptions, however. In New York City, the Association for Neighborhood and Housing Development serves as the trade association for about fifty nonprofit housing organizations. In Massachusetts, New Jersey, California, and elsewhere, CDCs and other nonprofits have formed trade associations to lobby state governments, lenders, and foundations to increase support for the nonprofit sector as well as to provide technical training for members. In some cities and states, they are also part of broader housing coalitions working on legislative issues.

At the national level, the National Congress for Community Economic Development serves as the CDCs' trade association in Washington. LISC, Enterprise, and Neighborhood Reinvestment Corporation also claim much of the same turf. Such competition is typical within social movements and within business sectors, particularly when participants envision a growing pie. In the case of the nonprofit housing sector, some might argue that competition is evidence of an explosion of community organizations and opportunities and that such tensions are healthy. At the same time, turf competition makes it more difficult for the nonprofit sector to mobilize its constituency around a common political agenda and strategy for expanding the resources devoted to low-income housing.

Despite the new emphasis on voluntarism, America's families should not have to depend on corporate or foundation largesse to produce affordable housing. Even the most penny-pinching nonprofit groups acknowledge that the federal government will have to resume a major role if their local success stories are to be repeated on a broad enough scale to relieve the national housing crisis. The growing fiscal crisis of cities and states makes it increasingly difficult to squeeze housing resources out of mayors and city councils, governors and state legislatures. Most states are cutting their housing budgets. It is only at the federal level that enough resources exist to solve the housing crisis. This makes it more imperative than ever for nonprofit housing organizations to work together to change federal housing policy.

Legislative Victories

During the 1980s, the nonprofit sector was relatively impotent in mobilizing political pressure to expand federal housing funds. But some groundwork was laid, so that in the early 1990s, the nonprofit sector won three small but important legislative victories in Congress. These include:

Community Housing Partnerships. In 1987, at the request of Boston Mayor Ray Flynn, Representative Joseph Kennedy (Democrat of Massachusetts) sponsored legislation, the Community Housing Partnership Act, to provide federal funding specifically to help community-based nonprofit groups build and rehabilitate affordable housing for families. A variety of organizations—including the U.S. Conference of Mayors, the National Low-Income Housing Coalition, and the nonprofit sector's various networks (LISC, Enterprise, NCCED)—lobbied on behalf of this legislation.

That same year, developer James Rouse (head of the Enterprise Foundation) and David O. Maxwell (chairman of Fannie Mae) convened a National Housing Task Force at the request of Senator Alan Cranston (cochair of the Senate Committee on Banking, Housing, and Urban Affairs). Composed of a prestigious panel of housing experts, the group issued a report, *A Decent Place to Live*, in March 1988 calling for an increased federal commitment to low-income housing and a specific set-aside for the nonprofit sector.

The Rouse-Maxwell report's recommendations were eventually translated into legislation, the National Affordable Housing Act, that was enacted by Congress in October 1990. This legislation included a new program, HOME, that directed new funds to state and local governments for affordable housing. Representative Kennedy's proposal, Community Housing Partnerships, was folded into the HOME program; it requires that a minimum of 15 percent of HOME funds be allocated to community-based nonprofit organizations.

Low Income Housing Tax Credit. In 1990, 1991, and 1993, the nonprofit sector also successfully mobilized support to extend the federal Low Income Tax Credit, a program that many CDCs use to get private investment in their housing projects. The tax credit is a limited tool: its complexity requires an army of lawyers, and its low-income requirements extend only fifteen years. But groups such as LISC and the Enterprise Foundation have successfully marketed it to major corporations, which derive both profits and high-profile "social responsibility" credit from investing in affordable housing.

Community Reinvestment Act. The nonprofit sector also successfully lobbied Congress in 1990 and 1991 to strengthen the Community Reinvestment Act (CRA), the antiredlining law that gives community groups and local government leverage to pressure banks to invest in inner cities. Under pressure from community activists, many banks have sought to demonstrate their commitment to the goals of the CRA by initiating or expanding support for CDC-sponsored developments. In 1991, out of these battles over the CRA, LISC and the Enterprise Foundation—along with activist groups such as ACORN and the Center for Community Change—formed a new Community Reinvestment Coalition that is funded by several large national foundations. The coalition will help to coordinate the work of the nonprofit sector and other housing advocacy groups around CRA-related issues.

All three legislative victories are important steps. But Congress has not restored housing even to the level of federal assistance of the pre-Reagan years. In 1981, the U.S. housing budget was $33 billion. By 1989, it had fallen to $9 billion. In 1992, it had increased only slightly, to about $11 billion. Federal housing policy continues to be both inadequate and distorted. Today, according to HUD, only 29 percent of eligible low-income renter households—4.07 million out of 13.81 million—receive any kind of federal housing subsidy (Casey, 1992). Even fewer low-income homeowners receive any subsidy.

In contrast, most affluent Americans—many living in mansions—get housing aid from Washington through the regressive homeowner income tax deduction. This tax expenditure cost the federal government more than $47 billion in 1991 alone. About one-third of this subsidy goes to the 3.8 percent of taxpayers with incomes above $100,000, and about 12 percent goes to the wealthiest 1 percent of taxpayers with incomes above $200,000. More than half of these tax breaks (51.6 percent) go to the 8 percent of taxpayers with annual incomes above $75,000. Yet half of all homeowners do not claim deductions at all. Tenants, of course, don't even qualify (Dreier and Atlas, 1992).

The closest thing to a Canadian-style social housing program is legislation sponsored by Representative Ron Dellums of California called the National Comprehensive Housing Act. This bill, drafted by an Institute for Policy Studies task force, calls for an annual expenditure of $50 billion (IPS, 1989). The federal government would make direct capital grants to nonprofit groups to build and rehabilitate affordable housing, as well as to purchase existing privately owned housing for transfer to nonprofits. These homes would remain in the "social" sector, never again to be burdened with debt. Occupants would pay only the operating costs, which would be dramatically lower than what poor and working-class families currently pay for housing. The Dellums bill is clearly a visionary program but not a winnable one in the current political climate.

A Constituency for Affordable Housing?

Currently, America's housing advocacy movement—and the nonprofit housing sector within it—lacks the political support to significantly reorder the nation's misguided housing priorities. The hard truth is that housing is still a marginal issue in American politics. It was not a major issue in the 1992 presidential campaign, and it is not a "win or lose" issue in congressional campaigns. When journalists write about key domestic issues, they include health care, child care, education, and usually crime and the environment, but rarely affordable housing.

Part of the housing advocacy movement's difficulty is that the current political climate is hostile to activist government. The conservative agenda—deregulation, privatization, reduced social programs, opposition to taxes, overt and subtle appeals to racism—has dominated the public debate. Federal housing programs are caught in the cross fire. Much of the public is convinced that government in general—and government housing programs, in particular—doesn't work. To most citizens, government housing programs mean publicly owned or publicly subsidized projects in poor repair. In fact, public housing is often used as a metaphor for the failure of activist government. The most recent HUD scandal fed this skepticism. Most people believe that low-income housing programs reward some combination of government bureaucrats, politically connected developers, and people who engage in antisocial or self-destructive behavior.

The housing advocacy movement has, for the most part, been unable to put forward an alternative vision with broad appeal. It has yet to find a way to frame the issue so that it appeals to middle-class people and suburbanites. Community-based nonprofit housing has the potential to remedy this situation. It is an alternative to "government housing" that plays into conservative themes of self-help, voluntarism, and entrepreneurship. For example, a *New York Times* story of March 8, 1992, about an Enterprise Foundation–assisted project in Brooklyn carries the headline: "How to Build Low-Cost Housing the Private Way." But whether this approach will succeed is still not clear because ultimately even the nonprofit sector requires more government money to succeed.

Politically, the constituencies engaged in the housing issue are extremely narrow. The coalitions that promoted government-assisted housing from the 1940s through the 1970s—builders, mortgage bankers, unions, and housing activists—fell apart in the 1980s. During the past few years, there has been some effort to broaden the housing constituency, but it has been only marginally successful.

Some sectors of the business community have begun to recognize the importance of the housing problem in terms of the nation's business climate (Dreier, Schwartz, and Greiner, 1988). As with health care and child care, high costs in housing are increasingly becoming a barrier to business profits. If the American work force is to be competitive in an increasingly global economy, some argue, individual employers cannot be burdened with subsidizing housing, health care, child care, and other living costs. The success of some of America's competitors is due, in part, to the role their governments play in subsidizing these costs. In recent years, a growing segment of the American business community has become sympathetic to some version of government-sponsored universal health care and child care. Housing may be the next item on this agenda.

A few unions are beginning to focus more seriously on affordable housing. For the building trades unions, the reason is obvious: the poor housing industry is causing high unemployment among building trades members. More housing means more jobs and a jump-start for economic recovery. Nevertheless, this recognition has not yet galvanized the Building Trades Council, much less the AFL-CIO, to focus attention on a national housing policy as it has, for example, on national health care.[4]

Other activist constituencies—women's groups, seniors, civil rights organizations, and environmentalists—also have a stake in the housing struggle. Among environmentalists, there is a natural alliance around such issues as lead paint. Women's groups rally around the feminization of homelessness and the importance of linking subsidized housing with human services. Civil rights groups respond to the persistence of redlining and housing discrimination. All may eventually find common cause with the hundreds of nonprofit developers that have been struggling for over a decade not only to provide affordable housing, but to make the issue of affordable housing a higher priority of United States policy.

CONCLUSION

What housing lessons can the United States learn from Canada? The Canadian experience demonstrates that it takes time to build the capacity of the nonprofit sector. There are no quick fixes. It cannot be done if housing policies zigzag, making it impossible to build up the staffing and organizational infrastructure needed to make the nonprofit sector a real player in the housing business. Canada has spent almost thirty years developing and investing in a nonprofit housing *system* with clear guidelines, dependable funding, and strong (often community-based) nonprofit developers and managers. In the United States, it will take at least a decade to move the country's nonprofit housing sector from the margins to the mainstream. But Canada shows that the incubation process pays off down the road.

Canadians have recognized that for a social housing program to be successful, nonprofit *production* is not enough. It must also be accompanied by social *ownership* that provides for long-term affordability and keeps the housing in the social sector.

Both the U.S. and the Canadian experience shows that there are no cheap or easy solutions to the housing problem. Housing is expensive. There is no way around this fact. No magic formula is going to lead to low-cost provision of high quality housing for lower-income people. Good, affordable housing for everyone, just like good, affordable, universal health care, is fundamental to human well-being. The commitment of society—through government spending—is necessary.

More broadly, Canadians still believe that government can help solve social and economic problems—and they are more willing than their U.S. counterparts to pay taxes to make government work. Canada's third sector housing movement, moreover, is part of a strong progressive movement (including community-based organizations, churches, and labor unions) supporting candidates and policies that address the needs of working-class and middle-class populations. Further, because Canada's social programs are broad based, they are not stigmatized as targeted solely to the poor. In the United States, the view that subsidized housing is a welfare program primarily serving inner-city minorities undermines its support among the economically pinched white middle class. Canada has its share of racial and ethnic hostility, but these tensions have not become an excuse to dismantle government social programs.

Canada's housing policy is part of its overall progressive approach to social policy. The distribution of income is similar in the two countries. As in the United States, about one-seventh of the Canadian population is poor. Housing subsidies do not alone account for the comparatively better living conditions of Canada's poor and working-class families. A universal health insurance program, a good unemployment insurance program, and a variety of family support programs play roles in creating a relatively better housing and urban quality of life for Canadians than for Americans (Hanratty and Blank, 1992).

This progressive approach is also reflected in the tax system. Canada does not allow mortgage interest or property tax deductions for homeowners. In the late 1970s, when inflation and interest rates were very high, a proposal to introduce such a tax deduction for Canadian homeowners was defeated and is no longer seriously discussed because of its inequity and its potential impact on the federal deficit. Even though Canadians do not enjoy this tax benefit, the homeownership rates in the United States and Canada are virtually identical.

A major reason why Canada can afford strong housing and other social programs is that only a very small portion of the federal budget goes for defense. Housing advocates in the United States hope that the collapse of communism and changes in their country's competitive position in the world economy will result in a "peace dividend"—cuts in the bloated Pentagon budget—that can translate into expanded budgets for affordable housing and other social needs. Some members of Congress are likely to view defense cuts as an opportunity to reduce the budget deficit rather than to address the domestic agenda. But the Clinton administration and the present Congress have pledged to address domestic concerns. To do this will require a major shift from military to civilian spending.

As America's housing crisis deepens, it could become an explosive political issue. Policymakers will be looking for new approaches and solutions.

The recent HUD scandal provides an opportunity to rethink how housing is delivered for the many U.S. citizens who are not well served by the marketplace. Clearly, the nation must spend much more on housing if it is to address the growing housing needs of its people. But even if Congress were willing to find the funds—by cutting defense spending or raising taxes on the wealthy and big business—it would be difficult to convince the public that its money had been well spent if it wound up lining the pockets of politically connected builders.

The nonprofit approach provides an alternative. It should appeal to Republicans who emphasize self-help, entrepreneurship, and grassroots initiative. And it should make sense to Democrats who want to show that government programs can serve the needy without getting entangled in wasteful bureaucracy or political favoritism. Canada has demonstrated that social housing can work on a major scale. The United States should learn this lesson from its neighbor to the north.

APPENDIX: COST CONSIDERATIONS IN CANADA'S SOCIAL HOUSING PROGRAM

In 1986, in order to encourage the provinces to become more active in housing, the federal government entered into agreements with each province whereby the province plays a more significant role in implementing federal social housing programs in its jurisdiction. In exchange, the provinces began paying a share (about 25 percent) of the program costs (Banting, 1990). Prior to that time, the federal government financed the full subsidy cost of the nonprofit program.

Attempts by political conservatives and the real estate lobby to replace Canada's social housing supply programs with a U.S.-style private rent supplement or voucher approach to housing subsidies have been vigorous at times. Canada has a small private rent supplement program, which dates back to 1970. Over the past decade new commitments have averaged about 1,500 units per year, mainly to address special situations in different regions of the country (CMHC, 1992b). Instead of any conclusive evidence about the comparative long-term cost-effectiveness of the options—analysis that is very difficult to carry out in a convincing and conclusive fashion—commonsense arguments have, in the end, carried a great deal of weight in the public debate.

The Ontario Government's Ministry of Housing recently examined the average per unit subsidy costs for its huge public housing portfolio (about 84,000 units), for its private sector rent supplement program (20,000 units), and for the monthly subsidy cost of the new nonprofit housing units it is providing this year (with a total of 117,000 nonprofit housing units in the province). These figures do not offer any conclusive proof in the debate between the cash transfer approach (rent supplements and/or vouchers) versus the in-kind transfers approach (social housing supply), but they do shed light on the issue of long-term versus short-term cost-effectiveness of each approach. The 1992–93 subsidy costs for public housing, which includes both the federal and provincial share of the subsidies, is under $300 Cdn. per unit, which includes the average capital costs per unit of a large-scale repair to the portfolio. These costs are less than the $400 to $500 per unit average for the private sector rent supplement units. The average monthly subsidy cost of the new nonprofit housing units is about $950 per month (Housing Policy Branch, Ontario Ministry of Housing, Toronto, Jan. 1993).

As in the case of homeownership, however, the monthly costs of the nonprofit housing units are the highest in the initial years. These costs decline over time. Like the public housing units, nonprofit units will eventually have a relatively low per-month subsidy cost. The nonprofit housing program, therefore, even with its higher initial costs, is eventually much more cost effective than the rent supplement program. This cost comparison data for the public sector only confirms what many people know at a personal level: owning a home is cheaper than renting over the long term. This conclusion was verified recently in a study carried out for the Canadian Home Builders' Association:

> In general, owners' shelter costs are greater than renters' for several years following the purchase of a home. However, over time, rents rise with inflation while the main component of owners' shelter costs (the mortgage payment) stays relatively constant (except when interest rates rise). As a consequence, over the long-term, owners' shelter costs are significantly lower than renters'. This is particularly true once the mortgage is repaid. (Clayton Research Associates, 1992: i)

The analogous choice in the housing subsidy cost effectiveness debate is between owning (public or nonprofit housing options) versus renting (rent supplement or housing voucher options).

Until the third major revision in the government's social housing funding formula, co-ops and other nonprofits had a similar funding formula. In 1986 the federal government and the cooperative housing movement agreed to experiment with a new mortgage instrument for co-ops, substituting the index-linked mortgage (ILM) for the equal payment mortgage (EPM). Interest rates on index-linked mortgages are based on a fixed "real" rate of return, the rate of return the lender wants after inflation, plus a variable rate that is adjusted according to inflation. Therefore no provision has to be built into the rate of interest to take account of inflation risk, as there is in equal payment mortgages. This makes the initial payments of ILMs much more affordable to potential borrowers. To maintain the "real" rate of return that the lender wants, the interest rate is adjusted periodically according to the rate of inflation over the previous year (CMHC, 1986). After five years the federal evaluation of the new mortgage instrument found that lower than real interest rates for comparable investments were realized by the ILM, making it "a more cost effective mortgage instrument than the EPM," resulting in savings that helped make the latest funding formula "a more cost effective way to deliver cooperative housing" than the previous formula (CMHC, 1992a: 329–330).

NOTES

1. We use the word "subsidized" to describe housing that receives direct government grants, loans, or insurance that lower the cost of that housing to below-market levels. We do not include housing whose owners receive tax breaks like mortgage interest deductions or accelerated depreciation and whose owners are not required to target that housing to lower-income residents.

2. The United States opted in the 1960s and 1970s to replace its public housing program with incentives such as tax write-offs, discount mortgages, and rent subsidies to induce for-profit developers to build housing for the poor. One such incentive was an escape clause that required developers to keep rents targeted for the poor for only twenty years. The public housing supply program was, in essence, privatized. The taxpayer still paid for the project, but a private developer built and managed it in exchange for owning it and being able to cash in on the land and building value twenty years later. The program thereby guaranteed a rolling depletion of private low-rent housing built at public expense. This American approach has created a highly unstable low-rent housing stock. At the bottom end, many subsidized units were thinly capitalized and badly managed. Many were abandoned by their owners; one-third of the projects in an early HUD rental subsidy program were ultimately foreclosed. At the opposite end of the market, the financially successful units were also at risk of being withdrawn from the supply of affordable housing, as landlords saw opportunities to convert them to market-rate rental apartments or condominiums, particularly in the hot 1980s housing market. Congress intervened in 1990 to restrict the landlords' options, but at the extremely costly price of providing further bribes to prevent them from withdrawing from the government subsidy program. In addition, the allocation of profitable housing subsidies has been chronically vulnerable to political favoritism. Scarce grants often went not to

the best developers but to the best-connected ones. The recent corruption scandal at HUD was popularly reported as a story of how Reagan administration officials steered scarce subsidies to political insiders. But the real issue at HUD concerns the roles that government, private developers, and community organizations ought to play in an effective national program for affordable housing.

3. During the early 1980s, CMHC sought to develop an improved method of determining housing need. What is now called the Core Housing Need Model is an indicator of total housing need combining measures of housing adequacy, suitability, and affordability. It is based on data collected every two years from a specially designed Shelter Cost Survey carried out for CMHC by Statistics Canada, a government agency (CMHC, 1991). Similarly, the Bush administration sought to undermine support for subsidized housing by targeting assistance exclusively to the poorest of the poor. For a discussion of targeting in the United States, see Nelson and Khadduri (1992) and the comments by Stegman (1992) and Cavanaugh (1992).

4. Indeed, there appears to be an emerging conflict between CDCs and unions. This controversy has been simmering for several years. It boiled over in a *New York Times* story (February 24, 1992) about a union picket of a single-room-occupancy project in Times Square sponsored by a nonprofit group (Common Group, Inc.) with funding from the City of New York. The issue was whether the contractor was nonunion. Nationwide, in the current recession, with very little new construction on large-scale projects, the building trades unions have begun to focus on smaller-scale projects, including housing. With the costs of financing, land, and materials relatively fixed—and limited subsidies for tight budget housing projects—many nonprofit groups look to save money on "labor costs." This puts them in direct conflict with unions, which fought hard over the years to raise the working conditions and wages of their members. This is not a problem in Canada, where the labor movement is strongly supportive of social housing programs and where unions and social housing developers are allies within the NDP. As a result, most social housing projects use union workers.

REFERENCES

Affordable Housing: The Years Ahead. Manual. New York: Ford Foundation, 1989.

Apgar, William, et al. *The State of the Nation's Housing*. Cambridge, Mass.: Harvard University Joint Center for Housing Studies, 1991.

Bacher, J. "Canadian Housing Policy in Perspective." *Urban History Review* 15, no. 1 (1986): 3–18.

Banting, Keith G. "Social Housing in a Divided State." In George Fallis and Alex Murray (eds.), *Housing the Homeless and the Poor: New Partnerships among the Private, Public, and Third Sectors*, pp. 115–163. Toronto: University of Toronto Press, 1990.

Birch, E. L., and D. S. Gardner. "The Seven Percent Solution: A Review of Philanthropic Housing, 1870–1910." *Journal of Urban History* 7 (1981): 403–438.

Bishop, Catherine M. *Building on Success: A Report on State Capacity-Building Programs Targeted to Nonprofit Housing Developers*. Washington, D.C.: National Support Center for Low-Income Housing, 1991.

Bratt, Rachel. "Dilemmas of Community-Based Housing." *Policy Studies Journal* 16, no. 2 (1987): 324–334.

Canada, Federal Task Force on Housing and Urban Development. *Report of the Federal Task Force on Housing and Urban Development*. Ottawa: January 1969.

Canada Mortgage and Housing Corporation. *The Federal Co-operative Housing Program—Featuring Index-Linked Mortgages*. Ottawa: CMHC, 1986.

———. *Public Housing Program: Program Evaluation Report, Summary*. Ottawa: CMHC, 1990.

———. *Core Housing Need in Canada*. Ottawa: CMHC, 1991.

———. *Evaluation of the Federal Co-operative Housing Program*. Ottawa: CMHC, 1992a.

———. *Urban Social Housing Programs Evaluation Assessment Report: Non-Profit, Urban Native and Rent Supplement*. Ottawa: CMHC, 1992b.

Carter, Tom, and Ann McAfee. "The Municipal Role in Housing the Homeless and Poor." In George Fallis and Alex Murray (eds.), *Housing the Homeless and Poor: New Partnerships among the Private, Public, and Third Sectors*. Toronto: University of Toronto Press, 1990.

Casey, Connie H. "Characteristics of HUD-Assisted Renters and Their Units in 1989." Washington, D.C.: U.S. Department of Housing and Urban Development, Office of Policy Development and Research, March 1992.

Cavanaugh, Gordon. "Comment on Nelson and Khadduri." *Housing Policy Debate* 3, no. 1 (1992): 67–75.

Clancy, Patrick, Langley C. Keyes, Edward Marchant, and Robert Whittlesey. "The Role of Nonprofit Organizations in the Housing Process." Mimeographed report to HUD, 1973.

Clayton Research Associates. *Homeownership as an Investment*. Report. Toronto: Canadian Home Builders' Association, 1992.

Community Information Exchange and United Way of America, *Raising the Roof: A Sampler of Community Partnerships for Affordable Housing*. Washington, D.C., 1988.

Cooper, M., and M. C. Rodman. *New Neighbors: A Case Study of Cooperative Housing in Toronto*. Toronto: University of Toronto Press, 1992.

Council for Community-based Development (CCD). *Expanding Horizons: A Research Report on Corporate and Foundation Grant Support of Community-based Development*. Washington, D.C., Fall 1991.

Deyle, C. J., and J. David Hulchanski. "The Housing Affordability Gap in Canada: The Need for a Comprehensive Approach." In Robert B. Katz (ed.), *Housing in the '90s: Common Issues*. Urbana: University of Illinois Press, 1989.

Dreier, Peter. "Progressive Housing Policy in Canada," *Shelterforce*, 13, no. 4 (1991): 12–15, 19.

———. "Redlining Cities: How Banks Color Community Development." *Challenge*, November/December 1991.

Dreier, Peter, and John Atlas. "How to Expand Homeownership for More Americans." *Challenge*, March/April 1992.

Dreier, Peter, and W. Dennis Keating. "The Limits of Localism: Progressive Housing Policies in Boston, 1984–1989." *Urban Affairs Quarterly* 26, no. 2 (1990): 191–216.

Dreier, Peter, David Schwartz, and Ann Greiner. "What Every Business Can Do about Housing." *Harvard Business Review* 66, no. 5 (September/October 1988): 52–61.

Hadrian, Ricanne. "Combining Organizing and Housing Development: Conflictive yet Synergistic." M.C.P. thesis, Department of Urban Studies and Planning, MIT, 1988.

Hanratty, Maria, and Rebecca Blank. "Down and Out in North America: Recent Trends in Poverty Rates in the United States and Canada." *Quarterly Journal of Economics* 48 (February 1992).

Hodgkinson, Virginia A., Richard W. Lymann, and Associates (eds.). *The Future of the Nonprofit Sector*. San Francisco: Jossey-Bass, 1989.

Hulchanski, J. David. "The Evolution of Property Rights and Housing Tenure in Post-War Canada: Implications for Housing Policy." *Urban Law and Policy*, 9, no. 2 (1988): 135–156.

———. "Canada's Housing and Housing Policy: An Introduction." School of Community and Regional Planning, University of British Columbia, Vancouver, June 1988.

———. "Canada." In Willem van Vliet (ed.), *International Handbook of Housing Policy and Practices*, pp. 289–325. New York: Greenwood Press, 1990.

Hulchanski, J. David, M. Eberle, M. Lytton, and K. Olds. "The Municipal Role in the Supply and Maintenance of Low Cost Housing: A Review of Canadian Initiatives." Vancouver: Centre for Human Settlements, University of British Columbia, 1990.

Institute for Policy Studies (IPS). *The Right to Housing: A Blueprint for Housing the Nation*. Washington, D.C., 1989.

Keating, W. Dennis, Keith P. Rasey, and Norman Krumholz. "Community Development Corporations in the United States: Their Role in Housing and Urban Redevelopment." In Willem van Vliet and Jan van Weesep (eds.), *Government and Housing*, pp. 206–218. Newbury Park, Calif.: Sage Publications, 1990.

Kelly, Christine, Donald Kelly, and Ed Marciniak. *Non-Profits with Hard Hats: Building Affordable Housing*. Washington, D.C.: National Center for Urban Ethnic Affairs, 1988.

Leonard, Paul, Cushing Dolbaare, and Edward Lazare. *A Place to Call Home: The Crisis in Housing for the Poor*. Washington, D.C.: Center on Budget and Policy Priorities and the Low Income Housing Information Service, 1989.

Mayer, Neil S. *Neighborhood Organizations and Community Development*. Washington, D.C.: Urban Institute Press, 1984.

———. "The Role of Nonprofits in Renewed Federal Housing Efforts." In Denise DiPasquale and Langley C. Keyes (eds.), *Building Foundations: Housing and Federal Policy*, pp. 365–388. Philadelphia: University of Pennsylvania Press, 1990.

Miron, John R. *Housing in Postwar Canada*. Kingston and Montreal: McGill/Queen's University Press, 1988.

National Housing Task Force. *A Decent Place to Live*. Report. Washington, D.C., March 1988.

National Congress for Community Economic Development (NCCED). *Against All Odds: The Achievements of Community-based Development Organizations*. Washington, D.C.: NCCED, March 1989.

———. *Changing the Odds: The Achievements of Community-based Development Corporations*. Washington, D.C., December 1991.

———. *Community-Based Development: Investing in Renewal*. Washington, D.C., September 1987.

National League of Cities. *A Time to Build Up: A Survey of Cities about Housing Policy*. Washington, D.C., 1989.

Nelson, Kathryn P., and Jill Khadduri. "To Whom Should Limited Housing Resources Be Directed?" *Housing Policy Debate* 3, no. 1 (1992): 1–56.

Nenno, Mary. *New Money and New Methods: A Catalog of State and Local Initiatives in Housing and Community Development*. Washington, D.C.: National Association of Housing and Redevelopment Officials, 1986.

Peirce, Neal R., and Carol F. Steinbach. *Corrective Capitalism: The Rise of America's Community Development Corporations*. New York: Ford Foundation, 1987.

———. *Enterprising Communities: Community-based Development in America*. Washington, D.C.: Council for Community-based Development, 1990.

Powell, Walter (ed.). *The Nonprofit Sector*. New Haven: Yale University Press, 1987.

Roberts, Benson F., and Fern C. Portnoy. "Rebuilding a New Low-Income Housing Industry: A Growing Role for the Nonprofit Sector." In Marshall Kaplan and Franklin James (eds.), *The Future of National Urban Policy*, Durham, N.C.: Duke University Press, 1990.

Rose, Albert. *Canadian Housing Policies (1935–1980)*. Toronto: Butterworths, 1980.

Selby, J., and A. Wilson. *Canada's Housing Cooperatives: An Alternative Ap-*

proach to Resolving Community Problems. Vancouver: University of British Columbia Planning Papers, 1988.

Skloot, Edward, and Margaret Seip. "The Activities and Accomplishments of New York City's Community Development Organizations." New York: New Ventures, January 1989.

Stegman, Michael A. "Comment on Nelson and Khadduri." *Housing Policy Debate* 3, no. 1 (1992): 57–66.

Suchman, Diane R. (ed.). *Public/Private Housing Partnerships*. Washington, D.C.: Urban Land Institute, 1990.

Vidal, Avis. *Rebuilding Communities: A National Study of Urban Community Development Corporations*. New York: New School for Social Research, Community Development Research Center, 1992.

Wekerle, G. R. "Canadian Women's Housing Cooperatives: Case Studies in Physical and Social Innovation." In C. Andrew and B. More Milroy (eds.), *Life Spaces: Gender, Households, Employment*, pp. 102–140. Vancouver: University of British Columbia Press, 1988.

Wolfe, J. M., and W. Jay. "The Revolving Door: Third Sector Organizations and the Homeless." In George Fallis and Alex Murray (eds.), *Housing the Homeless and the Poor: New Partnerships Among Private, Public, and Third Sectors*, pp. 197–226. Toronto: University of Toronto Press, 1990.

Zdenek, Robert. "Community Development Corporations." In Severyn T. Bruyn and James Meehan (eds.), *Beyond the Market and the State: New Directions in Community Development*, pp. 112–127. Philadelphia: Temple University Press, 1987.

2 Beyond the Market and the State: The Diverse Domain of Social Housing

JOHN EMMEUS DAVIS

Housing policy in the United States at every level of government has seldom been tenure neutral. It has, in fact, been tenure specific: tilted quite intentionally toward privately owned, market-priced homes or, as a somewhat reluctant second choice, toward privately owned, for-profit rentals. No other form of housing has received from the public sector anywhere near the amount of financial assistance, legal protection, and political support long lavished on this privileged pair.

Aside from the special case of military housing, the only form of *public ownership* that has received regular—though grudging—governmental support has been that embodied in locally chartered public housing authorities (PHAs). The ownership of housing by other governmental or quasi-governmental bodies has rarely been a subject of serious public debate, let alone a recipient of public largess. Until recently, alternative forms of *private ownership* have not fared much better. The American celebration of fee simple, market-priced homeownership and the American acceptance of unrestricted for-profit rentals have combined to force other forms of private tenure out of the spotlight of public policy and into the shadows of the underfunded and unfamiliar.

Despite such historic neglect, alternative models of private, nonmarket housing have proliferated during the last decade or two. They have even begun to attract a modicum of governmental support, especially at the municipal level. Such support has multiple causes, but none is more compelling than a dawning recognition that neither the traditional PHA-style housing of the public sector nor the traditional market-rate housing of the private sector is a very effective vehicle for community efforts to improve the housing situations of low- and moderate-income people. Particularly in the case of market-priced homeownership and for-profit rentals, a growing number of public officials and community activists have come to realize that neither of these market-driven forms of tenure are very well suited to preserving the scarce subsidies, public and private, that are necessary to bring private housing within the reach of persons of modest means; even less suited are they to preserving the hard-won affordability of this assisted housing.

By contrast, the retention of subsidies and the preservation of affordability are the forte of the many models of privately owned, socially oriented, price-restricted housing that have lately been winning wider acceptance in the United States. These third sector models of tenure, collectively known as *social housing*, are becoming quite numerous—and quite diverse. Indeed, new models of social housing, along with innovative mixtures or modifications of old models, have been appearing on the American scene with surprising regularity in recent years.

Although a hopeful sign of the continuing search for new ways of meeting the housing needs of poor and moderate-income people, such intense innovation can be a bit problematic. Multiple models of social housing can be confusing for someone searching for the best way of promoting and preserving affordable housing. Such a crowded, varied, and changing landscape can make it difficult to know which direction to take, which model to pursue. What is needed is an overview of the current scene. What is needed is a conceptual map, one that identifies not only the major landmarks within the diverse domain of social housing but the differences and distances among them.

A SOCIAL HOUSING CONTINUUM

Six models of social housing may conveniently serve as points of reference for all the rest. They are: the deed-restricted, owner-occupied house; the community land trust; the limited equity condominium; the limited equity (or zero equity) cooperative; the mutual housing association; and multiple forms of nonprofit rental housing. All are differentiated from the more traditional tenures of the market and the state by providing housing that is privately owned, socially oriented, and price restricted.[1] They are differentiated *from one another* by variations in the legal and organizational means by which the affordability of social housing is maintained and by variations in the "bundle of rights" to which the occupants of social housing are entitled.

The affordability of social housing is perpetuated legally and organizationally by means of:

1. a *pricing formula*, which defines the maximum price at which the housing may be rented or resold; a cap intended to maintain rents and resale prices at an affordable level for some targeted class of low-income or moderate-income persons;
2. a *legal mechanism* by which the pricing formula is contractually imposed on the housing's current (and future) owners; and
3. an *administrative structure* for monitoring and enforcing any restrictions on price (and use) imposed on the housing.

Although common to all models of social housing, these three elements can vary quite significantly. The second and third, in particular, help to distinguish one model of social housing from another.[2] Each model employs a different legal mechanism in imposing rent and resale restrictions. Each establishes a different administrative structure for enforcing these restrictions over time.

These models are distinguished from one another as well by the type of tenure that each establishes for the people who occupy social housing. For each model, there is a unique distribution of a residential property's "bundle of rights" between its current occupants and some other entity, such as a nonprofit corporation with a legal interest in that property.[3] For each model, the rights reserved for the residents—what might be called the "occupant's interest"—are different and distinct.

The "occupant's interest" not only *differentiates* these models of social housing but *positions* each in relation to the rest along a tenurial continuum stretching between owner-occupied housing and tenant-occupied housing (see Figure 2-1). Toward the homeowner end of this tenure line, most of a property's bundle of rights are held by its occupants: only a few "sticks" have been removed from those traditionally possessed by the individual homeowner; only a few "sticks" of use and control have been conveyed to someone else. Toward the other end of the tenure line, most of these rights are held by someone other than the occupants—typically a corporate landlord. Only a few "sticks" of the property's bundle of rights are possessed individually and exclusively by those who make that property their home.

The continuum that is formed when all six of these "landmark" models of social housing are placed on the tenure line represents a series of cumulative changes in the "occupant's interest." Turned on its side with tenant-

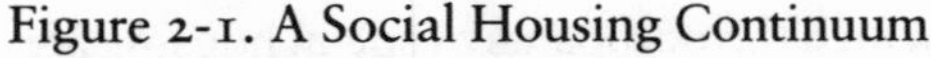

Figure 2-1. A Social Housing Continuum

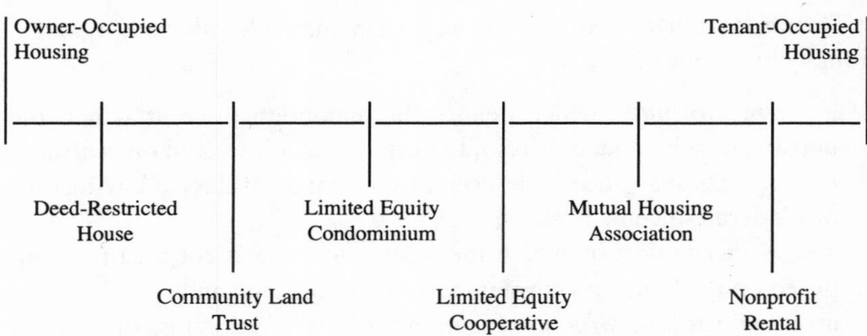

occupied housing at the bottom, this social housing continuum looks more like a "tenure ladder," an ascending series of small steps between tenancy and homeownership. But there is a connotation in this latter term of one model being "higher" or "better" than another that I would prefer to avoid. After examining each model more closely, I will return to the question of comparative advantage, asking which model might be best in a general policy promoting social housing.

Deed-restricted, Owner-occupied House

Occupant's Interest. This model could just as well be called "resale restricted house" or "limited equity house." I have chosen "deed-restricted, owner-occupied house" to highlight its two most distinctive features. The first is the common use of a *deed*, encumbered by a covenant or option, to restrict prices and preserve affordability. The model's other distinctive feature is that the occupants of a single-family house are also its *owners*, though at least one important "stick" is removed from an owner-occupant's traditional bundle of rights: the right to resell that house at market value.[4] The owner-occupant has an exclusive interest in a parcel of land, in the structural improvements on that land, and in any mineral, water, or development rights accompanying that land.

Legal Mechanism. This interest in real property is evidenced and secured by the occupant's possession of a deed for both the land and the improvements. Embedded in the owner-occupant's deed is either a preemptive option or a restrictive covenant that contractually controls the property's future affordability. A *preemptive option* gives a nonprofit corporation, a public agency, or some other party the first right to repurchase the homeowner's property at a restricted price determined by a formula that is part of the option. A *restrictive covenant* imposes an obligation on the owner-occupant to resell the property at the restricted, formula-driven price to someone from a specified pool of income-eligible buyers. In either case, these resale restrictions run with the land and bind any subsequent owners.

On occasion, these same restrictions have been embedded not in the property's deed but in either a mortgage or a free-standing contract. Instead of running with the land, these contracts bind only the current owner-occupant and must be renegotiated and renewed with each subsequent buyer. In the case of restrictions inserted into a mortgage—whether the first mortgage or a subordinate one—these affordability controls are binding upon the current owner-occupant only so long as the mortgage itself remains in effect. Paying off the mortgage releases the homeowner from any continuing obligation to resell the property at a restricted price.

Administrative Structure. It is not unusual for the sponsors and proponents of single-family housing encumbered with restrictive covenants to claim that this model is "self-enforcing." Their assertion is that covenants running with the land ensure perpetual affordability and that administrative oversight is unnecessary. Should the current owner-occupant attempt to resell the property in violation of the covenants contained in the deed, so the argument goes, either the buyer, the buyer's lender, the buyer's lawyer, or the company being asked to issue insurance on the property's title will block the sale. These outside agents function, in effect, as the ultimate enforcers of long-term affordability.

The confidence put in outside agents has often proven, in practice, to be misplaced. Interested sellers and interested buyers have found ingenious ways to circumvent the scrutiny of the outside parties presumed to enforce affordability at the time of sale. "Self-enforcing" deed restrictions have also failed, in some states, simply because state law either limits the duration of such affordability covenants or requires some party with a real interest in the property (and its covenant) to publicly and periodically assert that interest—or else the covenant lapses.[5]

Learning from past failures, most sponsors of deed-restricted housing have turned over the task of enforcing affordability to either a nonprofit organization or a public agency. This administrative entity oversees all subsequent sales of the price-restricted houses, purchasing the properties at the formula-determined price and reselling to other income-eligible buyers or monitoring the direct transfer of the properties from seller to buyer. Under either arrangement, an interested organization or agency is there to ensure that the house is actually sold to the "right" buyer at the "right" price.

Variations. As a final note on this model, it should be pointed out that detached, single-family, owner-occupied houses are neither the only type of housing nor the only tenure for which continuing affordability has been achieved through a preemptive option or restrictive covenant embedded in a property's deed. Deed restrictions have been used to preserve the affordability of townhouses, row houses, and multiunit apartment buildings. They have also been used as a second line of defense in protecting the long-term affordability of limited equity condominiums, limited equity cooperatives, and nonprofit rentals.[6]

Community Land Trust

The community land trust (CLT) is a dual ownership model: one party holds the deed to a parcel of land; another party holds the deed to a house (and to any other structural improvements) located upon that land. The owner of the land is a nonprofit, community-based corporation. The owner of the improvements is usually a single family but may be an individual, a cooperative, a nonprofit corporation, or any other legal entity.

Occupant's Interest. The occupant of a land trust house—or, more accurately, the occupant of a house located on land trust land—is the owner of that house. Most of the "sticks" in the bundle of rights traditionally held by the American homeowner are held by the occupant, including those associated with security of tenure, privacy of use, (some) equity on resale, a legacy for one's heirs, and the right to control and change one's own living space according to personal tastes and needs. The occupant also holds a long-term lease for the land lying beneath the house. This lease typically runs for ninety-nine years, unless a shorter term is indicated by state law. It is renewable and inheritable. It conveys to the homeowner/leaseholder a possessory interest in the parcel of land on which his or her home is located.

Legal Mechanism. The ground lease is also the means by which several important "sticks" are removed from the homeowner's usual bundle of rights. Restrictions are typically imposed on the uses to which the house and land may be put. The most common of these regulate the right to rent and the right to improve the property. The homeowner/leaseholder may not sublet either house or land without prior permission of the nonprofit landowner—i.e., the CLT—and a cap is set on the monthly rent. Prior permission from the CLT may also be required for any structural additions or improvements.

The most significant restrictions from the point of view of perpetuating affordability are those that pertain not to use but to resale. Embedded in the ground lease is a pricing formula and a preemptive option granting the CLT the first right to repurchase the house at a restricted price should the current leaseholder/homeowner decide to sell. This option may be backed up by a right of first refusal, which is also embedded in the ground lease.

Administrative Structure. Responsibility for enforcing these restrictions on use and resale rests with the CLT, the owner and lessor of the land.[7] Because the CLT is the owner, as well, of the option to repurchase all structural improvements, it typically acts as buyer or broker for any housing resold by the current occupants. Either the CLT repurchases the property itself from the departing homeowner at the restricted price set by the option's formula, reselling it soon after for approximately the same price to another income-eligible homeowner, or the CLT arranges for the property to be sold by the departing homeowner directly to another income-eligible homebuyer selected from the CLT's waiting list. Thus does the CLT ensure both the *initial eligibility* of the housing's occupants and the *perpetual affordability* of the housing itself.

The CLT is a community-based organization, with membership open to any adult who lives within the geographic area that the CLT defines as its "community." All of the CLT's homeowners/leaseholders are also members. One-third of the CLT's board of directors are elected by the membership to represent the interests of members who are *not* leaseholders. One-third are elected to represent the interests of members who *are* leaseholders. The final third are appointed by the two-thirds who have been elected. Within this appointed third, seats are sometimes reserved for representatives of other community-based organizations. This tripartite structure is intended to balance the short-term interests of those who occupy CLT housing—those who may someday have the greatest economic interest in removing the restrictions on use and resale—with the long-term interests of the larger community.[8]

Variations. While nearly all CLTs have tripartite boards with at least a third of the seats reserved for leaseholder representatives, there is much diversity among the hundred CLTs that currently exist in the United States with respect to the composition and election of their boards. There is even more diversity in the type and tenure of the structures that are commonly located on CLT land. Some CLTs lease out land—and preserve affordability—for buildings with commercial uses. Many do the same for multiunit buildings with residential uses. Thus CLTs have been, on occasion, the lessors of land beneath limited equity condominiums, limited equity cooperatives, and mobile home parks. CLTs have also served not only as the lessors of land beneath owner-occupied housing but as the developers, owners, and managers of rental housing.

This last variation is, of course, a marked departure from the original model situated toward the homeowner end of the social housing continuum. Many CLTs have discovered, however, that the practical task of providing housing for the urban poor often requires a more mixed organizational agenda, one that promotes homeownership for some and secure tenancy for others.[9]

Limited Equity Condominium

Occupant's Interest. The condominium *without* price restrictions is already a deviation from the American ideal of individual, fee-simple ownership of a single-family, detached house. Significant "sticks" have already been removed from the homeowner's traditional bundle of rights. A condominium project is typically a cluster of dozens, or hundreds, of attached townhouses or apartments, although in cities such as Boston two-unit or three-unit condominium projects are common. Each of the project's homeowners holds a "unit deed" for a separate apartment; each holds a separate mortgage; each pays the taxes and insurance on the unit. What is owned by each has sometimes been described, somewhat derogatorily, as a "box of air." What is individually, exclusively owned by the condominium's owner-occupants, in other words, is the apartment's interior space, including the surface treatments of walls, floors, and ceilings. The structural elements lying just beneath those surfaces—studs, joists, rafters, etc.—are *not* individually owned; they are not a part of the unit deed. Nor are the exterior hallways, systems, sidewalks, or lands that surround and service individual apartments. They are jointly owned by all who individually own the project's units. They are common property.

This common property is operated by the condominium association, which is composed of all who own individual units within the same project.[10] This association pays taxes and insurance on the land and other common property, collects fees for the maintenance of common areas, and enforces any rules governing the use of common areas and individual units. Some of these rules can be quite restrictive and intrusive, dealing as they often do with the kind of improvements that may be made to individual units, the kind of commercial or recreational activities that may be pursued on site, and the kind of subletting that may be allowed.[11]

Although many restrictions may be placed on the *use* of market-rate condominiums, there are no restrictions on *price*. Individual owners may sell their units to whomever they choose for whatever the market will bear. The condominium association neither approves nor regulates these sales.

Legal Mechanism. By contrast, restrictions on price are the hallmark of the *limited equity* condominium. The owners of individual units must resell their units for a restricted price and must resell to a particular buyer (or eligible class of buyers). This requirement is enforced through a pricing formula and preemptive option (or restrictive covenant) embedded in the unit deed. These same resale restrictions may be referenced in the master deed for the project's common property and in the bylaws of the condominium association.

Administrative Structure. Conceivably, the condominium association could be given control over every conveyance of a condominium unit by being assigned the option to repurchase the unit at its limited equity price. In practice, this has seldom been considered an effective method for preserving long-term affordability. Many limited equity condominiums have been developed as a result of some municipally imposed "linkage" or "inclusionary zoning" requirement setting aside a small percentage of the total units within a newly constructed residential project as "affordable" housing. Since the majority of the project's units are market-priced condominiums, most members of the project's condominium association have little interest in monitoring and enforcing the affordability of the project's nonmarket units. Even less protection for long-term affordability may exist in those few projects in which the *majority* of the units are price restricted because homeowners with an economic interest in removing the limits on their equity are being asked to ensure that those limits are rigorously and regularly enforced.

The task of monitoring and enforcing the resale restrictions on limited equity condominiums, therefore, is commonly assigned to an *outside* party, either a municipal agency or a nonprofit corporation. The condominium association retains responsibility for enforcing any restrictions on use. The municipal agency or nonprofit corporation is assigned responsibility for enforcing restrictions on price, including the price at which the condominiums may be resold or sublet by current (and future) owners.[12]

Limited Equity Cooperative

Cooperative housing, like condominium housing, is operated and governed by an organization whose members are drawn exclusively from those who occupy the apartments in a multiunit housing project.[13] Unlike the condominium association, however, the cooperative housing corporation is the *owner* of the project's real estate: land, building(s), and the individual apartments themselves. It is the corporation that owns the deed, holds the mortgage, and pays all municipal taxes and fees.

Occupant's Interest. The occupants of cooperative housing are *tenants*, albeit tenants of a special kind. An occupant's exclusive use of an individual apartment is secured by a proprietary lease between the co-op corporation and the apartment's occupant(s). Occupancy under the terms of this lease is far more secure than is typically the case under the standard landlord-tenant agreement; for example, occupants may be evicted only for cause. What is more unusual about this particular form of tenancy, however, is the fact that co-op tenants are also shareholders and members of the same corporation from which they lease their apartments. They do not own their individual apartments, but they do own shares in the corporation that owns their apartments (as well as the rest of the project's real estate). They are, moreover, voting members of that corporation, with direct control over its assets, its operations, and its enforcement of any restrictions on the value of individual shares or the use of individual apartments.[14] The occupant of cooperative housing, in short, is simultaneously a tenant, a shareholder, and a member. These rights and roles are inseparable (see Figure 2-2).

Legal Mechanism. There is considerable complexity to the legal means by which these rights and roles are spelled out and tied together. The only aspects of this legal structure needing elaboration here, however, are those that distinguish the limited equity cooperative from its market-rate counterpart—those that make long-term affordability a reality. The most important of these distinguishing features is the financial cap placed on

Figure 2-2. Limited Equity Housing Cooperative: Rights and Roles

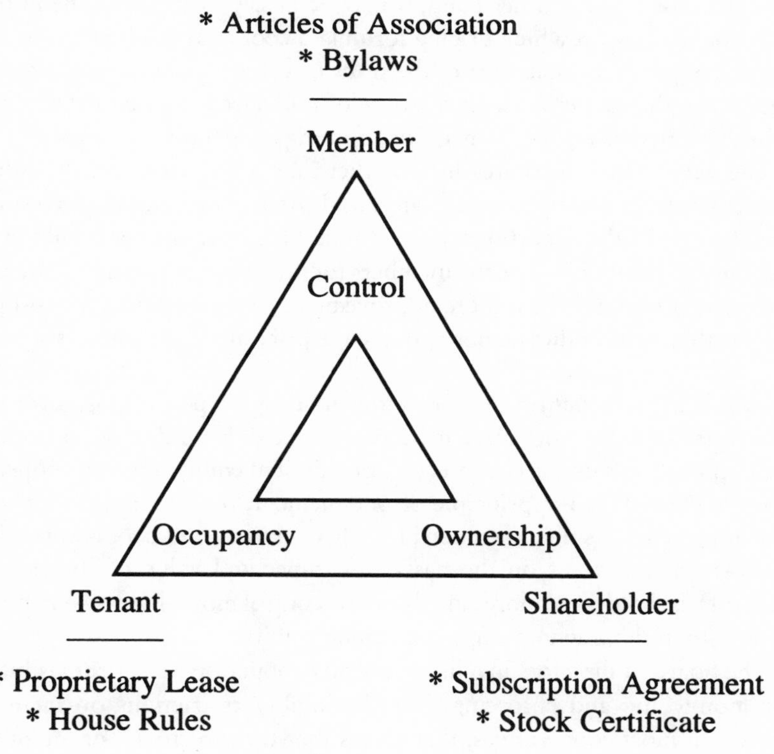

the transfer value of co-op shares. An occupant's ownership interest in the co-op corporation cannot be resold for more than the maximum price determined by a formula embedded in three documents: the *subscription agreement*, which serves as both a "buyer beware" disclosure document and a purchase-and-sale contract for the prospective purchaser of co-op shares; the *stock certificate*, which evidences the occupant's ownership of a specified number of co-op shares; and the *bylaws* of the corporation itself. These documents impose a legal limit on the amount of equity to which tenant-shareholders are entitled upon vacating their apartments and reselling their shares. They also grant the cooperative corporation a preemptive right to repurchase these shares at their limited equity price.

Limited equity cooperatives restrict the transfer value of members' shares to a level below their full market value. This limited equity price may be considerably higher than the price the departing member paid upon joining the co-op; on the other hand, it may be nearly identical to the initial price, depending on which pricing formula a cooperative adopts. Limited equity cooperatives that restrict the transfer value of members' shares to little more than their value at the time of purchase are often called "par value," "zero equity," or "nonequity" housing cooperatives.

The value of co-op shares in a market-rate cooperative, on the other hand, is determined by a market appraisal. At transfer, the shares are resold directly by the departing tenant-shareholder to whomever is willing to pay the asking price. While the members (or directors) of a market-rate cooperative often have the right to approve prospective buyers of the co-op's shares, they neither dictate nor approve the price at which a unit is sold.[15]

Administrative Structure. A cooperative housing corporation is governed by a board of directors elected by the tenant-shareholders who occupy the corporation's units. The directors of a limited equity housing cooperative are elected on the principle of one member, one vote; each housing unit represents a single membership. Most market-rate cooperatives, by contrast, assign votes on the basis of number and value of shares; the tenant-shareholders of more valuable units control more shares—and more votes—than those who occupy less valuable units.

The board of directors in a limited equity cooperative has responsibility for monitoring and enforcing the affordability restrictions on member shares. In most cooperatives, this means that the directors—or, in larger projects, the co-op's management company or staff, acting on behalf of the directors—repurchase the share(s) of a departing tenant at a below-market price and resell those share(s) to an incoming tenant at the same restricted price. Since the cooperative housing corporation is directly involved in both transactions, there is little risk of the cooperative apartment changing hands at a cost exceeding the limited equity price.

A risk to affordability is, however, inherent in the organizational structure of the cooperative itself. It is the same risk discussed in connection with the limited equity condominium—namely, that the task of preserving the long-term affordability of a project's units is assigned to residents with a personal stake in the long-term profitability of those units. Over time, if the difference between the market value of a cooperative's shares and the restricted price grows considerably, the economic incentive for the cooperative's members to amend the corporation's bylaws, relaxing or removing restrictions on the transfer value of their shares, can be enormous. Many cooperative housing corporations that were limited equity cooperatives when founded are market-rate cooperatives today.

Variations. Learning from these cases of lost affordability, some proponents of cooperative housing have begun to experiment with organizational variations that mix the co-op model with other models of social housing. The most common of these "mixed models" have used deed restrictions to safeguard the long-term affordability of limited equity cooperatives or have developed cooperatives on land leased from a CLT.

Other variations endeavor to preserve a cooperative's original commitment to long-term affordability by changing the composition of the governing board. Thus, instead of a board made up exclusively of members residing in the co-op's units, some cooperatives have boards with a block of seats occupied by people who are neither members nor residents. These "outside" directors, in some cases, are directly appointed by the nonprofit organization that developed the cooperative in the first place. The purpose behind all such tinkering with the cooperative's governing structure is to make it more difficult for a temporary majority of self-interested shareholders to amend the corporate charter and to remove the affordability controls on the members' shares.[16]

Mutual Housing Association

There is great diversity in what has been called mutual housing in the United States. Consequently, there is little agreement as to what exactly a mutual housing association (MHA) might be. I will describe one basic form that an MHA may take and immediately acknowledge several variations.

The mutual housing association may be described, most simply, as an "organization of organizations."[17] Separate residential buildings on scattered sites are owned by a single nonprofit corporation, the MHA. Each building contains another formal or informal association, controlled by that building's occupants, which accepts a degree of responsibility for operating that building on the MHA's behalf.

Occupant's Interest. The occupants of each of the MHA's buildings are tenants who have signed a fairly standard landlord-tenant agreement. They lease their individual apartments from the MHA, although in some cases they may lease their apartments from the organization that controls and manages their building. They are not merely the tenants of the MHA, however, or of the building-level organization; they are voting members of both. The board of directors of the MHA is made up of resident representatives from the building-level organizations, along with "outside" representatives not residing in any of the MHA's buildings. The board of directors of the building-level organization, if a formal organization actually exists, is democratically elected by the building's occupants. In smaller buildings, this building-level organization may simply be composed of all who reside in the building. Thus the occupants of these buildings are simultaneously tenants, members, and directors of the "umbrella" nonprofit that owns their building (the MHA), as well as members and directors of the building-level organization that may help in the operation of their building.

Legal Mechanism. The long-term affordability of units owned by the MHA is preserved through the MHA's bylaws and through any operating agreement that may exist between the MHA and the building-level organizations. These documents define and dictate an on-going corporate commitment to maintain rents at a level that low- and moderate-income residents can afford.

Administrative Structure. The MHA is the monitor and enforcer for the long-term affordability of its units. Day-to-day management may sometimes be delegated to building-level organizations, but the structural integrity, economic viability, and on-going affordability of *all* the buildings and *all* their units is overseen by the MHA. The MHA's commitment to affordability is underwritten, in turn, by its 501(c)(3) tax exemption and by the diversity of interests on its board. The MHA board is made up of resident representatives from its separate buildings, prospective residents from the MHA's own waiting list, and nonresident representatives drawn from the larger community. The self-interest of none of these groups is served by overturning the MHA's organizational commitment to long-term affordability.

Variations. Having described the MHA in this way, I must reiterate that many proponents of this model would describe it rather differently. Some would delegate no operational control from the MHA to the building-level organizations. Some would dispense with the building-level organizations altogether, preferring that house rules and other building-level issues be decided by MHA staff in consultation with the tenants in each building.

Another variation, created in Madison, Wisconsin, combines a nonprofit MHA, acting as developer and owner of scattered-site buildings, with a limited equity cooperative that manages these buildings with oversight from the MHA. A more federated structure has been created in Burlington, Vermont, where the MHA owns no buildings at all but holds in trust the replacement reserves and vacancy reserves for a number of small, separately incorporated, separately managed cooperatives. The federation also holds a durable power of attorney to intervene in the internal affairs of its member co-ops in cases of financial instability. The California MHA, by contrast, possesses neither property nor reserves but acts as a state-wide organizer, educator, and lobbyist for various forms of resident-controlled housing.

What is common to all of these variations is a nonprofit organization with four elements: a governing board composed of residents and nonresidents; a corporate commitment to resident security and resident control over their "own" homes; a corporate commitment to continuing affordability; and a corporate commitment to the continued development of additional affordable housing. This last is particularly important in distinguishing MHAs from co-ops. As Lisa Schwartz (1992: 4) has pointed out: "Cooperative development and management has . . . been marked by a tendency toward 'one-shot' efforts, with cooperative sponsors failing to use the expertise they have gained to create additional cooperatives." By purpose and design, MHAs are expansionist developers of affordable housing. Cooperatives usually are not.[18]

Nonprofit Rental Housing

So great is the diversity of nonprofit rental housing in the United States that the only common traits are (1) ownership or control of residential buildings by a nonprofit corporation, (2) occupancy of that residential property by tenants, and (3) stabilization of residential rents, where rent increases are tied directly to a building's actual cost of operations. Landlord profits are removed from the picture, even if the landlord is not.

Occupant's Interest. Rights of occupancy are secured for the property's tenants through a standard landlord-tenant agreement between individual tenant households and the nonprofit corporation. Tenants are granted an exclusive right to occupy and use an individual apartment for one year at a time, as long as they pay their monthly rent. They have no other rights of ownership or control. Although tenant-managed nonprofits are not unknown, the tenants of nonprofit landlords are typically granted no more control over their apartments or their building(s) than the tenants of for-profit landlords.

Legal Mechanism. The nonprofit status of the landlord, institutionalized in the nonprofit's organizational bylaws, in its state charter, and (perhaps) in a 501(c)(3) tax exemption from the federal government, provides some protection for the long-term affordability of its holdings.[19] Such corporate documents do not ensure that rents will never rise beyond the reach of lower-income tenants, but they do remove most of the personal economic incentives that help to drive up rents in housing owned by for-profit landlords.

A more certain guarantee of long-term affordability in nonprofit rental housing may be found in rent stabilization contracts between nonprofit landlords and some outside funder, often a public agency. Such contracts typically define the target population that the nonprofit landlord must serve, the "affordable" rent that must be charged, and the procedure for increasing rents over time. These terms are usually spelled out in a separate contract, although they may also be embedded in a subsidy covenant running with the land or in a mortgage between the nonprofit landlord and the outside funder. Although few of these rent stabilization contracts with public agencies have lasted beyond twenty years in the past, there is no reason they cannot be made to endure far longer.

Administrative Structure. Nonprofit corporations that own and operate rental housing have been established and structured in many different ways. They may be affiliates of a church, a union, or a social service organization. They may be subsidiaries of a for-profit organization or a public housing authority. They may be community-based organizations with members drawn exclusively from a particular neighborhood or tenant-based organizations with members drawn primarily from the occupants of a particular housing project. They may be coalitions having a board of directors composed entirely of representatives from other nonprofit organizations. They may (or may not) be recognized as charitable, tax-exempt organizations by the IRS. Whatever its form, the nonprofit corporation is responsible for maintaining the affordability of the units it owns. This responsibility may be imposed or reinforced by a rent stabilization contract with some outside party, but it is carried out day to day by the nonprofit corporation.[20]

Variations. Nonprofit rental housing has numerous variations, including multiple forms of tenant management and multiple "mixtures" with other models of social housing. One common variation, in which a nonprofit organization is partnered with for-profit investors to produce affordable housing for low-income tenants, deserves special mention. Such partnerships have become quite widespread since 1986, as a result of the federal Low Income Housing Tax Credit program. They raise important questions about what is really meant by "social housing."

The ownership or participation of a nonprofit organization does not, by itself, turn rental housing into social housing. Indeed, for many nonprofit housing developers the perpetuation of affordability is neither a conscious nor a consistent goal. Many others readily embrace this goal but quickly abandon it at the altar of financial necessity as soon as private capital is needed to make a project happen. Attracting such private investment, using either Low Income Housing Tax Credits or some other profit-oriented vehicle, does not always mean the loss of affordability. Housing produced in this way does not have to revert to the market in fifteen to twenty years when tax benefits run out.[21] Some nonprofits have, in fact, become quite skillful in structuring deals with for-profit investors that ensure both the on-going control of the project's administration by the nonprofit organization and the on-going affordability of the project's units.

Such partnerships have been the exception, however, rather than the rule. More commonly, nonprofits have surrendered both short-term control and long-term affordability in order to maintain investor confidence in a project—or simply because long-term affordability was never part of their corporate mission. Not only does the housing produced by these partnerships not deserve to be called social housing, it should probably not even be called nonprofit housing. Michael Stone (1993), for one, has suggested "quasi-nonprofit" and "compromised nonprofit" as more appropriate designations.[22]

What is key, in other words, is not only the presence of a nonprofit organization but the prospect for continuing affordability. Nonprofit rental housing that is price restricted for ten or fifteen years is only temporarily a part of the social sector—a sojourner, not a permanent resident. Such housing replicates a short-sighted solution of the past that has become a long-term problem today.

ON-GOING INNOVATION: IMPETUS AND ISSUES

These six models of privately owned, socially oriented, price-restricted housing generally describe the tenurial landscape lying beyond the more familiar tenures of the market and the state. They do not exhaust the field, however. Many variations have not been mentioned. Many others are still unfolding, as housing activists across the U.S. mix and modify the basic models reviewed above or start from scratch with their own conceptions of how the rights and responsibilities of private property should be rearranged.

The impetus for such on-going innovation has sometimes been the pressing need to tailor more exactly a particular project to the specific conditions of whatever financing happens to be available, or the practical need to apportion more effectively the many tasks involved in developing and managing affordable housing. More frequently and fundamentally, however, this on-going process of innovation and experimentation has been rooted in one or more of three enduring concerns: the pursuit of perpetual affordability; the quest for greater accountability; and the desire to make mutuality more prominent a part of these private, nonmarket models of housing.

Affordability

By custom and by law, privately owned housing in the United States is a commodity. It is bought and sold for the highest price a willing buyer will pay to a willing seller. Anything that unduly interferes with this market transaction—anything that unduly restricts for any significant length of time the price an owner may receive from this transaction—runs contrary to the general course of common law in the United States. Much experimentation in social housing has originated, therefore, out of various schemes for sidestepping possible legal challenges to contractually imposed restrictions on the pricing and conveyance of such privately owned housing.[23]

Real though the risk of legal challenge may be in some jurisdictions, a more serious threat to the continuing affordability of price-restricted housing has long been recognized by activists working with models of limited equity homeownership: the economic self-interest of the people who own and occupy that housing. The very people who are most supportive of price controls when they are first trying to buy a home can become the least supportive when facing the prospect of reselling a home for less than its fair market value. They have the greatest material interest in taking over the board of the sponsoring organization and in removing any contractual restrictions imposed on the resale price of their property.

Recognizing this economic fact of life, proponents of social housing have attempted to buttress the affordability of their projects by three means. They have tried (not always with success) to create perpetual interests that run with the land, attempting to protect affordability by imposing "self-enforcing" mechanisms not dependent on administrative bodies that might be subverted in the future. They have attempted to make the administrative structure of their models more accountable to prospective homebuyers—or to the community at large—than to current homeowners. Or they have given outside parties who cannot profit from the property extraordinary powers in monitoring and enforcing long-term affordability. The outcome of these efforts has been a number of organizational variations designed to protect the precarious affordability of privately owned, price-restricted housing.

Accountability

Other variations arise out of a continuing quest to make social housing—and the nonprofit sponsors of such housing—more responsive to the needs and wants of two constituencies: those who occupy the housing, and those who reside in the surrounding neighborhood. It is not enough to grant occupants more control over their individual units, argue many proponents of social housing; they must be granted a degree of control as well over any sponsoring organization that develops, owns, or manages their housing. How such control should be structured—and whether occupant control should be granted at all, given the threat it can pose for continuing affordability—are issues of considerable controversy within social housing circles.[24]

Similarly, it is often argued that some larger community outside of the occupants' ranks should exercise control over social housing. This outside "community" is defined, most often, as other interested residents of the geographic locale (i.e., the neighborhood) in which the social housing is located. More narrow or more expansive definitions have also been used, however. Thus the "community" incorporated into the governing structure of a social housing organization has sometimes been people who are currently on the organization's waiting list for affordable housing, or people with economic, physical, or mental handicaps who have a need for affordable housing, or people of goodwill anywhere in the region who are supportive of the organization's mission. How this "community" should be defined, how it should be involved, and how the competing demands of "community control" and "occupant control" might be reconciled within the same organization, are issues that provoke continuing debate and continuing innovation.

Mutuality

Finally, innovation continues because new ways are being devised to interconnect and support organizationally the individual occupants of social housing. Many would-be occupants of social housing possess neither the income nor the skills to function successfully as self-sufficient homeowners. Many others lack the ability even to function successfully as self-sufficient tenants. New ways are being sought, therefore, to make mutual aid as much a part of the "social orientation" of these private, nonmarket models of housing as the creation and perpetuation of affordability.

An organizational commitment to mutuality assumes that housing must serve not only as a means of individuation, but as a means of solidarity, especially in times of calamity and distress. Such a commitment assumes limits to the kind of residential autonomy typically expected in most market-driven forms of housing. Not every household can find its separate way to safe, decent, and affordable housing. Not every household can bear individually the costs, risks, and responsibilities of gaining—and retaining—secure occupancy in separate residential units.[25]

Challenging this "every-household-for-itself" approach to housing, most models of social housing embrace a more supportive, collaborative approach in which the burdens and risks of housing are shared, scarce resources are pooled, separate households are linked together in common cause, and collective security makes individual security both possible and real.

This organizational commitment to mutuality has tended, in the past, to be more fully developed at the tenant end of the social housing continuum. Models having more of a homeowner focus and feel have tended to emphasize autonomy over mutuality. But this is changing. Across the entire social housing continuum, there is a new awareness that security of tenure may require more than a guarantee of lasting affordability. As the proponents of these models look for new ways to put mutuality more on a par with affordability, social housing continues to change.

COMPARATIVE ADVANTAGE: WHICH MODEL SHOULD PUBLIC POLICY SUPPORT?

Is there one model of social housing with a clear advantage over all the others? Should public policy single out one model for special support, while ignoring the rest? My own answer would be that the best policy is one that promotes *multiple* models of social housing, establishing as many as possible in the same locale.

This is not to ignore the advantages that certainly exist from one model to another. Different models have different strengths in developing particular types of housing, in using particular forms of financing, in serving particular classes of people, or in meeting particular requirements for long-term affordability, accountability, and mutual aid (see Table 2-1). Some models of social housing, for example, are better suited to single-family housing; some to multifamily housing. Some can make use of Section 8 rental assistance; some cannot. Some require occupants to qualify for individual mortgages; some do not. Some expect a high degree of self-sufficiency from the housing's occupants in managing and maintaining their units, while others promote a more collaborative sharing of burdens, risks, and responsibilities. Some are controlled by their occupants, some by the surrounding community, and some by a self-perpetuating board. Some have a better chance than others of preserving affordability for many years.

Obviously, there are advantages to selecting the right model of social housing for the situation at hand. What should be just as obvious, however, is that the "best" model is not everywhere and always going to be the same. Indeed, the real advantage would seem to lie in having a *choice* of models to meet a variety of changing situations, conditions, and needs.[26] The "best" model of social housing, in short, may be two, three, or even more of these models in the same community.

Multiple models of social housing enable public officials and community activists not only to find the most *compatible* fit between a particular model and a particular set of circumstances but to build a *complementary* fit among the models themselves. Multiple models narrow the gaps that customarily exist among different forms of tenure, making the transition

Table 2-1. Comparative Advantage: Six Models of Social Housing

Deed-restricted, Owner-occupied House

Advantages:
- Maximal autonomy for homeowner
- Tax deductions for interest and taxes
- Marketability: close to "traditional" homeownership
- Few administrative costs for sponsoring agency
- Financial system designed to assist first-time homebuyers (banks, FmHA, FHA, and state HFAs)

Disadvantages:
- Single house on a single lot has a high per-unit cost; difficult to serve lower-income households
- Rental assistance (Section 8) cannot be used
- Affordability may be lost because "self-enforcing" deed restrictions prove unenforceable
- Maximal autonomy means maximal responsibility; little sharing of burdens or risks
- Household must be "bankable"; poor credit history or uneven income will disqualify for mortgage

Community Land Trust

Advantages:
- High autonomy for homeowner
- Buy-in price reduced by removing cost of land
- Tax deductions for interest and taxes on building
- Financial system designed to assist first-time homebuyers (banks, FmHA, FHA, and state HFAs)
- Nonprofit sponsor's ownership of land enhances enforceability of affordability restrictions
- Nonprofit sponsor's tri-partite board protects sponsor's long-term commitment to affordability
- Support of first-time homebuyers by nonprofit sponsor eases transition from renting to owning
- Sponsoring organization is "expansionist" developer
- Sponsoring organization can get 501(c)(3) status

Disadvantages:
- Single house on a single lot has high per-unit cost even with land removed; hard to serve very poor
- Household must be "bankable"; poor credit history or uneven income will disqualify for mortgage

- Rental assistance (Section 8) cannot be used
- Financial system not yet fully familiar with mortgaging houses on leased land
- Marketability: removing land from homeowner's interest causes concern, especially in rural areas
- High administrative costs for nonprofit sponsor
- Individual risk and responsibility for house

Limited Equity Condominium

Advantages:
- Lower per-unit cost gives greater initial affordability than a detached house
- Tax deductions for interest and taxes on units
- Financial system designed to assist first-time homebuyers; system familiar with condominium model
- Popular familiarity with condo model as well
- Pooled risk and responsibility for common property

Disadvantages:
- Household must be "bankable"; poor credit history or uneven income will disqualify for mortgage
- Rental assistance (Section 8) cannot be used
- Continuing affordability may be jeopardized by use of "self-enforcing" unit deed restrictions or by outside enforcer not having "touch and concern"
- Where lower-income units are in the minority, the condo association may assess unaffordable fees
- Condominium associations are not "expansionist" developers (though a sponsoring nonprofit may be)
- Individual risk and responsibility for unit

Limited Equity Cooperative

Advantages:
- Lower per-unit buy-in cost gives greater initial affordability than detached house or condo
- Individual "bankability" not required
- Tax deductions for interest and taxes
- Rental assistance (Section 8) *can* be used
- Corporate ability to enforce continuing affordability of shares will withstand legal challenge
- Maximum pooling of burdens and risks
- Better maintenance: peer pressure and corporate oversight maintain units in good repair
- One member one vote gives occupants great control
- "Schools of democracy," teaching group skills
- A ready-made community for those who desire one

Table 2-1. Continued

Disadvantages:
- Members may amend corporate bylaws to repeal protections over long-term affordability
- Less autonomy; less "feel" of homeownership
- Not everyone has the time, desire, or skills to devote so much time to participatory democracy
- Pooling of risk can mean that everyone goes down together; a few deadbeats can drag it down
- System of affordable share loans not available in many places; buying into older co-ops can become difficult for lower-income households
- Co-ops are seldom "expansionist" developers
- Co-ops are not eligible for 501(c)(3) status
- Need for constant board training can be costly

Mutual Housing Association

Advantages:
- A lower per-unit "buy-in" cost than detached house, condo, or co-op
- Individual "bankability" not required
- Rental assistance (Section 8) *can* be used
- Board with balanced interests ensures lasting affordability
- Risks and burdens shifted to nonprofit sponsor from individual households
- Management oversight by MHA keeps units repaired
- Occupants have direct control via building-level assn. and indirect control via reps on MHA
- Nonprofit sponsor (MHA) is "expansionist" developer
- Maximum horizontal mobility of occupants
- Nonprofit sponsor can get 501(c)(3) status

Disadvantages:
- Occupants are tenants, with neither the autonomy nor benefits of homeownership
- Occupants may only have as much security as ensured by annual lease and landlord-tenant laws
- Occupants have only indirect—and minority—control over the nonprofit sponsor (MHA)
- Conflicts can occur among tenants and between individual houses and the MHA

Nonprofit Rental Housing

Advantages:
- Lower per-unit "buy-in" cost than detached house, condo, or co-op
- Individual "bankability" not required
- Rental assistance (Section 8) *can* be used
- Risks shifted from individual households to nonprofit sponsor
- Management and maintenance by nonprofit sponsor

- Nonprofit sponsor is often "expansionist" developer
- Maximum horizontal mobility of occupants
- Nonprofit sponsor may get 501(c)(3) status

Disadvantages:
- Occupants are tenants, with neither the autonomy nor benefits of homeownership
- Occupants have only as much security as ensured by annual lease and landlord-tenant laws
- Occupants generally have no voice in decisions affecting their housing
- Traditional landlord-tenant disputes may be common
- Governing board may later decide to abandon its commitment to long-term affordability

---

from one to another less daunting and difficult than before. Because the needs and resources of residents differ, people should be able to choose freely among a range of models with different benefits, risks, and demands. Because the needs and resources of residents change, people should be able to move easily from one form of tenure to another. Every model of social housing provides security and affordability over time. But when several of these models are developed in the same locale, people of modest means are provided not only a choice of tenure, but a chance to move—opportunities that are increasingly rare in housing provided by public policy and the private market alike.

Twenty-five years ago, Catherine Bauer looked back on the "dreary deadlock of public housing" in the United States and reviewed some of the mistakes she believed she and others had made in establishing this *publicly* owned form of price-restricted housing. She concluded with the following words:

> What is primarily needed, not only for low-income slum dwellers and minority groups but for the great mass of middle-income families in all their infinite variety of taste and need, is more choice in location, dwelling type, and neighborhood character. The kind of home best suited to a given American family can never be decided by officials. Their highest responsibility, rather, is to make sure that public policies keep the "effective market" broad enough to provide some real selection at all economic and social levels. (Bauer, 1985: 284)

As community activists and public officials throughout the United States begin directing more resources toward *privately* owned, price-restricted housing, they would do well to heed Bauer's advice. A continuum of tenures is not only a convenient way of classifying the many models of social housing. It is also a practical way of combining these models into a single system of affordable housing offering more diversity—and more mobility—than less affluent households normally enjoy. Housing needs come in many varieties. Housing tenures should too.

NOTES

Acknowledgments: This review of social housing's "diverse domain" benefited greatly from close and critical readings given to earlier drafts by Carol Baldassari and Kirby White. Their assistance is gratefully acknowledged. Any mistakes or omissions that remain in the presentation of these models are the responsibility of the author alone.

1. More detail on these three characteristics of social housing, along with a longer discussion of the differences between social housing and more traditional tenures of the market and state, can be found in the Introduction to the present volume.

2. Although variations of pricing formula can also be quite significant, they do not necessarily differentiate one model of social housing from another. The *same* pricing formula used by a community land trust, for example, might be used by a limited equity cooperative or by the nonprofit owner of rental housing. Alternatively, each model might use a different formula. More information on pricing formulas can be found in ICE (1992; 1991) and Baldassari (1988: 43–46).

3. Property in land or buildings is often described as a collection of separate—and separable—"rights." Each right (e.g., the right to the exclusive use of a parcel of land, the right to develop it, the right to bequeath it, the right to rent or sell it for a profit, and so forth) is portrayed as a single "stick" in this collection (or "bundle") of rights.

4. Other "sticks" may be removed (or regulated) as well, especially the homeowner's traditional right to become an absentee landlord by subletting the house to another occupant. In most models of social housing, the owner's continuing occupancy of a price-restricted home is given as high a priority as the property's continuing affordability.

5. It should be noted that many deed restrictions protecting the affordability of single-family housing are intentionally designed by their sponsors to lapse after a specified number of years, *not* to last in perpetuity.

6. For further details on the deed-restricted, owner-occupied house, see Keeley and Manzo (1992), Kirkpatrick (1990), Baldassari (1988; 1989), NRC (1987), and Stone (1986).

7. The CLT may—and often does—perform other functions, such as land assembly, housing construction, housing rehabilitation, housing finance, and various training and service roles for new homeowners. Since my focus here is on preserving long-term affordability, this "preservationist" role is the only one discussed.

8. Additional information on the community land trust model can be found in Abromowitz (1992), ICE (1982, 1991), Baldassari (1989), White and Matthei (1987), and Davis (1984).

9. Among the 1992 amendments to the National Affordable Housing Act of 1990 is a definition of community land trusts that embraces the original model while allowing some variation. This definition, appearing in Section 213 of the Housing and Community Development Act of 1992, reads in part: "The term community land trust means a community housing development corporation . . . that (A) acquires parcels of land, held in perpetuity, primarily for conveyance under long-term ground leases; (B) transfers ownership of any structural improvements located on such leased parcels to the lessees; and (C) retains a preemptive option to purchase any such structural improvements at a price determined by formula." *Primarily* is the operative word here, one that anticipates and allows some deviation from the original CLT model.

10. It is important to note that the condominium association does not own any of the project's real property. All real property is owned by the *members* of the association, either individually or jointly.

11. Since many lenders prefer to write mortgages only on condominiums within projects with at least 70 percent of the units occupied by owners, an increasing number of condominium associations have begun closely monitoring and controlling the subletting—and, in some cases, the resale—of individual units. Their concern is not to protect the project's affordability, of course, but to protect the marketability (and value) of its units.

12. For further details on the condominium model, see Baldassari (1989), Kaufman and Corrigan (1987), Silverman and Barton (1987), and Mallach (1984).

13. Although a single, multiunit apartment building is the most common type of housing cooperative, a cooperative housing corporation may own and operate several apartment buildings on the same site, single-unit or multiunit buildings on scattered sites, or the land and improvements in a mobile home park. (In a "leasing co-op," the cooperative housing corporation may not be an "owner" at all.) In other words, a fifty-unit apartment building in a downtown neighborhood, owned and operated by a cooperative housing corporation, is not the *only* kind of co-op housing that exists in the United States.

14. Most restrictions on the use of individual apartments are imposed through the proprietary lease. Additional use restrictions, affecting both individual apartments and the project's common areas, are imposed by the cooperative's "house rules." These rules, originally adopted and periodically amended by the members themselves (or by their representatives on the board), establish the cooperative's standards for parking, repairs, guests, noise, use of common areas, and so forth.

15. There are two other "value" differences between a limited equity cooperative and a market-rate cooperative. In the former, there is a limit to the dividends

that may be distributed in the event of an operating surplus, and the total value of members' shares is a minor percentage of the total value of the corporation's assets. Most of the equity in a limited equity cooperative is owned by the corporation. In a market-rate cooperative, there is no limit on dividends, and most, if not all, of the equity is owned by the members.

16. Additional information on limited equity housing cooperatives can be found in Liblit (1964), Blais (1977), Coughlan and Frank (1983), Kirkpatrick (1981, 1992) and Zimmer (1977). Recent efforts to organize housing cooperatives in Los Angeles and New York City are documented by Heskin (1991) and Leavitt and Saegert (1990). Stories of Canadian co-ops are presented in Cooper and Rodman (1992) and Helman (1986). British co-ops are examined in Birchall (1987) and Henry (1983).

17. The MHA model has also been described as a "cooperative of cooperatives" or a "scattered site cooperative" because some MHAs issue capital shares that members must purchase as a condition of occupancy. The corporate entity that issues these shares, however, is a state-chartered nonprofit with a 501(c)(3) tax exemption, not a cooperative housing corporation. The minimal cost and nominal rate of interest paid on these shares, moreover, make the residents' contribution more closely equivalent to a renter's security deposit than to a cooperative's membership share. For these reasons, I believe that using cooperative language to describe the MHA adds unnecessary confusion, although some of the forms this model can take look very much like cooperative housing. (Others can look very much like nonprofit rental housing with an added dose of tenant control.)

18. Additional information on MHAs can be found in Bratt (1991), Kirkpatrick (1992), Schwartz (1992), Sutemeier (1989), and Neighborhood Reinvestment Corporation (1985).

19. Not every nonprofit is granted a federal tax exemption. When 501(c)(3) status is granted, however, strict limits are placed on the uses to which the property may be put and the parties who may derive financial gain from the property's lease or sale.

20. Additional information on the nonprofit development and ownership of rental housing can be found in Mayer (1990, 1991), Keating, Rasey, and Krumholz (1990), Clay (1989), and NCCED (1989, 1991).

21. The prospect of these units reverting to market-rate rentals at the end of fifteen years is, in fact, the most telling criticism of the federal Low Income Housing Tax Credit (LIHTC) program, whether nonprofits are involved or not. There is a special irony here for those who come to social housing via painful experience with the failed federal programs of the past. As Chester Hartman (1992: 12) has pointed out, "This system for the most part is building an exact replica of the 'expiring use restriction' problem we're all grappling with now, with respect to those 1960s and 1970s projects built under the Sec. 236 and 221(d)(3) programs."

22. Stone's purpose in proposing these labels is not to disparage either the mo-

tives or the dedication of those nonprofits who enter into partnership with private investors but to indicate how the meaning and mission of nonprofit ownership can be distorted by financing projects with profit-driven sources of equity and debt.

23. These legal obstacles to price-restricted housing are embodied in two common law principles known as the "rule against perpetuities" and the "rule against unreasonable restraint on alienation."

24. The entire issue of occupant participation, especially for models of social housing that lie toward the tenant-occupied end of the continuum, is complicated not only by the need to preserve affordability, but by basic questions such as: What are the purposes of participation? Which forms of participation achieve such purposes? Do occupants want "control," or is "involvement" enough? An excellent discussion of these questions can be found in a little-known paper by Peter Marcuse (1970). See also Neidhardt (1993).

25. The importance of balancing "autonomy" with an equal commitment to "mutuality" is discussed more fully in Davis (1990). After this 1990 article appeared, I discovered that Emory Bogardus had long ago included "the mutuality principle" in his reformulation of the original Rochdale Principles. Bogardus wrote (1964: 27): "The principle of mutuality repudiates the often-expressed doctrine of 'everyone for himself and the devil take the hindmost,' a practice which developed where a theory of competition dominated human thinking, where pioneering conditions compelled everyone to depend largely on himself."

26. Despite our present focus on social housing, it is important to remember that public housing should be included among this "mix" of choices for lower-income people, along with publicly assisted, private housing. Public policy must ensure that the affordable, price-restricted housing operated under these "old" models is not lost to the marketplace while additional resources are being directed toward "new" models of social housing.

REFERENCES

Abromowitz, David M. "Community Land Trusts and Ground Leases." *ABA Journal of Affordable Housing and Community Development Law* 1, no. 2 (1992): 5–6, 15–17.

Baldassari, Carol. *A Catalogue of Methods for Preserving Affordable Housing*. Boston: Metropolitan Area Planning Council, 1988.

———. *Limited Equity Homeownership: Programs that Create and Protect Affordable Housing*. Boston: Metropolitan Area Planning Council, 1989.

Bauer, Catherine. "The Dreary Deadlock of Public Housing." In J. Paul Mitchell (ed.), *Federal Housing Policy and Programs: Past and Present*, pp. 277–285. New Brunswick, N.J.: Center for Urban Policy Research, Rutgers University, 1985.

Birchall, Johnston. *Building Communities the Cooperative Way*. London: Routledge and Kegan Paul, 1987.

Blais, Saundra (ed.), *Cooperative Housing: A Handbook for Effective Operations*. Ann Arbor, Mich.: Midwest Association of Housing Cooperatives, 1977.

Bogardus, Emory S. "Seven Principles of Cooperation." In Jerome Liblit (ed.), *Housing the Cooperative Way: Selected Readings*. New York: Twayne, 1964.

Bratt, Rachel G. "Mutual Housing: Community-based Empowerment," *Journal of Housing*, July/August 1991, pp. 173–180.

Clay, Phillip L. *Mainstreaming the Community Builders*. Cambridge: Department of Urban Studies and Planning, MIT, 1989.

Cooper, Matthew, and Margaret Rodman. *New Neighbors*. Toronto: University of Toronto Press, 1992.

Coughlan, William, and Monte Frank. *Going Co-op*. Boston: Beacon Press, 1983.

Davis, John Emmeus. "Reallocating Equity: A Land Trust Model of Land Reform." In Charles Geisler and Frank Popper (eds.), *Land Reform, American Style*, pp. 209–232. Totowa, N.J.: Rowman and Allanheld, 1984.

———. "Reconcilable Differences: Housing and Human Rights in the USA." *Peace and Democracy News* 4, nos. 1, 2 (1990): 7–8, 39–45.

Hartman, Chester. "Debating the Low Income Tax Credit: Feeding the Sparrows by Feeding the Horses" *Shelterforce* 14, no. 1 (1992): 12, 15.

Helman, Claire. *The Milton Park Affair*. Montreal: Vehicle Press, 1986.

Henry, Stuart. *Private Justice*. London: Routlege and Kegan Paul, 1983.

Heskin, Allan David. *The Struggle for Community*. Boulder, Colo.: Westview Press, 1991.

Institute for Community Economics (ICE). *The Community Land Trust Handbook*. Emmaus, Pa.: Rodale Press, 1982.

———. *The Community Land Trust Legal Manual*. Springfield, Mass., 1991.

———. *Designing Resale Formulas for Homeownership Programs*. Springfield, Mass., November 1992.

Kaufman, Phyllis, and Arnold Corrigan. *Understanding Condominiums and Coops*. Stamford, Conn.: Longmeadow Press, 1987.

Keating, W. Dennis, Keith Rasey, and Norman Krumholz. "Community Development Corporations: Their Role in Housing and Urban Development." In Willem van Vliet and Jan van Weesep (eds.), *Government and Housing*, pp. 206–218. Newbury Park, Calif.: Sage Publications, 1990.

Keeley, Michael, and Peter Manzo. "Resale Restrictions and Leverage Controls," *ABA Journal of Affordable Housing and Community Development Law* 1, no. 2 (1992): 9–11.

Kirkpatrick, David. "Limiting the Equity in Housing Cooperatives: Choices and Tradeoffs." *Economic Development and Law Center Report* 11, no. 1 (1981): 1–9.

———. "Resale Controls: Tools for Preserving Affordability," *Economic Development and Law Center Report* 20, Summer/Fall, 1990: 9–14.

———. "Cooperatives and Mutual Housing Associations," *ABA Journal of Affordable Housing and Community Development Law* 1, no. 2 (1992): 7–8.

Leavitt, Jacqueline, and Susan Saegert. *From Abandonment to Hope*. New York: Columbia University Press, 1990.

Liblit, Jerome (ed.). *Housing the Cooperative Way: Selected Readings*. New York: Twayne, 1964.

Mallach, Alan. "Creating and Maintaining Lower-Income Occupancy in Inclusionary Housing Programs." In his *Inclusionary Housing Programs: Policies and Practices*, pp. 133–165. New Brunswick, N.J.: Center for Urban Policy Research, Rutgers University, 1984.

Marcuse, Peter. "Tenant Participation—For What?" Working Paper 112-20. Washington, D.C.: Urban Institute, 1970.

Mayer, Neil S. "The Role of Nonprofits in Renewed Federal Housing Efforts." In Denise DiPasquale and Langley Keyes (eds.), *Building Foundations: Housing and Federal Policy*, pp. 365–388. Philadelphia: University of Pennsylvania Press, 1990.

———. "Preserving the Low-Income Housing Stock: What Nonprofit Housing Organizations Can Do Today and Tomorrow," *Housing Policy Debate* 2, no. 2, 1991: 499–533.

National Congress for Community Economic Development (NCCED). *Against All Odds: The Achievement of Community-based Development Organizations*. Washington, D.C., 1989.

———. *Changing the Odds: The Achievements of Community-based Development Corporations*. Washington, D.C., 1991.

Neidhardt, Frank S. "Cooperative Housing and the American Dream." M.C.P. thesis, Department of Urban Studies and Planning, MIT, May 1993.

Neighborhood Reinvestment Corporation (NRC). *The Mutual Housing Association: An American Demonstration of a Proven European Concept*. Washington, D.C., 1985.

———. *Resale Strategies*. Boston, 1987.

Schwartz, Lisa. "Three Mutual Housing Association Types Present Opportunities and Options." *Cooperative Housing Journal*, 1992: 3–9.

Silverman, Carol, and Stephen Barton. "Common Interest Communities and the American Dream." Working paper no. 463, Institute of Urban and Regional Development, University of California, Berkeley, September 1987.

Stone, Michael E. "Homeownership without Speculation." *Shelterforce* 9, no. 4 (November/December 1986): 12–14.

———. *Shelter Poverty: New Ideas on Housing Affordability*. Philadelphia: Temple University Press, 1993.

Sutemeier, Debbie. "Mutual Housing: Resident Control without Ownership." *Shelterforce* 11, no. 6 (1989): 7–9.

White, Kirby, and Charles Matthei. "Community Land Trusts." In Severyn T. Bruyn and James Meehan (eds.), *Beyond the Market and the State*, pp. 41–64. Philadelphia: Temple University Press, 1987.

Zimmer, Jonathan E. *From Rental to Cooperative: Improving Low and Moderate Income Housing*. Beverly Hills, Calif.: Sage Publications, 1977.

3 Diminishing Returns: A Critical Look at Subsidy Recapture

HELEN S. COHEN

Long-term protection of the public's investment in affordable housing is gradually becoming a credo among municipalities—even a litmus test for public policy. Whether the result of obvious economic constraints or lessons gleaned from poorly planned programs of the past or conclusions derived from a far-reaching analysis of private property and publicly assisted housing, it is slowly dawning on many municipal officials that public dollars should be safeguarded against the whims of the market and the speculative desires of individual investors. There is a growing agreement that cities have a responsibility to somehow *recycle* their scarce subsidies for affordable housing.

But there are questions: How should cities accomplish this? Which programs most effectively protect the public's investment while providing low- and moderate-income people decent, affordable, secure places to live? How long should the public's investment be protected? Which mechanism is most fair? Most efficient? Most marketable? And, more fundamentally, should permanent affordability be a municipality's bottom-line requirement, or is the recapture of public subsidies enough?

In spite of widespread agreement on the need to preserve public dollars, municipal officials in different regions of the country have answered these questions in different ways and have arrived at different conclusions about how to proceed. The basic policy debate has been framed around two options:

1. *Subsidy recapture.* A municipality's investment in affordable housing is recycled through a "shared equity" type of program, whereby the City subsidizes the initial purchase of a home for a low- to moderate-income buyer and gets back its subsidy plus a percentage of the appreciation when the unit is resold. With this technique, homes are resold at the highest value the market will bear, with no restrictions on price. The City then uses its "recaptured" capital to finance the next eligible buyer in the same or in another home.
2. *Subsidy retention.* The affordability of publicly assisted, privately owned housing is preserved through price restrictions on future sales (or rents), which ensure that the units do not escalate in price beyond what might be affordable for a low- or moderate-income buyer. With this approach, municipal subsidies are locked in place, creating and retaining a permanent stock of affordable housing.

The relative effectiveness of subsidy recapture versus subsidy retention is the subject of the present chapter. I provide both a descriptive overview of these programs and a critique of their financial, social, and political consequences, drawing on examples from several municipalities with very different market conditions. My focus is on homeownership programs, though my conclusions extend to rental housing as well.

Although subsidy recapture and subsidy retention are both enormous improvements over housing programs requiring *no* recycling of the public dollar, subsidy retention is the more effective policy. It simply makes more sense, economically and socially, to use scarce public resources to produce and preserve a permanent stock of affordable housing. This is particularly true in urban or suburban areas with rapidly inflating real estate markets, limited access to land, and median incomes that lag behind a rapid rise in housing costs. In these settings, affordability is difficult to achieve at the outset, but once that feat has been accomplished, it can be—and should be—perpetuated for as long as possible. What is needed is not simply a program that recycles a municipality's housing dollars but one that invests those dollars in the kind of housing that is itself recycled from one owner-occupant to another without losing any of its publicly subsidized affordability.[1]

SUBSIDY RECAPTURE

Subsidy recapture or equity-sharing programs vary in structure, mechanics, and scale, depending on the demographics of the city, the goals of the particular program, available sources of financing, and various political and legal realities. These programs also go by a variety of names: homeownership co-investment (HCI), equity participation, shared appreciation, and equity partnership, among others. They may be administered by various entities: public, private, or nonprofit. I will concentrate here solely on programs administered by a municipal agency that subsidize homeownership for low- or moderate-income residents.

Despite the variation among subsidy recapture programs, most of them adhere to a few key features:

- Public or private subsidies are co-invested with the funds of a prospective homebuyer to reduce the principal of the homebuyer's mortgage.
- Repayment of all or part of this subsidy—both principal and interest—is deferred until the property is resold. Because repayment is deferred, the homeowner's monthly mortgage payments are reduced, enhancing the affordability of the housing unit.
- The homes are sold and resold at their highest market value.
- Co-investors share in the home's appreciation, usually in proportion to the amount of their initial investment. The financial commitment of the municipal agency is treated as an investment made with the goal of getting back a proportionate "fair return" on the municipal dollars put into the property.
- Subsidies that are recaptured are used again by the municipal agency to refinance the same home with a new buyer or to finance another home.

A simple example helps to illustrate the financial obligations of each party. Say municipal agency *X* lends $20,000 at a simple annual interest rate of 5 percent to help finance a $100,000 home. Repayment of principal and interest is deferred until the home is resold. At the time of resale, the homeowner/borrower owes the agency $20,000 plus interest—plus 20 percent of the home's appreciation. If the home resells for $150,000 after five years, the homeowner/borrower pays back the $20,000 subsidy, plus $5,000 in interest, plus $10,000 (20 percent of $50,000 appreciation). The municipal agency then uses its $35,000 to subsidize the next purchaser of that same home, which now costs $150,000, or to locate another unit to finance with the recaptured and augmented subsidy.

The goal of most subsidy recapture programs is twofold: to assist lower-income households in purchasing homes they could not otherwise afford, and to preserve and recycle the public's investment in housing. Continuing affordability of the housing itself has historically not been a goal. Equity-sharing programs directly assist homebuyers in purchasing homes at prevailing market rates, enabling them to get into the market and to profit from the deal, if and when they resell. These programs also serve as a mechanism for the City to recoup at least some of its investment. According to advocates of this approach: "With an equity sharing program, units can be sold and resold at market value without artificial controls or restrictions. Agencies can place the return on their investments in a revolving fund and then use those resources to help other potential buyers. Recycling public resources in this way is consistent with the current realization that both resources and the tax base are finite."[2]

Recycling funds in this way is also consistent with the common belief that cities should not unreasonably intervene in the market or unduly restrict an individual's rights as a homeowner. There is a premise that all parties involved should get their "fair return," based on whatever the market can generate and allocated according to whatever each party has invested in the deal.

Unfortunately, these same premises and practices compromise efforts to preserve the affordability of housing over time, particularly in inflating markets. The subsidy recapture model assumes that the market will stay flat enough for the pool of recycled funds to keep pace with rising housing costs. As the constant dollars available for housing shrink, however, and as housing costs escalate relative to household income, many cities are faced with the troubling reality that they cannot maximize the return on their investment without minimizing the affordability of the housing they subsidize. Conversely, they cannot ensure the affordability of the subsidized housing, as it changes hands at an unrestricted price, without assisting fewer and fewer buyers or adding more and more dollars to their original investment. This is the paradox at the heart of subsidy recapture: the preservation of the public subsidy is incompatible with the preservation of affordability, and vice versa.

SUBSIDY RECAPTURE IN ACTION: SAN FRANCISCO'S FIRST-TIME HOMEBUYER PROGRAM

San Francisco is a prime example of a city whose housing costs have escalated at an astronomical rate in the last decade while average incomes have lagged far behind. In the Bay Area between 1980 and 1990, median household income increased by 76 percent (not adjusted for inflation), while the median value of owner-occupied units increased by 162.8 percent and median rents increased by 131.8 percent. In the city of San Francisco between 1980 and 1990, the median home value increased from $104,600 to $298,900. This profile is typical of many West Coast cities where real estate values are still soaring—cities like Seattle, which is currently experiencing some of the same inflationary trends that swept California in the middle to late 1980s.

San Francisco was one of the first cities in California to institute a homeownership program using a subsidy recapture model based on shared equity. The San Francisco First-Time Homebuyer Program, begun in 1984, is administered by the Mayor's Office of Housing and Community Development. The program is targeted to first-time homebuyers earning up to 120 percent of the median income for San Francisco; it is not exactly a "low-income" housing program, but it makes a highly inflated homeownership market more accessible to moderate-income residents.[3]

Through the First-Time Homebuyer Program, the City provides deferred payment, shared appreciation, and second mortgages ranging from $35,000 to $65,000. The City will make a loan to an eligible buyer if his or her downpayment, combined with a conventional loan from a local bank, does not cover the cost of the home. The City's loan is subordinated to the conventional financing, and payment of the principal is deferred until the unit is sold or rented.

The deferred loan from the City serves to write down the initial cost of the property and thus to reduce the amount of debt the homeowner(s) must cover. When the unit is resold to another homebuyer, the subsidy must be repaid, along with a percentage of the appreciation proportionate to the City's initial investment in the property, plus an additional 10 percent of the appreciation.

The directors of the First-Time Homebuyer Program have tried to adapt the terms and policies of the program to accommodate changing market conditions. When the program first began in 1984, the City either collected a simple 6 percent annual interest rate on its loans or recaptured 20 percent of the appreciation, whichever was less. The high rate of inflation of land and housing costs in San Francisco quickly convinced the City that it needed to increase the percentage of recaptured appreciation. Otherwise, the program would never keep pace with the market, and the amount of subsidy needed to make the housing affordable to subsequent buyers would have to be increased substantially with each transfer. Since 1988, the City has taken back a portion of the appreciation that is equivalent to its proportionate share of the initial investment plus an additional 10 percent. Interest on the City's investment is no longer charged to the homeowner.

To preserve the affordability of these publicly subsidized homes, the City has tried to enforce contractual obligations of owners to sell to other eligible buyers. When buying into the shared equity arrangement, property owners must agree to restrictions that either limit the sale of the property for thirty years to another low- or moderate-income household or grant the City a right of first refusal to repurchase the property at the market rate if the homeowner decides to sell. The City may then assign its purchase right to another entity or individual, or it may repurchase the property and refinance it for another eligible buyer.

Despite these restrictions, assisted homeowners have been able to sell their homes at the highest possible price. An inflationary market and the lack of municipally imposed restrictions on profits or prices have meant that they could repay the City both the deferred loan and a share of their homes' appreciated value and still walk away with a substantial windfall. Many of the program's homeowners have done just that. Consequently, the subsidized homes themselves have become less and less affordable to subsequent moderate-income buyers, who require greater amounts of subsidy from the City.

The First-Time Homebuyer Program was established on the assumption that the City's initial investment of $35,000 to $65,000 would be "recycled" with little erosion and little need of replenishment as long as the rate of appreciation in housing costs was not 4 percent higher than the rate of increase in median income. This assumption proved way off the mark. As noted earlier, there has been a much larger gap between housing costs and household incomes in the Bay Area over the last decade.

The City of San Francisco responded by revamping the program's terms and conditions to capture a greater portion of an assisted property's equity upon resale, but this has not prevented the gradual depletion of the original subsidy pool. According to Joe LaTorre, director of the mayor's Office of Housing and Community Development, it now takes the recycled subsidy from *two* homes, on average, to finance each new homebuyer in the current market. In a market like San Francisco's, simply recycling a portion of the market appreciation does not ensure the preservation of affordability or the preservation of the original subsidy pool.

The most glaring weakness of San Francisco's First-Time Homebuyer Program is its inability to fulfill its own objective of preserving a pool of public subsidies for affordable housing. The recapture mechanism, while allowing initial homeowners to reap the benefits of traditional homeownership, simply does not keep pace with the cost of housing. Without any limits on resale prices or profits, individual homeowners walk off with huge equity windfalls while the pool of public dollars for future deals steadily shrinks.

Even when the original homeowner sells to another eligible buyer (of which there are many on a long waiting list), the sale price is still at the highest possible market rate. The City must compensate for an ever-widening affordability gap with an ever-higher subsidy, reducing the total subsidy pool over time; this is precisely what subsidy recapture programs profess, or at least aim, to avoid. The City gets something back on its original investment, but it must reach into its pockets again and again to refinance other homes (or the same homes) at inflated prices. These outcomes have led policy analysts and the managers of these publicly financed loan programs to question the benefits resulting from the subsidy recapture approach.

DOES SUBSIDY RECAPTURE WORK?

Are there circumstances under which a subsidy recapture program might work? Is the paradox—and failure—I have noted in San Francisco unique to that city's particular homeownership program, or is it intrinsic to subsidy recapture itself? While many market conditions and political constraints affect the success of any municipal housing program, my own conclusion is that there is a fundamental problem with the recapture approach to preserving public dollars. Under inflating market conditions, in particular, it is ineffective, judged solely by the standards that most subsidy recapture programs set for themselves.

The San Francisco scenario of spiraling housing costs and shrinking recaptured subsidies has, in fact, been played out in a number of other communities in California, as well as in other parts of the country. Two studies from other cities, one on the West Coast and the other on the East, further illuminate the concerns I have raised and support my conclusion that, in most cases, subsidy retention, rather than subsidy recapture, is a more effective means of recycling public dollars invested in affordable housing.

San Mateo, California

The Community Development Department of the City of San Mateo, California, commissioned an analysis of different shared appreciation models in 1990 to determine whether the recapture approach would be an effective use of municipal resources for a first-time homebuyer program. A careful analysis led to the conclusion that only by intervening in the market and restricting the resale prices of subsidized housing would the City be able to maintain the initial level of affordability and to recycle its subsidy efficiently.[4] The study showed that if no resale restrictions were imposed, the City would have to recapture almost all of the appreciation in order to maintain affordability with the same level of subsidy (see chart in Appendix showing diminishing returns of subsidy relative to housing costs).

Given the high inflation rate of housing in the area, even a fifty-fifty split in the appreciation between the City and the homeowner would not allow the City to recapture enough funds to sustain the unit's affordability (that is, its affordability to another buyer at the same relative income level). The City would be obliged either to pump additional dollars into the unit for a new eligible owner or to lose the unit to the market when it resold. According to the City's assumptions, only if the rate of inflation in housing prices dropped significantly below the twenty-year historical trend of 12.31 percent would the fifty-fifty split be sufficient to maintain the unit's affordability.

Based on the above analysis, the Community Development Department of San Mateo concluded that the only model that would maintain the affordability of assisted units and not require the City to continue to refinance units with ever-greater amounts of public money would be one in which resale prices were restricted to the rate of increase of San Mateo's median income. Applying such a resale restriction, homeowners would be allowed to resell their homes only for an amount equal to what would be affordable for a moderate-income buyer.[5] The units themselves would remain affordable to the low- to moderate-income group for whom the program was originally designed.

Boston

In Boston, Massachusetts, a similar conclusion was reached in 1988 by the Public Facilities Department (PFD) in its analysis of different options for the use of municipal housing subsidies. PFD concluded that programs that attempt to recapture City subsidies and then rebuild or refinance new units are not self-sustaining and are not efficient from an economic standpoint. Without restricting resale prices, such programs would require significant additional public investment to maintain the initial affordability level over time. According to PFD's assistant director at the time, "Restricting resale prices to a fixed 5–6 percent increase is at least twice as efficient at maintaining the availability of an affordable housing stock as options that rely on the recapture and recycling of funds."[6]

Tables 3-1 and 3-2, developed by PFD, give an indication of the level of additional subsidy required over a ten-year period using a simple recapture mechanism.

Given projected inflation in the Boston housing market, PFD's conclusion was that it would cost the City $79,422 per unit in subsidy to make homeownership affordable to a low-income buyer in 1998, compared to $25,000 per unit in 1988. Even if the full $33,597 of City funds were recaptured, there would still be a funding gap of $45,825 in 1998. In other words, unless the City were to continue to pump additional subsidy into the program, there would be a dramatic reduction in the affordable housing stock. Under this "recycle and rebuild" scenario, for every one hundred units lost through resale, only forty-two new homes could be rebuilt with the remaining funds. More than half (58 percent) of the units financed with municipal funds would be permanently lost when the first owners decided to sell.

Cost efficiency is even poorer in programs that recapture funds from assisted units resold at market rates and then use these funds to refinance the *same* home for the next buyer. Using a finite allocation of public funds, only thirty-eight units out of every one hundred that were initially subsidized would remain affordable.

Compared to the above, the option of restricting resale prices, as shown in Table 3-2, was found to be a much more efficient mechanism for maintaining affordability and preserving public funds.

Using this "restrict and retain" approach, limiting appreciation to an income growth rate of 5.62 percent (the average neighborhood growth rate over fifteen years), *no additional subsidy would be required* over time. One

Table 3-1. Subsidy Recapture: "Recycle and Rebuild"

	1988	*1998*
Construction cost	$100,000	$208,997
Affordable price	75,000	129,575
Subsidy required	25,000	79,422
Recapture, 1998 (lend at 3%)	N/A	33,597
Resubsidy required in 1998	N/A	*45,825*

Source: Public Facilities Department, City of Boston, unpublished paper, 1988.

Table 3-2. Subsidy Retention: "Restrict and Retain"

	1988	*1998*
Construction cost	$100,000	$208,997
Affordable price	75,000	129,575
Restricted price	75,000	129,575
Recapture 1998	N/A	10,914
Resale price for homeowner, 1998	N/A	118,661
Subsidy required	*25,000*	0

Source: Public Facilities Department, City of Boston, unpublished paper, 1988.

hundred units subsidized by the City would result in one hundred units of affordable housing even after resale. Not only would the City not need to replenish its original subsidy pool, but additional revenue would be generated for the City to finance more homes. Though the homeowner would not get the maximum appreciation that the home could produce, linking the return to average income growth would still yield significant annual increases in equity for the homeowner, well above what might be earned, for example, had that money been placed in a conventional investment such as a CD or government bond.

CONCLUSION: PITFALLS AND POPULARITY OF SUBSIDY RECAPTURE

The success of a subsidy recapture program, in terms of financial efficiency, depends to a great extent on the local real estate market, the availability of developable land, and the amount of subsidy a municipality is able to recapture when homes are resold (that is, the percentage of appreciation that accrues to the municipality with each resale). In rural areas or more depressed urban areas, where inflation in real estate is relatively low, subsidy recapture may be a financially viable model for assisting first-time homeowners and recycling scarce public dollars.

The economics of this program simply do not work, however, in urban and suburban areas where steady appreciation in land and housing prices is the norm. Public subsidies will eventually be depleted and private affordability will eventually be compromised. Municipalities will be in the position of continually pumping additional funds into the same (or similar) units in order to keep them within the financial reach of potential low- to moderate-income buyers. Without price restrictions, initial homeowners will walk off with substantial equity due to market appreciation. Prospective homebuyers of modest means will walk into closed doors—priced out of the appreciating market altogether.

Subsidy recapture does nothing to limit the endlessly spiraling cost of real estate that makes affordable housing a more and more remote dream for most lower-income people in this country. Instead of controlling the cost of housing, the municipality with a subsidy recapture program is actually given a stake in the kind of petty speculation that helped create its housing problem in the first place. It also, inadvertently, is given a stake in all the antisocial consequences of our national obsession with appreciating property values: the temptation to weigh in on the side of anyone who resists the "invasion" of minorities, the siting of public facilities, the development of homeless shelters, or any event perceived as a "threat to property values."

Subsidy recapture also does nothing to expand the *supply* of affordable housing—and may do just the opposite. Housing that may have been relatively affordable when first purchased with a public subsidy tends to become less and less affordable over time. Indeed, many subsidy recapture programs should not really be called affordable housing programs at all because they eventually lose affordable units to the market rather than preserve them.

In addition to these problems associated with the cost and supply of housing, subsidy recapture is flawed in its underlying assumption of limitless growth. The proponents of recapture programs seem to assume that there is an infinite amount of land on which to build new housing as homes are sold off and subsidies are recycled. But the economic, social, and environmental conditions most communities face do not allow for the ongoing development and loss of affordable housing, compromising the integrity and accessibility of existing neighborhoods. The limitless growth mentality becomes particularly problematic as more and more cities and rural communities institute strict antigrowth and infrastructure regulations.

With all the problems accompanying the subsidy recapture approach, why is it embraced by so many cities? Why does subsidy recapture seem an attractive and justifiable alternative to subsidy retention?

The first answer is that subsidy recapture programs are easier to sell politically—to city councils, to financial institutions, to current homeowners, and to potential homeowners alike. These programs tend to be perceived as "fair," with each party getting a fair return on its investment, and as a way to help moderate-income families get a "foot in the door." Tampering with the market—or the right to profit from it—is a more difficult policy for most municipalities to contemplate or defend.

Public officials are more likely to view appreciation through the eyes of bankers than through the eyes of low-income communities. The idea of using public money to push up property values is often perceived as positive—a way to "improve" local properties and neighborhoods. Appreciating property values are seen by bankers and public officials alike as a welcome opportunity to share in the action rather than as a dreaded threat to neighborhood stability and the long-term affordability of housing.

These prejudices and preconceptions aside, subsidy recapture does not measure up, not even to the minimal standard that it sets for itself of "recycling" and protecting a pool of public subsidies. Public dollars are better protected through subsidy retention, leveraged over time into greater and greater *community* wealth. A permanent pool of affordable housing can, in the end, assist many more first-time homebuyers than a typical recapture program without additional infusions of capital. Subsidy retention yields a perpetual return on the public dollar in the form of a permanent—and expanding—stock of affordable housing. This is a lasting benefit that is enhanced, not diminished, with the passage of time.

San Mateo Analysis

*Model 1: Shared Appreciation (No Resale Price Control)**

	At 12.31%	*At 9.5%*
Resale price 2000	$574,721	$446,081
First mortgage 1990 (repaid)	$157,184	$157,184
City subsidy 1990 (repaid)	22,816	22,816
Deferred city interest	36,363	36,363
Subtotal A	($216,363)	($216,363)
Total appreciation (Resale minus subtotal A)	$358,357	$229,718
50% Owner share	$179,179	$114,859
50% City share	179,179	114,859
	$358,357	$229,718
Funding available for unit		
50% City share	$179,179	$114,859
Mortgage differential	146,858	146,858
Subtotal A	$216,363	$216,363
Total funding for unit	$542,400	$478,080
FUNDING GAP (city surplus in parentheses)	$32,321	($31,999)

*Model 2: Subsidy Retention (Resale Price Control)**

	At 12.31%	*At 9.5%*
First mortgage 2000 (paid to owner)	$304,042	$304,042
First mortgage 1990	(157,184)	(157,184)
Owner's share of appreciation (mortgage differential)	$146,858	$146,858
City's share:		
Resale price 2000	$574,721	$446,081
First mortgage 2000	(304,042)	(304,042)

San Mateo Analysis, Continued

Model 2: Subsidy Retention (Resale Price Control) *

	At 12.31%	*At 9.5%*
City's share	$270,679	$142,039
% Owner's share	35	51
% City's share	65	49
FUNDING GAP	0	0

Assumptions for Both Models:

Sales Price 1990: $180,000
Resale Price 2000: @12.5% appreciation = $574,721
@ 9.5% appreciation = $446,081

110% Median income 1990: $50,160
110% Median income 2000: $97,020
Income increase: 6.28%
First mortgage 1990: $157,184
First mortgage 2000: $304,042
City subsidy: $22,816

Source: Analysis prepared for the Community Development Department of the City of San Mateo by the law firm of Goldfarb and Lipman, San Francisco, 1990.
*In model 1, the city receives 50% of the appreciation plus 10% compounded interest. In model 2, the city guarantees affordability; the owner's share of the appreciation is equal to the amount that is affordable to a new buyer at the same relative income level.

NOTES

1. The choice between subsidy retention and subsidy recapture has become very real for every municipality that is a "participating jurisdiction" under the National Affordable Housing Act of 1990 (NAHA). Title II of NAHA, the so-called HOME program, originally required resale restrictions on assisted owner-occupied units. Section 209 of the Housing and Community Development Act of 1992, however, amended NAHA to allow participating jurisdictions the option of either restricting the resale prices of HOME-assisted, owner-occupied units or recapturing the

HOME subsidy upon resale of the assisted units. No restrictions on price are required under the latter option.

2. See *Equity Sharing Handbook*, State of California Department of Housing and Community Development, Division of Community Affairs, Sacramento, Calif., June 1982.

3. The City also administers a first-time homebuyer program for condominium purchases for moderate-income residents. Price restrictions are set on these properties, and no City financing is provided. This price-restricted variation is not a part of the First-Time Homebuyer Program discussed here.

4. This analysis assumed twenty-year historical trends in housing costs and median incomes. It also assumed individual expenditures of 33 percent of gross income on housing costs.

5. The City would have to add an additional subsidy to these units only if the first homebuyer resold the house to someone earning less—for example, if a homeowner earning 120 percent of median income sold to someone earning 110 percent. The City would make up the difference.

6. Memo from Kevin McColl, Public Facilities Department, City of Boston, February 26, 1988.

4 Community-based Housing: Strengths of the Strategy amid Dilemmas that Won't Go Away

RACHEL G. BRATT

For the past four decades there has been an increasing belief in the United States that neighborhood residents should play some role in community development activities. Initiatives have ranged from the rather mild provisions for citizen participation in the federal Urban Renewal program to the more powerful (although not necessarily more productive) calls for "maximum feasible participation" during the 1960s. As community residents have become frustrated with the results of citizen participation mandated from above, as federal programs and funding have been cut back, and as the neighborhood agenda has gained momentum, nonprofits and community-based groups have taken more initiative in housing and community development.

Nonprofits recently have gained visibility in policy debates and have won some important legislative victories at the national level. The Financial Institutions Reform, Recovery, and Enforcement Act of 1989 (FIRREA), the savings and loan bailout legislation, provides nonprofits the first right to purchase distressed S & L properties from the Resolution Trust Corporation. A similar provision, aimed at properties owned by failed commer-

A shorter version of this chapter first appeared in *Policy Studies Journal* 16, no. 2 (1987–1988): 324–334. This chapter is a revised and updated version of Rachel G. Bratt, "Community-based Housing: Strengths of the Strategy amid Dilemmas That Won't Go Away," in Naomi Carmon (ed.), *Neighborhood Policy and Programmes: Past and Present*, pp. 181–200 (London: Macmillan Academic and Professional Ltd., and New York: St. Martin's Press, 1990). Reprinted with permission of The Macmillan Press Ltd.

cial banks, was included in the Comprehensive Deposit Insurance Reform Act of 1991, the Federal Deposit Insurance Corporation (FDIC) bailout legislation. Also significant is the provision under Title VI of the Cranston-Gonzalez National Affordable Housing Act of 1990 that gives nonprofit organizations and other "priority purchasers," as a way of permanently solving the "expiring use" problem, the first right to make a bona fide offer to purchase a federally subsidized development whose owner has announced an interest in prepaying the mortgage.

But perhaps the major victory for community-based housing advocates is the Community Housing Partnership set-aside contained in Title II of the 1990 act, as part of the HOME program. At least 15 percent of each participating jurisdiction's HOME funds must be earmarked for use by nonprofit producers of affordable housing. Although this may be viewed as a step in the right direction, it is only a step. For FY1993 a total of only $150 million for the set-aside was appropriated (a reduction of 33 percent from FY1992). For locales receiving the minimum HOME allocation, $500,000, this translated into only $75,000, hardly enough to make a major dent in meeting a community's needs for affordable housing. Funds to meet the *operating* expenses of nonprofit Community Housing Development Organizations, a critical need, are restricted to 5 percent of each jurisdiction's overall HOME allocation. (In the original legislation, no such funding was earmarked.)

The newness of all these programs precludes any type of evaluation. However, it is relevant to note that federal support for community-based housing efforts has grown substantially over the past few years, lending legitimacy to the overall strategy.

Community-based housing programs can be defined as efforts in which members of a community group or tenants group join together to produce, rehabilitate, manage or own housing. The central feature is that control and often ownership of the housing is in the hands of the individuals who live in the housing or the community. These efforts can be distinguished from other forms of community action that have resulted in legislative or regulatory initiatives (for example, the Community Reinvestment Act, local rent control, and condominium conversion ordinances). Community-based housing programs actually provide housing or some services or resources that are needed for housing; legislative or regulatory initiatives depend on other actors to change their mode of operation to make housing more available or affordable.

Community-based housing organizations are generally nonprofits whose primary orientation is toward low- and moderate-income people in their neighborhoods. Although some community-based housing groups may form for-profit subsidiaries, the latter operate as facilitators of the overall goals of the parent nonprofit, community-based organization.

Community-based housing programs usually rely on considerable funding and technical assistance from outside sources, public and private. In this sense, they are not strictly self-help. Self-help efforts that are dependent on individuals helping themselves or each other in an informal context—such as through home repairs or renovations—are not considered community-based programs; the latter are carried out through a formal or semiformal arrangement or organizational framework. Finally, because outside resources are provided to community-based housing initiatives and the organization does not operate for profit, the net cost of the housing to renters or owners is usually below prices on the private, unsubsidized market.

Proponents from all political perspectives have heaped praise on community-based programs. Conservatives hail these efforts as signs that self-help and voluntarism can work and that public intervention is unnecessary; liberals see the potential in the community-based movement for better allocating resources and enabling citizens to enter the mainstream of society and thus to become more active participants in the democratic process; the left both lauds the empowerment and community control aspects of these efforts and warns that they can divert community leaders from demanding more sweeping and systemic changes.

Ideological arguments aside, the community-based housing stratgegy has some positive and some negative attributes. As summarized in Table 4-1, the positive attributes are persuasive and the negative attributes can largely be countered with convincing explanations. Community-based groups must be viewed as both logical and competent housing providers.

HOUSING AS A COMMUNITY DEVELOPMENT STRATEGY

Part of the reason why community-based groups emerge as good vehicles to produce low-income housing is that there are few other options at the present time. However, with respect to the broader issue of community development, housing rehabilitation and production is only one of the possible alternatives. The key competitor to a housing-oriented community development strategy is economic development, which entails job creation, assistance to new and existing small businesses, and occasionally facilitating a community buy-out of a firm threatening to leave the area. Yet many experiences with economic development to date have been problematic.

First, agencies experienced with economic development have reported difficulty in finding the right kinds of business ventures and entrepreneurs to support. A good idea does not evolve into a good business deal without management experience and expertise, as well as substantial personal commitment and involvement. Unfortunately, locating entrepreneurs with this mix of characteristics has turned out to be much harder than anticipated. Moreover, deals that were eventually funded often ended in default (Bratt and Geiser, 1982).

Second, economic development attempts to do something that the private market has already decided is unprofitable. Although the judgment of a bank not to invest in a local business or the decision of a firm to leave an area may be based on false notions of neighborhood decline and unprofitability, it may rest on an accurate assessment. In particular, firms that leave an area usually do so *after* profits have fallen. Residents in low-income neighborhoods, by definition, have little money with which to support businesses and services. In fact, a business venture in almost any neighborhood is faced with an uncertain market once it is operational.

Third, economic development is usually an invisible activity that does not have a direct neighborhood impact. A venture that creates a handful of jobs does not have a visual presence and does not represent a tangible sign that the community is rejuvenating itself. In short, community economic development appears to be dependent on factors that operate outside the neighborhood, and successful initiatives can be hidden from the community's view.

In comparison to the obstacles associated with using economic development as the vehicle for community development, housing emerges as a much more viable strategy. Most important is the very strong demand for decent, affordable housing in most market areas. There is little chance that such housing would languish unrented on the marketplace. In addition, housing is an extremely satisfying, visible indication of a community development process. Unlike job creation or business development, there is nothing "behind the scenes" about transforming a vacant lot into new housing units or rehabilitating an abandoned or deteriorated building. Housing development changes a neighborhood in observable, "concrete" ways.

For all these reasons, the vast majority of community-based organizations are predominantly engaged in housing activities (NCCED, 1991;

Table 4-1. Positive and Negative Attributes of the Community-based Housing Strategy

Positive	*Negative*	*Response to Negative*
1. Housing problems that probably would not be addressed are alleviated. 2. Community-based housing programs can provide important personal benefits both to local citizens who are active members in the community-based organization and to residents. The former gain useful experience in housing development and management; the latter usually gain some control over their living environments. 3. Community-based housing groups often branch out to provide social service programs, such as day care, job training, or elderly services. 4. Community-based housing developments can help stabilize a neighborhood, serving as a hedge against displacement and gentrification.	1. Volume of production is too low to be significant.	a. Some housing is better than no housing. b. Little low-income housing is being produced in any other way, and the demand is acute. c. Volume could be increased with sufficient publicly provided financial and technical supports.
	2. Many neighborhoods with serious housing problems but without organizational capacity might be left out.	Low-income housing should also be produced by other sponsors, such as local public housing authorities.
	3. Community groups are too inexperienced to assume responsibility for the complexities of housing development.	Many community-based housing groups have demonstrated their ability to do housing production, rehabilitation, and management. Newer groups could be assisted with sufficient public supports.
	4. It is very difficult to replicate a successful community-based housing program.	Replication has been accomplished for several programs, notably the Neighborhood Housing Services program.
	5. Predecessors of present-day community-based housing groups, the nonprofits of the 1960s and early 1970s, had a mixed record of	a. The "mixed record" also included many successes, some of which are detailed in this chapter.

Positive	Negative	Response to Negative
	achievement; developments owned by nonprofits defaulted at a higher rate than developments owned and operated by for-profit entities (also see note 5).	b. Nonprofits were allowed to participate in federally subsidized programs even if they had minuscule financial resources and reserves. c. Technical assistance and funding from the federal government and other agencies was minimal. d. The financing formula of the subsidy programs used by early nonprofits, Section 221(d)(3) and Section 236, did not provide for increases in operating expenses. This was also problematic for for-profit owners.
	6. The community-based housing strategy plays into conservative thinking that self-help can solve the housing problem and that the government need not provide additional resources.	Proponents of the community-based housing strategy must emphasize that self-help overtones do not mean that funding from other sources is unnecessary. Community-based housing advocates need to work for a comprehensive public support system.

Source: This table is condensed from information presented in two previous publications (Bratt, 1986, 1989a).

Vidal, 1992). But in spite of the relative advantages of the housing strategy, it is still important to consider how the broader economic needs of a community can be met. Increasingly, organizations that have successfully developed and managed housing have been revisiting the economic development agenda. Hopefully, the lessons from past economic development efforts will result in more promising programs and outcomes. There also has been growth in the importance and visibility of a handful of neighborhood-based comprehensive community development initiatives, which are being implemented in many cities across the country. Although housing is invariably an important component of such efforts, they also include planned or actual improvements in child and family services, recreational programs, and health care (Eisen, 1992). These types of programs, in which the citizen role is central, warrant continued support and study.

In summary, housing is a good approach, albeit a partial one, to neighborhood improvement and community development, and community-based sponsors appear to be in a good position to initiate and manage such projects. But before we can fully embrace community-based housing as both a housing and a community development strategy, six major dilemmas inherent in the approach should be examined.[1]

Dilemma 1. Unrestricted Private Ownership and Accumulation versus Social Control and Access

Some community-based housing programs involve transfering ownership to residents or assisting individuals to purchase or rehabilitate their own homes, with no continuing restrictions on resales or rents. However, much of what is generally thought of as community-based housing is dependent on long-term ownership, management, or control by a community-based organization. In advocating a community-based housing strategy, we are, therefore, implicitly supporting a social housing agenda over one that advances unrestricted private ownership and accumulation.

In this country, homeownership has been called the "American Dream." It is no accident that at two key points in recent history—during the economic upheavals of the 1930s and during the urban riots of the 1960s—homeownership was used as a vehicle to subdue unrest and discontent. First by providing mortgage insurance to lenders through the Federal Housing Administration and later by offering the poor opportunities to become homeowners through the Section 235 program, the government has supported the homeownership ideal. In addition, the homeowners' deduction—the ability of home-owning taxpayers to deduct from income the interest portion of their mortgage payment as well as the total amount of property taxes paid when calculating their tax liability—is a critical way in which the government actively reinforces the dream and reality of homeownership. Whether these initiatives have created a zeal for homeownership, thereby shaping consumer demand, or whether they simply have responded to deep-seated aspirations "to own a place of one's own," may be debatable. But particularly in the absence of competitive alternatives to ownership, most people in the United States—two-thirds of all households—choose to own their own homes, and many of those who do not often state that ownership is a dearly held goal (Tremblay and Dillman 1983; Fannie Mae, 1992; NAR, 1992). In view of this, a policy that supports social ownership in favor of unrestricted, individual ownership would seem to be severely out of step with the preferences of most individuals. Thus, the first part of this dilemma questions on what grounds, if any, it makes sense to advocate a community-based housing strategy instead of a traditional homeownership approach?

First, a comprehensive policy to assist low-income households could include a homeownership component (such as the Nehemiah program), with price restrictions that keep owner-occupied homes affordable for future generations. Proposing a community-based strategy does not mean choosing only one form of housing tenure. Public policy ought to supply alternatives that reflect the range of consumer needs and choices. For some households, however, aside from their income level, homeownership is simply not the optimal tenure. Whether because the household has no interest in home maintenance, because the desire to live in a certain location may be short-lived, or because income is so limited or unpredictable that even subsidized homeownership may be too costly, rental units are still a necessary option for many people. In addition, to the extent that homeownership is most often associated with single-family homes, as opposed to cooperatives or condominiums, a physically handicapped or elderly individual may find owning a home an unwanted burden.

Second, much of the multiunit rental housing developed by community-based organizations actually appears to offer some of the most important attributes of individual ownership, such as the feeling of control over one's immediate environment and a sense of security.[2] For example, a community-based development can include tenants in management decisions, such as budgeting issues and repair and improvement priorities, and can foster a sense of shared ownership. Reporting on the feelings of tenants who live in housing built by a community-based organization in Boston, one observer noted: "Because of the large role the tenants had in designing it, and because, as members of Inquilinos Boricuas en Accion [a community-based organization] they own it, there is the pride of homeownership, of keeping it attractive" (Rivas, 1982). Similarly, a tenant in a building owned by Jubilee Housing, a community-based organization in Washington, D.C., described her perceptions: "How has the building changed since Jubilee took over? Well, I would say it is much better because we work together—we work with Jubilee to get the building in better shape. Now everybody takes their share of the work and we are getting along O.K." (Jubilee Housing, n.d.: 13).

Additional evidence that residents in community-based housing developments can have many of the same feelings about security and control over their living environments as homeowners comes from a 1988 survey for which I was responsible, under contract to the Neighborhood Reinvestment Corporation. Thirty-nine of the forty-nine residents living in a mutual housing development in Baltimore were surveyed by staff of the Cosmos Corporation. The survey found the following:

> Nearly two-thirds of mutual housing residents . . . think of themselves more as owners than as renters. . . . They also indicated that some of the best features about the Association are ones that are related closely to the homeownership experience.
>
> For instance, the two features of mutual housing that received the highest ratings pertain to financial and personal security . . . [Mutual housing residents understand that] increases in monthly payments are directly related to increases in real costs . . . and [they have] security against displacement.
>
> Also highly valued by over 40 percent of the respondents is the sense of having a monetary investment in the property, the low monthly payment, and the opportunity for another family or household member to succeed them in occupancy of the unit. Taken together, these data provide a good indication that some of the key attributes of homeownership, as well as the feeling of being a homeowner, are clearly experienced by [Alameda Place] residents. (Bratt, 1990b: 41–42)

Although a tenant in a community-based development may face a loss of security through eviction, the reasons for this happening are likely to be limited to nonpayment of rent and extreme disruptiveness. In contrast, tenants in for-profit developments also may be evicted or have to leave because rents undergo a larger than expected increase or because the building is converted to high-priced cooperatives and condominiums. Thus, although a sense of empowerment and security may be greater in a home of one's own, community-based housing appears to offer these advantages, at least to some extent.

Third, community-based housing, in which tenants have more control than in a traditional rental situation, may provide a good opportunity to develop some of the skills in property management and budgeting that are useful if the household assumes home ownership at some later time.

Although most housing produced by community-based housing groups is multifamily rental housing, many organizations have also developed units for sale. The second aspect of the dilemma of unrestricted private ownership and accumulation versus social control and access relates to the desirability of placing limitations on the amount the housing can appreciate. If the housing is owner-occupied, as in a cooperative or traditional one-family home, is it appropriate to limit the return on the household's equity to some fixed standard, which would be below what would be obtained if the unit were sold privately, without any restrictions?

Arguing that it is unfair to a low- to moderate-income household who has bought its own unit in which equity appreciation is limited, one could question why this household should be prohibited from enjoying an inflationary housing market while more affluent cooperators or homeowners are not? Is it fair to advocate a policy that puts a ceiling on the monetary benefits an individual can derive from housing when greater benefits are commonplace in the rest of the housing system?

In response, on the assumption that public subsidies were used to develop, rehabilitate, or reduce the purchase price or operating costs of the housing, it seems rational that the appreciation should not be exclusively the property of the occupant. Assuming that the lower-cost housing is needed by future households, then it may be unconscionable as a public policy to allow units that were supported with a public subsidy to disappear as a public resource. The point of an equitable housing policy is not to reward households that are lucky enough to obtain a low-cost unit but to make sure that the overall public good is enhanced by providing access to that housing by needy households for as long into the future as possible or necessary.

But there is yet another perspective on this issue. If one compares the indirect public subsidy through the IRS code, which allows homeowners to deduct the interest portion of their mortgage payments from their incomes when calculating their tax liabilities, with the direct public subsidies received by community-based housing groups, one could argue that it is unfair to restrict appreciation of equity for owners in the latter subsidy program but not for those in the former program.

Both aspects of this dilemma, unrestricted private ownership versus social control and private accumulation versus social access, encompass two sets of provocative arguments. Advocating a community-based housing strategy implies a willingness to accept the strong social objectives inherent in the community-based approach. But to the extent that these may clash with private goals or preferences, the dilemma is likely to be debated over and over again.

Dilemma 2. Targeting Local Residents versus Open Access or Occupancy According to Need

A large part of a community-based organization's agenda usually involves an explicit focus on improving conditions in the neighborhood or preserving existing resources for local residents. In short, community-based development, by definition, involves a strategy of targeting improvements to the indigenous population.

At first glance, this appears both logical and straightforward. However, the community-based approach can create some interesting conflicts, pitting two seemingly legitimate views against each other. Opposing the directing of resources to local citizens are advocates both for low-income residents in general, who happen to live outside the targeted area, and for racial groups who do not comprise the dominant group in the community and have no representation in the community-based organization.

Two brief examples illustrate the conflict. Several years ago when Inquilinos Boricuas en Accion (IBA), a prominent Hispanic community-based organization in the South End of Boston, completed a new federally subsidized housing development, it was charged with discriminating against eligible non-Hispanic applicants, particularly African Americans. Although the units had been developed by the Hispanic organization, African American community leaders argued that limiting occupancy to Hispanics was in violation of civil rights laws. Subsequently, IBA agreed to set aside a proportion of its units for non-Hispanic tenants (Rivas, 1982).

More recently, the Massachusetts Commission against Discrimination in Housing (MCAD) issued a complaint against the bricklayers' union, which had developed eighteen low-cost houses for sale, for limiting eligibility to existing residents in the neighborhood in which the new houses were built. Because only 15 of the neighborhood's 31,000 residents are African American and there are few other minorities, the targeting would have had a discriminatory effect. Since the City had sold the land to the union for $1, any form of discrimination, whether intentional or not, could not be permitted. As the MCAD chairman noted: "The point is access" (*Boston Globe* editorial, 12 March 1986).

Although these two cases were resolved relatively easily and promptly, the underlying dilemma is likely to be played out in many similar circumstances. Whether the community-based approach will be able to sustain support from neighborhood residents while accommodating to the legal and ethical demands of outsiders remains to be seen.

Dilemma 3. Ability to Maintain Community and Tenant Orientation versus Need to Act like a Developer and Landlord

It is widely accepted that the goals of for-profit landlords in producing, owning, and managing housing differ from those of tenants. For the owner, there is a desire to reduce costs as much as possible, even if maintenance and repairs are sometimes compromised, and to keep rents as high as the market will bear. Clearly, for tenants, the reverse is true. To what extent are community-based developers and owners in the identical position as their for-profit counterparts? They, too, must be concerned with the "bottom line" and must make sure that their costs can be met by rental income. Moreover, whether as a general partner in a limited partnership, as a landlord, or as a manager, the community-based sponsor is required to accept the basic operations of the housing finance and real estate system. It is somewhat ironic that most community-based housing has been developed by a nonprofit group entering into a for-profit limited partnership (Schuman, 1986).

While there is a great deal of truth to these observations, several responses can be made. First, despite the need for community-based groups to become players in the market economy, they still are much more likely to undertake nonmarket types of projects and to behave in more socially conscious ways than strictly for-profit developers. In terms of targeting their housing to low-income people, charging low rentals, and being willing to undertake projects in neighborhoods that for-profit developers would avoid, nonprofit community-based developers have traditionally been much more concerned with social issues than those operating for profit. From several studies done during the late 1960s and early 1970s the following patterns emerged:

- Nonprofit sponsors used the rent supplement and the leased housing programs proportionally more frequently than for-profit developers, thereby making units more affordable and available to lower-income people (Disario, 1969; Keyes, 1971).[3]
- A comparison of nonprofit and for-profit developments in Boston revealed that tenants in the former paid lower average rentals (Disario, 1969).
- Research conducted by HUD disclosed that projects built by nonprofit sponsors served needier families than those built by limited dividend sponsors (HUD, 1975).[4]
- Based on an evaluation in twenty-four cities, it was learned that nonprofit sponsors of 221(d)(3) housing were more likely than for-profit developers to undertake projects in urban renewal areas (Keyes, 1971).
- Many community-based sponsors openly confronted the toughest housing issues: central city rehabilitation, utilization of minority contractors and developers, and involvement of tenants in management decisions (Keyes, 1971).
- The Urban Institute found that cooperatively owned and nonprofit housing was, in general, more effectively managed than for-profit developments (cited in U.S. Comptroller General, 1978).

In addition to these concrete accomplishments indicating that community-based sponsors do not operate in the same ways as for-profit developers, nonprofits "break the rules" of the real estate system outright if they have to. For example, when confronted with the choice of defaulting on mortgage payments or reducing services to tenants, many nonprofits have chosen to provide housing services to tenants for as long as possible rather than to pay debt service to financial institutions.[5] A manager in a community-based development that had defaulted on its mortgage loan put it this way: "We had to make a decision, do you let people stay cold or do you pay the mortgage? Who[m] are we to serve, the government or the tenants?" (Urban Planning Aid, 1973: 41).

Although it is apparent that a nonprofit, community-based group is more likely than a for-profit owner to assume protenant positions, it is also clear that certain built-in conflicts between tenant and landlord are likely to persist no matter who the owner is. As long as community-based organizations stay in close contact with their tenants, these conflicts are likely to be minimal. But if the community-based group loses touch with its constituency, its tendency to act like a "regular" landlord could become problematic for tenants. Whether or not community-based groups will be able to stay in tune with resident needs while operating in a fiscally responsible manner will become clear only with time.

Dilemma 4. Advocacy versus Project Development

Many community-based development groups were originally organized around advocacy issues such as rent control, antiarson, mortgage disinvestment, tenants rights, and urban renewal. After years of protest and fighting both city hall and powerful real estate interests, many organizations went on to do housing development. A key reason for this shift was frustration with limited gains and the compromises that had to be made in order to get any type of change or regulation.

For example, Kathy McAfee, a Boston housing activist, explains her annoyance with the enactment of a rent control measure sponsored by the Massachusetts Tenants Organization (MTO):

> When Boston's weak rent control ordinance was due to expire at the end of 1982, the MTO decided not to push for strong rent control or even reinstatement of the moderate, pre-1976 version. Instead, the MTO came up with a proposal for a Rent Grievance Board to which tenants could appeal rent increases. It was a measure that appeared to have a chance of passage precisely because it would not impinge significantly on the interests of most landlords and developers, and indeed, after an intensive lobbying campaign, a watered-down version of the grievance board was adopted.
>
> This pathetically weak measure has done little to stem the tide of rent increases. Most MTO members would agree, but they say they lacked the power to squeeze anything better out of the council at the time. (McAfee, 1986: 422)

Many protest organizations began to feel that this type of watered-down victory was worse than no victory at all. Instead, they began to focus on ways to take direct control of the production, ownership, and management of housing. Rather than trying to "change the system," they would try to leverage it to gain the resources and assistance needed to provide decent housing themselves. But herein lies a possible dilemma. For a protest organization, "fighting city hall" is both expected and considered a key strategy of change. However, a development organization needs to cultivate good relations with city hall as well as with members of the banking and development community. A group cannot easily picket the mayor's office in support of a rent control ordinance or lodge a protest against a bank for redlining and also apply for a Community Development Block Grant from the City or a mortgage loan from the bank. The two—protest and leveraging the system—simply do not go together easily.[6]

But maybe the change from protest to development is good. Maybe there is no need for a group to do both. This is plausible, but there are still persuasive reasons why a strong community group organized around protest is also likely to be essential.

First, while development is enormously satisfying, it directly benefits only a relatively small number of people. In contrast, while a strong rent control ordinance or condominium conversion law may be difficult to enact and problems in implementation may occur, the measure can assist thousands of households.

Second, organizing around an issue that directly affects people's lives is an extremely good way to foster resident participation. There is no way to have a mass protest movement without strong community support. A development organization, on the other hand, may become so immersed in the details of housing development and finance that it may quickly lose its grassroots support and find it impossible to engage many people in hours of technical conversations or in stacks of complex legal and financial documents. To what extent is a community-based housing development organization able to stay representative of citizen interests and concerns while struggling through a maze that often baffles even the most seasoned real estate entrepreneur? One might argue that unless a group remains active in advocacy and protest, it will quickly lose its base of support in the community. But unless it becomes familiar with the technicalities of development in a serious and professional way, the group will neither achieve credibility in the community nor be able to build, rehabilitate, own, or manage any housing.

The choice of how to balance advocacy activities and project development, therefore, presents itself as a critical dilemma facing community-based housing development organizations. Maintaining a vigorous protest agenda has clear advantages but exacts a price.

Dilemma 5. Maintaining a Good Staff versus Low Salaries and Few Opportunities for Advancement

One of the major factors determining the success of community-based housing development organizations is the quality and expertise of the staffs. In a study of ninety-nine neighborhood development organizations funded through the federal Neighborhood Self-Help Development Program,[7] Neil Mayer cited the importance of an executive director who is skillful in a wide variety of activities: providing overall direction and leadership, maintaining good relationships with the community, and being able to raise funds for project work. In addition, he underscored that the staff should have expertise in specific technical areas relevant to the development work, such as project financial feasibility and marketability (Mayer, 1984).

In short, the successful executive director of a community-based organization must be a first-rate entrepreneur. But while the private, for-profit sector pays such individuals handsomely, nonprofit salaries are usually meager. Often, a community-based organization is able to attract an individual who grows into being a good executive director. However, after several years, burnout can occur. Long hours, low pay, a constant scrambling for resources, problems with board members, and frustration getting projects off the drawing boards are some of the usual factors causing personnel to wear down and finally resign. An executive director of a successful organization often has many job options, but they almost always involve leaving the community. The high salaries offered by for-profit developers or the lure of private consulting may become too attractive to turn down. After years of gaining experience "in the trenches" and developing invaluable relationships, an executive director's skills are extremely marketable.

For staff members who want to advance in the agency, there are likely to be few, if any, positions to fill. The most recent data on the size of nonprofit community development corporations comes from a survey performed under the direction of Avis Vidal at the New School for Social Research. The results are clear: community development corporations are relatively small organizations with a median staff size of five professionals and two clerical or manual support workers, for a total of seven full-time paid employees (Vidal, 1992: 43–44).[8] This means that opportunities for promotion within the agency are slim. For example, a project director likely has no place to go besides the executive directorship, and if that position is filled, the career path hits a dead end, particularly if the area has no other similar organizations. For someone willing to relocate to another part of the country, there would be more opportunities, but the low pay and the importance of community familiarity often make this type of move unattractive.

Also, over the past decade, as state and local governments have increasingly supported community-based development organizations (Goetz, 1992), jobs with state and local government programs have become more prevalent. The growth of national intermediaries that support community-based development, moreover, such as the Local Initiatives Support Corporation, the Enterprise Foundation, and the Neighborhood Reinvestment Corporation, have provided additional career opportunities for nonprofit staff. But this can amount to a "brain drain" at the local level.

Thus an important dilemma facing community-based development organizations is how, in view of the critical importance of a good staff, to both attract and keep well-qualified personnel when their skills can be marketed elsewhere and when the community-based organization provides few opportunities for advancement? Both the comparatively low wage scale and the lack of good career paths in nonprofits appear to be structurally linked to community-based development work. Salaries in nonprofits will never be competitive with those offered by for-profit developers, the small size of most nonprofits precludes easy advancement, and the growth in technical assistance providers and in public programs targeted at nonprofits has created some lucrative job opportunities, with the unintended consequence of siphoning off experienced nonprofit staff.

Dilemma 6. Need to Provide Services to Original Target Group versus Potential for Neighborhood Change and Redefinition of the Organization's Objectives and Clientele

The most likely reason for a community-based organization to adopt a housing development agenda is to alleviate housing problems, particularly for low- and moderate-income households living in the area. Once the housing is built or rehabilitated and occupied by qualified households, at least some of the organization's objectives have been fulfilled. As long as the membership and board composition of the community-based group is oriented toward improving housing, the broad goals of the organization and of the original target group—low- and moderate-income households—are largely consistent with each other.

As time passes, however, the neighborhood may go through a period of rejuvenation and possibly gentrification. This could, in turn, result in a change in the organization's membership, its board, and ultimately its original objectives. It is possible, for example, for a new group of more affluent residents to assume control of the organization and to change its goals to reflect the interests of the newcomers. One way to avoid potential conflicts with future tenants may be for existing community-based organizations to place long-range restrictions as to occupancy on the deeds of properties owned by the organization.

Since change of some type is virtually inevitable and since an area in which a strong community-based group is operating may stand a good chance of becoming upgraded, this dilemma can pose serious problems for low-income neighborhood residents. Its resolution has a great deal to do with the long-range viability of a community-based housing strategy.

POSTSCRIPT AND FUTURE DIRECTIONS FOR COMMUNITY-BASED HOUSING

Since the original versions of this chapter were published (Bratt, 1987–1988, 1989a, 1990a), additional problems and dilemmas facing nonprofits have begun to surface that likely will have major implications for the success of the fledgling movement. For example, development groups are under constant pressure to show development outputs, while less measurable needs or problems facing the community may go unmet. Although this is partially an extension of dilemma 4, the concern here goes beyond whether the organization is involved with advocacy and whether the group is directly focusing on the array of social, political, and economic components that contribute to a viable neighborhood.

The two major surveys of outputs of community-based development organizations, carried out by Vidal (1992) and NCCED (1991), focus on the activities that are most easily quantified: number of housing units produced, commercial projects undertaken, jobs created, or small businesses assisted. While these are extremely valuable efforts, and the data are enormously helpful, they go only part of the way toward providing a full understanding of the outputs of community-based development organizations. Less easy to measure, but ultimately at the core of the judged success of the movement, are changes in the neighborhood's overall attractiveness, both to existing residents and to potential newcomers, the level of public and private investment in the neighborhood, the quality and availability of social services, changes in resident behavior and attitudes, and the political strength of the community.[9]

Another critical concern facing the community-based housing movement is whether organizations will be able to maintain existing housing developments, both physically and financially. In the end, the success of nonprofit production programs will be measured more by whether the developments remain viable and affordable over the long term rather than by whether needed units can be produced over the short term. At present, there is no program aimed specifically at the existing stock of nonprofit-owned affordable housing. Long-term management issues, unless aggressively addressed, may prove to be the Achilles heel of the community-based housing movement.[10]

At the start of this chapter, the several ways in which nonprofit groups recently have gained national recognition were outlined. The HOME program with the 15 percent set-aside for nonprofits, enacted as part of the Cranston-Gonzalez National Affordable Housing Act of 1990, was briefly mentioned. Although this program has been widely supported by housing advocacy groups, such as the National Low-Income Housing Coalition, it is only a partial response to the needs of nonprofit housing developers and managers. Overall funding is quite limited, the amount going to some jurisdictions is very small, and funds for operating expenses are minimal. The set-aside, while better than nothing, goes only a short way toward building the kind of comprehensive support system for nonprofits advocated by those writing about the issue (Bratt, 1989a and 1989b; Clay, 1990).

Nonprofits need to be aggressive in articulating the problems they face both in managing their stock of housing and in producing affordable units. They need to be clear about the inadequacies of the system in which they have been asked to function and to underscore that they are making the best of an extremely tough situation. As Koebel (1992) has noted: "If the nonprofit housing sector becomes identified as a supporter and benefactor of this inefficiency, it runs the risk of being branded as inefficient once again." Further, when problems arise, there will be a strong tendency to blame the nonprofits rather than to see the problems as outcomes of a flawed system. A "blaming the victim" scenario could prove seriously damaging to the struggling nonprofit housing movement.

Although many states and locales have done a great deal to support nonprofit, community-based housing development (Bratt, 1989a and 1989b; Clay, 1990; Goetz, 1992), these efforts go only part of the way toward building a comprehensive program to support nonprofits. Furthermore, while these state and local funds were crucial during the Reagan-Bush era, they are not secure. As many states and locales face their own fiscal crises, cutbacks have become commonplace.

Strong federal policies, programs, and financing are absolutely critical to community-based housing, but it remains to be seen whether the election of President Bill Clinton will signal a new phase in federal support for such housing. The federal government should also support low-income housing through a revitalized public housing program, as well as through new forms of public-private partnerships in which lessons from the past are incorporated into the new initiatives (Bratt, 1989a). We must work toward the creation of a well-funded and multifaceted federal housing agenda that enables state and local governments, along with nonprofit organizations, to create programs that truly address and alleviate the housing needs of low-income people.

The many dilemmas of community-based housing will likely be the subject of numerous debates in the years ahead as local residents develop their own community-based programs and as mature organizations grapple with growth and development. While these dilemmas shed light on some of the conflicts facing nonprofit, community-based development, they do not undermine the overall approach. Community-based housing offers considerable advantages over other options for increasing the supply of low-cost housing (Bratt, 1985, 1989a). The past contributions of nonprofit housing developers have been significant. The potential of these developers is great. Public policy, at all levels of government, should support their growth.

NOTES

1. For an interesting parallel discussion of problems and options confronting neighborhood planning and development organizations, see Checkoway (1985) and Clay (1990).

2. Although security against unwanted displacement is thought to be a right of homeownership, Hartman, Keating, and LeGates (1982: 94) have pointed out that this widely touted benefit can be illusory: "Homeownership is no guarantee of housing security anymore, if it ever was. Sometimes displacement comes at the hands of speculators. . . . Sometimes . . . it is from government economic development policies. Sometimes . . . it is from public works projects that offer inadequate reimbursements and relocation assistance. Sometimes regressive property taxes are

the cause. And sometimes it is greedy credit institutions that feed on the incomes of people already run down by inflation." Similarly, a *New York Times Magazine* article in 1982 was titled, "Foreclosing on a Dream," and stated: "Owning a house used to be the goal of most American couples. But as a troubled economy forces record numbers to lose their homes to foreclosure, their dream has come to a painful end" (Brooks, 1982).

3. Clancy et al. (1973: 49) pointed out that a "high level of rent supplement or leased housing units in a Section 236 project, creates a more difficult management situation requiring much greater input of management staff time."

4. However, the same report also noted that "limited dividend sponsored units serve minorities more than nonprofit sponsored units do." It added: "No plausible explanation can be suggested for this situation" (HUD, 1975:7).

5. During the early 1970s the foreclosure rate among all subsidized housing developments, notably those built under the Section 221(d)(3) and Section 236 programs, was high. For the reasons behind this see Bratt (1989a). However, the foreclosure rate for nonprofit developments was two to four times higher than for for-profit developments. One reason for the financial problems facing nonprofits was their desire to operate the buildings as well as they could with their limited resources.

6. Some community-based groups have reputations for merging advocacy and development (e.g., the Coalition for a Better Acre in Lowell, Massachusetts). Vidal (1992) reports that a majority of community development corporations in her survey are involved with some form of advocacy work.

7. The Neighborhood Self-Help Development Program, enacted in 1978, provided $15 million in direct federal grants to neighborhood development organizations during 1979 and 1980.

8. For earlier data on the size of nonprofit development organizations see Mayer (1984) and Cohen and Kohler (1983).

9. Additional research is currently underway at the New School for Social Research, which is, in fact, attempting to assess the record of community development corporations in these areas.

10. This conclusion is based on numerous conversations with people involved with community development corporations in various parts of the country.

REFERENCES

Bratt, Rachel G. "Housing for Low-Income People: A Preliminary Comparison of Existing and Potential Supply Strategies." *Journal of Urban Affairs* 7, no. 3 (1985): 1–18.

———. "Community-based Housing Programs: Overview, Assessment and

Agenda for the Future." *Journal of Planning Education and Research* 5, no. 3 (1986): 164–77.

———. "Dilemmas of Community-based Housing." *Policy Studies Journal* 16, no. 2 (1987–1988): 324–334.

———. *Rebuilding a Low-Income Housing Policy*. Philadelphia: Temple University Press, 1989a.

———. "Community-based Housing in Massachusetts: Lessons and Limits of the State's Support System." In Sara Rosenberry and Chester Hartman (eds.), *Housing Issues of the 1990s*, pp. 277–306. New York: Praeger, 1989b.

———. "Community-based Housing: Strengths of the Strategy amid Dilemmas That Won't Go Away." In Naomi Carmon (ed.), *Neighbourhood Policy and Programmes: Past and Present*, pp. 181–200. London: Macmillan Academic and Professional Ltd., 1990a.

———. "Neighborhood Reinvestment Corporation–sponsored Mutual Housing Associations: Experiences in Baltimore and New York." Washington, D.C.: Neighborhood Reinvestment Corporation, 1990b.

Bratt, Rachel G., and Kenneth Geiser. "Community-based Economic Development: The Massachusetts Experience." Tufts University Unpublished manuscript, 1982.

Brooks, Andree. "Foreclosing on a Dream." *New York Times Magazine*, 12 September 1982.

Checkoway, Barry. "Neighborhood Planning Organizations: Perspectives and Choices." *Journal of Applied Behavioral Science* 21, no. 4 (1985): 471–486.

Clancy, Patrick E., Langley C. Keyes, Jr., Edward H. Marchant, and Robert B. Whittlesey. "The Role of Non-profit Organizations in the Housing Process." Report to HUD (mimeo), 1973.

Clay, Phillip L. "Mainstreaming the Community Builders: The Challenge of Expanding the Capacity of Non-profit Housing Development Organizations." Cambridge, Mass.: Department of Urban Studies and Planning, MIT, 1990.

Cohen, Rick, and Miriam Kohler. "Neighborhood Development Organizations after the Federal Funding Cutbacks: Current Conditions and Future Directions." Paper prepared for Division of Policy Development and Research, U.S. Department of Housing and Urban Development, Contract Order No. HUD 7177-82, 1983.

Disario, Rita Michele. "Non-profit Housing Sponsors: An Evaluative Study." M.C.P. thesis, MIT, 1969.

Eisen, Arlene. "A Report on Foundations' Support of Comprehensive Neighborhood-Based Community-Empowerment Initiatives." New York: New York Community Trust, 1992.

Fannie Mae. "Fannie Mae National Housing Survey." Washington, D.C., 1992.

Goetz, Edward G. "Local Government Support for Non-profit Housing: A Survey of U.S. Cities." *Urban Affairs Quarterly* 27, no. 3 (1992): 420–435.

Hartman, Chester, Dennis Keating, and Richard LeGates. *Displacement: How to Fight It*. Berkeley, Calif.: National Law Project, 1982.

HUD (U.S. Department of Housing and Urban Development). "Housing Production with Non-profit Sponsors." Staff study, 1975.

Jubilee Housing, Inc. "The Making of a Jubilee Co-op: The Ontario Court." Washington, D.C., n.d.

Keyes, Langley. "The Role of Non-profit Sponsors in the Production of Housing." In "Papers Submitted to Subcommittee on Housing, Panels on Housing Production, Housing Demand, and Developing a Suitable Living Environment," Part 1, Committee on Banking and Currency, U.S. House of Representatives, 92d Congress, 1st session, 1971, pp. 159–181.

Koebel, Theodore C. "International Comparisons of Nonprofit Housing in the Post–Welfare State." Paper presented at 1992 AREUEA/USC School of Business Administration, International Conference on Real Estate and Urban Economics, Redondo Beach, Calif., October 23, 1992.

Mayer, Neil S. *Neighborhood Organizations and Community Development*. Washington, D.C.: Urban Institute, 1984.

McAfee, Kathy. "Socialism and the Housing Movement: Lessons from Boston." In Rachel G. Bratt, Chester Hartman, and Ann Meyerson (eds.), *Critical Perspectives on Housing*, pp. 405–427. Philadelphia: Temple University Press, 1986.

National Association of Realtors (NAR). "Survey of Homeowners and Renters: Key Findings." Washington, D.C., 1992.

National Congress for Community Economic Development (NCCED). *Changing the Odds: The Achievements of Community-based Development Corporations*. Washington, D.C., 1991.

National Low Income Housing Coalition (NLIHC). "A Community-based Housing Supply Program." *Low Income Housing Round-Up* 108 (May, 1987).

Rivas, Maggie. "Villa Victoria: Where Families Stay." *Boston Globe*, April, 1982.

Schuman, Tony. "The Agony and the Equity: A Critique of Self-Help Housing." In Rachel G. Bratt, Chester Hartman, and Ann Meyerson (eds.), *Critical Perspectives on Housing*, pp. 463–473. Philadelphia: Temple University Press, 1986.

Tremblay, Kenneth R., Jr., and Don A. Dillman. *Beyond the American Dream: Accommodation in the 1980s*. Lanham, Md.: University Press of America, 1983.

U.S. Comptroller General. "Section 236 Rental Housing: An Evaluation with Lessons for the Future." Report to the Congress, PAD 78-13. Washington, D.C.: General Accounting Office, 1978.

Urban Planning Aid. "Community Development Corporations: The Empty Promise." Cambridge, Mass., 1973.

Vidal, Avis C. "Rebuilding Communities: A National Study of Urban Community Development Corporations." New York: Community Development Research Center, New School for Social Research, 1992.

5 Will All Tenants Win?

WOODY WIDROW

What do tenants want? Are most tenants satisfied or dissatisfied with the places they live? Do all tenants want the same thing? Do tenants want to own their current rental units or would they be satisfied as resident managers dealing with the day-to-day responsibilities and decision making of operating rental housing—collecting and setting rents, selecting tenants, and maintaining properties? Is their dream to own a single-family home in the suburbs or country? Is making a profit from the sale of their housing very important?

These are some of the key questions that must be answered by housing advocates and policymakers as they attempt to improve the housing situation of the nation's tenants, many inadequately housed and paying more than 50 percent of their income for rent. This chapter begins to answer some of these questions.

INTRODUCTION TO PRIVATE LANDLORD-TENANT RELATIONS

> The facts of life are simple: When you rent, you do not own. When you do not own, you do not dictate. It makes no difference whether the rental is a violin, a car, or an apartment. When you rent, you implicitly recognize the right of the owner to control his property. If you don't like it, don't rent.
>
> Letter to the Editor, *New York Magazine*, 6 January 1986

Before addressing what tenants want, it is important to place the desire for homeownership in this county in a larger context. The first point relates to the perceptions and problems of renting and renters in this country.

Tenants in the United States have always been viewed as second-class citizens. The lack of property ownership has profoundly affected American citizens in many ways, ranging from disenfranchisement in the nation's early years to deprivation of federal income tax deductions to lack of standing in their communities.

Tenants are viewed by homeowners and government officials as transients with little or no interest in their housing or their community. Viewed as having no vested interest, they are excluded from community issues.

Even housing advocates see renting in a negative light. An attorney for the New Jersey Public Advocate's Office recently stated that it was preferable to encourage homeownership over rental housing for low- and moderate-income families. He went on to say that it was "desirable for people to own the unit, if we don't want to re-create slums."[1] This lowly perception of tenants has existed for hundreds of years. It is a bias that is succinctly described by Constance Perin: "Homeowners are full-fledged citizens. Renters are not."[2]

Landlord-Tenant Relations Historically

The reason for the poor perception of tenants in the United States becomes clear when we look at history. The relationship between landlord and tenant is based on English feudal law. Since at least 1400, land has been valued as a person's most important possession. The amount of land one owned determined one's wealth and social status. The tenant's life was under the control of the landlord (the lord of the land). The tenant worked on the lord's land raising crops and caring for the property. In exchange, the tenant was allowed to live on the land. At the end of each month, the tenant paid rent from the crops grown or from money received by selling them. Once the land was turned over to the resident—giving the tenant temporary possession—the tenant was allowed to construct appropriate buildings for his own use.

The United States adopted most of the English feudal principles, which prevailed here until the 1960s. Basically, a landlord's obligation to a tenant remained unchanged for 550 years.[3] Once a housing unit was rented, the landlord had almost no responsibility to maintain a livable facility.

The tenant, however, was obliged to pay rent whether the landlord made repairs to the property or not.

Although landlords today are legally responsible for repairs, tenants continue to be blamed—rather than seen as victims—when property decays. Even when it is in good repair, rental housing is perceived as "bad."

The law turns this perceptual bias against tenants into an institutional bias. Although many laws reflect and reinforce this social prejudice against renters, zoning is the worst offender. Indeed, from the beginning, the legal basis for zoning embodied a prejudice against tenants.

The following opinion, handed down by the United States Supreme Court in 1926, provided the legal foundation for zoning—and for more than sixty years of exclusionary practices:

> With particular reference to apartment houses, it is pointed out that the development of detached house sections is greatly retarded by the coming of apartment houses, which has sometimes resulted in destroying the entire section for private house purposes; that in such sections very often the apartment house is a mere parasite, constructed in order to take advantage of the open spaces and attractive surroundings created by the residential character of the district. Moreover, the coming of one apartment house is followed by others, interfering by their height and bulk with the free circulation of air and monopolizing the rays of the sun which otherwise would fall upon the smaller homes, and bringing, as their necessary accompaniments, the disturbing noises incident to increased traffic and business, and the occupation, by means of moving and parked automobiles, of larger portions of the streets, thus detracting from their safety and depriving children of the localities until finally, the residential character of the neighborhood and its desirability as a place of detached residences are utterly destroyed. Under these circumstances, apartment houses, which in a different environment would be not only entirely unobjectionable but highly desirable, come very near to being nuisances.[4]

Strained Relations between Landlords and Tenants

The landlord-tenant relationship was once described as the second most passionate relationship in most people's lives. The sense of powerlessness many renters feel, especially when no legal remedies are available, arouses anger and causes confrontations rivaling lovers' quarrels. It is a volatile relationship.[5]

Two examples highlight the potential for conflict between landlords and tenants and the precarious situation of renters. The first comes from a 1986

Texas Tenants Union newsletter. "The good news is that . . . childrens' toys have been added to the list of items that a landlord is not allowed to take under the 'landlord's lien' when a tenant falls behind on the rent."[6] Before the law referred to was passed, landlords held children's toys as collateral against unpaid rent.

The second example is from a 1982 lease renewal sent to tenants of an apartment building in Chicago. Among the new provisions were:

> Occupancy by an invitee or guest of Tenant for a period in excess of ten days, without Lessor's prior written consent, shall constitute a breach hereof. . . . In the event of the death of the Tenant (provided no other Tenants are parties to the Lease), such Tenant's heirs, administrators, executors or duly appointed personal representatives may terminate this Lease (i) by giving 60 days written notice of termination measured from the last day of the month in which the notice is served and (ii) by serving such notice upon Lessor within 30 days after the Tenant's death and (iii) by paying all rent due: and (iv) by paying a sum equal to one month's rent as liquidated damages.[7]

A lease dictating guests' length of stay and requiring payment of three months' rent after you die is hardly conducive to warm feelings between tenants and landlords.

Raising Rents Shows Economy on the Rise?

There is an additional way that tenants occupying rental housing lose out. While lower rents and high vacancy rates usually create the most advantageous situation for tenants, mainstream economists and most government officials consider these conditions indications of a local economy's ill health. Indeed most policymakers applaud rising rents and falling vacancies and use the resources of government and the powers of the press to spur on these antitenant market conditions.

A recent article in the *New York Times* illustrates my point.

> Several statistical barometers suggest how far the Texas economy has recovered in the last four years. Apartment occupancy rates in Houston climbed 90 percent this year [1990] for the first time since 1982 and in Dallas for the first time since 1984. The average monthly rent in Houston last spring was $401, as against $372 in 1982. . . . Monthly rents in Dallas were an average of $459 in the last three months that ended in September, 1990 as against $430 in the last quarter of 1984.[8]

The obvious inference is that rising rents and low vacancy rates are signs of a growing economy, which benefits everybody. What is not discussed is how tenants will pay large rent increases without equally large increases in income.

HOMEOWNERSHIP IN AMERICA

Given the powerlessness and precariousness of the landlord-tenant situation, many advocates across the political spectrum have looked for alternative ways of giving tenants more security and more control over their housing. Since control seems synonymous with ownership in mainstream opinion—an equation that ignores both the hidden pitfalls of homeownership for lower-income people and the existence of alternative forms of tenure that enhance security and control—homeownership becomes the Holy Grail for tenants and their advocates.

"When people talk of the American dream, they mean, more often than not, homeownership. Most Americans are raised from infancy to believe that they will be able to grow up and own their own home; and that if they do not, they have failed themselves and their families in some fundamental way."[9]

" 'The only way to control housing is to own it,' says Marie Nahikian, former diretor of the Washington, D.C., city government program to help tenants buy their apartment buildings and convert them to housing cooperatives."[10]

Ownership and control are used interchangeably in the United States. The argument goes: you are either a tenant with little control over your rent, your length of stay, or the condition of your unit, and you cannot make any profit from its sale; or you own and control your unit.

As Alan Mallach notes,

> There is [an] important difference between rental and homeownership, an intangible but crucial difference: the way each is perceived in American society, and the association between them and social values. Homeownership is associated with stability, pride, and achievement, rental with impermanence, indifference, and failure. Furthermore, because it is so closely tied to social values, the process of becoming a homeowner is widely believed to be capable of transforming people; giving people a stake turns them from transient drifters into responsible community-minded folks. This is a major part of the ratio-

> nale for lower-income homeownership, since being poor is linked with much the same values, in many people's minds, as being a renter.[11]

And in a survey on housing conducted by Jacqueline Leavitt one woman noted:

> Until we have a cooperative society [rather than a competitive one] and male/female relations are friendly, cooperative and power-equal, women need their own homes. My home ownership nourishes and strengthens me; it's central to my inner and outer life. My outer life, the face I put to the world, gets more respect if I am a property owner. This is invaluable to us women with our vulnerability in a male-dominated society. It announces our independent status as nothing else can. . . . My inner life is especially enriched by my own space. I'm a member of this culture and so I have more self-respect as a property owner.[12]

Given a limited familiarity with other ways of gaining security and control of their housing and given the social status associated with owning a single-family house or condominium, it is not surprising that traditional homeownership is the only form of tenure to which tenants aspire. It is not surprising that most tenants want to become homeowners.

Problems with Traditional Homeownership

Yet, traditional homeownership in the United States does not necessarily lead to nirvana. For families with limited, seasonal, or fixed incomes the belief that security of tenure and control are inherent in homeownership does not always pan out.

The purchase of a market-priced home seldom solves all housing problems and seldom guarantees the large profits that realtors promise (which is another expected advantage in homeownership). For many property owners—and especially for those with low incomes—homeownership is just the beginning of their difficulties.

Even if a tenant is able to put together funds for a downpayment and make monthly payments, a number of problems can arise that are outside the control of the low-income owner. An unanticipated job loss, a catastrophic illness, a precipitous rise in property taxes, or the costly failure of furnace or roof can push a homeowner toward foreclosure. A downturn in the local economy can render the property less valuable than its mortgage, resulting in the homeowner's loss of large sums of money. These are not unusual events. According to Michael Stone, Professor of Community Planning at the University of Massachusetts–Boston, the rate of mortgage foreclosures tripled during the 1980s, reaching an annual rate of over 1 percent of all mortgages. Since 1986, foreclosures have been higher than at any time since the Great Depression.

Partially as a result of these problems, community activists and public officials at the local level have developed additional alternatives to for-profit rental housing. These alternatives provide much of the package of housing goods that residents want and need in the places they live while removing many of the problems that can and do develop with traditional homeownership.

Debating the Housing Alternatives

This newer social housing agenda—using alternative models of nonprofit rental housing and limited equity homeownership—is at odds not only with the traditional notion of homeownership but with the new federal programs championed by former HUD Secretary Jack Kemp. The debate over competing agendas has intensified with the passage of the National Affordable Housing Act of 1990. The act contains two key programs, HOME and HOPE, each with its own set of advocates.

The HOME Investment Partnership Act is designed to expand a delivery system that relies on local initiatives involving public-private partnerships. Federal funds are distributed to local and state government agencies for low-income housing development. All HOME funds must benefit persons earning less than 80 percent of the area median income. At least 15 percent of the funds is set aside for nonprofit organizations. The affordability of any units created with HOME monies must be guaranteed, according to the act, "for the remaining useful life of the property."

HOPE (Homeownership and Opportunity for People Everywhere) was championed by Jack Kemp. These initiatives include monies for the conversion of public housing and publicly subsidized rental housing to private homeownership. Restrictions on the affordability of these newly purchased, owner-occupied units lapse after seven years.

The 1990s are setting the stage for two divergent philosophies: nonprofit community-based organizations and others stress the need to preserve the affordability of units—whether through limited equity ownership, nonprofit rental, or some hybrid model, whereas Jack Kemp and his followers sing the praises of traditional homeownership and the "empowerment" of low-income tenants enabled to buy a piece of the American Dream at last. With the change of party in the White House, it will be interesting to see which philosophy the new HUD Secretary Henry Cisneros will adopt.

This struggle will be fought in low-income neighborhoods, in publicly assisted housing projects, in city halls and state houses, and in the media. Public officials, low-income residents, and the public at large will see and hear HOPE advocates like Kimi Gray (Washington, D.C.) and Bertha Gilkey (St. Louis), both public housing tenants who eloquently describe their efforts to create positive living environments. Their talk will be about empowerment through full equity homeownership, providing residents with long-term incentives to preserve and upgrade their housing stock far into the future. Kemp targeted HOPE as the cornerstone of HUD policy; it was one of his political priorities. Money was spent on a small number of units to ensure the success of his showcase program. Despite Kemp's departure from HUD, the debate over his policies, priorities, and programs will continue.

Whenever possible the advocates of HOME and third sector housing must challenge the HOPE program and demonstrate that what is being promised is far short of what is being delivered. They must show that the resources given to the HOPE homeowners will be much less than what is needed for their long-term success. They must find leaders among the ranks of community development corporations, community land trusts, mutual housing associations, and other nonprofit housing organizations if they are to compete in this battle of visions. They must find their own Kimi Grays—resident leaders who are fighting to keep their units affordable over time.

Finally, the advocates of HOME and third sector housing need not only a vision but a workable program, along with the courage to face squarely and address effectively the kinds of questions being raised in this chapter.

A DIFFERENT DEFINITION OF OWNERSHIP

Can this alternative social agenda prevail? Yes, if we can articulate a compelling vision. Yes, if we ask what tenants want. Yes, if we face the flaws and problems of both the HOME approach and the community-based development organizations that are lining up to put HOME into effect.

What Do Tenants Want?

Tenants have a long list of wants in their search for better housing. For most, this search has focused on the benefits derived from traditional homeownership: security of tenure, control, and equity.

Tenants want security. Security of tenure includes freedom from the fear of arbitrary eviction or retaliation, freedom from exorbitant rent increases, and privacy—the right to decide who enters and when.

Tenants want control. Control is taking part in the key decisions that affect the day-to-day and long-term conditions of their housing.

Tenants want equity. Equity is the forced savings and profit from the ownership of the property. When homeowners sell their property, the money they receive after paying the lender back on the mortgage is the savings (down payment and principle payments) and profit (appreciation of housing unit), which together equal the equity.

When tenants are asked if they would prefer to rent or to own, most answer, "To own." But do they necessarily mean all three aspects of ownership: security of tenure, control, and equity? Are all of equal importance? Are tenants willing to give up any of them?

Ownership could be separated into its various components, and residents could be asked: Do you want to be involved in the day-to-day decisions and operations of your housing (resident management), or do you prefer to pay for someone else to provide these management services? If rents were controlled and a tenant could only be evicted for specific reasons, would you feel secure in rented housing? Are you looking for a place to live that offers you peace and control over your housing, or are you really seeking to make a profit from your unit? Would you be willing to give up profit for security and control if your unit remained affordable permanently?

If we open the discussion of housing options with a concept of homeownership different from the traditional one, then we may get answers like the one from a woman who wrote "that she wanted neighbors close enough to hear her scream if she needed help but distant enough 'so I can sing without embarrassment.' "[13]

What the woman wanted was a sense of privacy and a sense of community—a place away from the day-to-day headaches, problems, and concerns of others but not remote from people, activities, culture, recreation, and the support that others can bring. Fee-simple ownership and full equity ownership are not the only ways to control one's destiny.

Will Tenants Accept Equity Limitations?

While many housing activists would like resale prices to be controlled so that units remain affordable for future generations, others disagree sharply with this approach.

"Some people strongly attack any limitation on resale values, saying it is just another way to keep people poor."[14] Large profits can be made from the sale of properties. Some people think that lower-income families should be allowed to benefit from a once-in-a-lifetime opportunity to "make big bucks" when they sell their housing unit. An investment for retirement, a legacy for the children, collateral for a business or loan is what home-ownership means for many people. Limiting these benefits is often seen as taking away something to which the property owner is entitled.

On the other hand, such benefits come at the expense of future families who will not be able to afford the higher housing costs that result when appreciation is added to the selling price of a unit.

According to one housing advocate, "My experience in working with tenants seeking to become owners teaches me that equity—obtained through selling—is the least of their concerns. It's nice, but if told they can't achieve security of tenure and control unless they give up some equity, they'll gladly do so."

ARE NONPROFIT COMMUNITY-BASED ORGANIZATIONS A SOLUTION?

If tenants will accept something less than full equity ownership, one of the major players in the development of limited equity housing will be the community-based organization (CBO). "Across the country, in poor communities from Appalachia to Watts, locally based nonprofit groups are striving to restore economic vitality and social stability. . . . Despite limited funding, a national recession and in many communities, worsening physical, social and economic conditions, these organizations have emerged as the prime catalysts for change and renewal."[15]

According to the National Congress for Community Economic Development (NCCED), the approximately two thousand CBOs have developed almost 320,000 units of housing. Many of these units are owner-occupied housing with a limitation on the owner's equity. With CBOs playing an increased role in the creation of affordable housing over the next few decades, it is important to have a closer look at their characteristics, advantages, and strategies.

For this chapter, CBOs are characterized as private, nonprofit organizations serving low-income communities. They are governed by a community-based board and produce housing with tenures ranging from rental to ownership. Many of them are committed to long-term affordability. Other nonprofit developers (local housing authorities, municipally created nonprofits, community action agencies) are not CBOs by this definition.

Regarding the programmatic advantage of community-based organizations, Avis Vidal suggests that these organizations offer at least three advantages in the development of low-income housing. First, grounded in their communities, these organizations have first-hand knowledge of local problems, priorities, and opportunities. Their boards of directors typically include substantial representation from their communities. Second, unlike private sector developers, their mission is service to the disadvantaged. They have stronger incentives than private housing managers to provide tenants with support services and to involve them in some of the management issues that affect their lives. Third, these organizations work beyond the bricks and mortar of housing development and see their work in a broader community context as revitalizing and stabilizing the neighborhoods they serve.[16]

Beyond the general characteristics and advantages of CBOs, it is necessary to differentiate them according to whether the organizational strategies they pursue are successful or unsuccessful. Successful community-based development organizations produce housing units. Yet beyond this, they continue to be responsive to and directed by the community. Too often, organizations produce housing units and gradually become just "developers," losing their community direction and organizational mission.

In addition, successful CBOs balance the production of housing that serves immediate needs with a commitment to the management of housing and the preservation of affordability that serves long-term needs of the community. CBOs must be in for the long haul as producers and providers. Also, CBOs must continue to be sensitive to dilemmas of process versus product. They must balance the building of units against the building of the organization.

Successful nonprofit housing developers do not assume that the transformation of private tenants into fully participating residents in new housing alternatives requires only a dash of training. This assumption is not only erroneous but dangerous. Success requires long hours of staff involvement, helping residents master new responsibilities.

In addition, "it is not surprising that the most successful lower-income cooperatives and resident-managed properties are those that grew out of community or tenant organizations, through which relationships of cooperation emerged, rather than those in which the cooperative structure was imposed from without, whether by a public agency or a well-meaning nonprofit sponsor."[17]

Success must not only be judged by the first few years of a new housing project or a new housing organization but over the life of the housing and over many years of the organization's operation.

What Are Community-based Organizations' Problems?

Some CBOs have lost their former membership base; they are now guided mostly by their staff and board of directors rather than by residents of the community. Others still encourage citizen participation in setting broad goals and policies for neighborhood revitalization, but they exclude local residents from implementing projects and programs. This contradicts the goal of grassroots citizen participation and the empowerment of the poor.

The term *empowerment* has been used without explanation in this chapter. Former HUD Secretary Jack Kemp touts *empowerment* as a central component in the HOPE program and a key to solving the low-income housing crisis. CBOs and housing activists also talk of empowerment, but they mean economic redistribution, increased public resources, and community control of neighborhoods and resources. Kemp's definition deemphasizes both government's responsibility in aiding people it wishes to empower and a reduction in public investment.

For Kemp and his supporters, homeownership is synonymous with empowerment, and with homeownership the responsibility of government ends. Clearly what is not addressed is the government's long-term responsibility for affordable housing. Providing such housing is left to the marketplace.

Secondly, when CBOs become focused on developing capital projects like low-income housing, they are less likely to be engaged in community organizing beyond assisting clients who occupy that housing. "It has been argued that [CBOs] cannot simultaneously act as developers, property owners, and management firms and also organize residents because this might involve them in conflicts with their own constituents over issues such as the selection of owners and tenants in [CBO-owned] and managed housing projects, rent and eviction policies, location of projects, etc."[18]

The debate continues on whether a CBO can wear two hats, acting as developer and as an organizer and advocate. Some groups have decided that they need to create separate entities for these two functions, with different organizations handling development and advocacy; a few groups have combined both in the same organization. As the CBO movement continues to grow, the issue of whether a CBO can be a landlord and manager as well as an advocate for the residents and their community continues to be an open question.

A third problem might be called, "Congratulations, you're the landlord."[19] In 1973, Urban Planning Aid[20] produced a booklet about the potential problems of community-based housing development. One of its concerns was that nonprofit developers would begin thinking and acting in the same manner as landlords:

> The most serious conflict of interest between the community housing sponsor and the community comes when the sponsor assumes the role of landlord. Any landlord has certain responsibilities: to collect rent and to maintain the buildings. Being a landlord leads the community sponsor to think like a landlord: if people can't pay the rent they should be evicted. Because the rent payments are so important, the community sponsor can't afford to question where the rent goes. As landlords they have the choice of going into default on the mortgage payments or charging people rents they can't afford."[21]

Similarly, tenant leaders who have successfully converted their building into a cooperative have complained that residents expect more from them than they got from the previous for-profit landlord, but they don't want to have higher monthly payments. " 'Some people expect more to be done now than they did when this was a rental property,' [Robert] Simon [president of Benning Heights Cooperative] says of his co-op. 'Because of the lack of funds we haven't been able to do the kind of maintenance we've wanted to.' "[22] These unrealistic expectations and the problems revolving around money issues, evicting fellow residents for nonpayment, and keeping the property fully occupied can lead to burnout among overworked tenant leaders who have had to hold their associations together in the face of great uncertainty about their future.

Fourth, beyond conflicts over control and accountability there are sometimes conflicts over equity. With many CBOs working on limited equity models (co-ops, land trusts, and resale-restricted housing through inclusionary zoning), there is an ongoing tension between organizational members and residents who want limited resale prices to preserve affordability and those who want very liberal resale prices to promote upward mobility. This problem must be dealt with early by the organization and with new residents or owners as they move in. Conflict over lost or potentially lost money can rip an organization apart.

PUBLIC POLICY CONCERNS AND QUESTIONS

I turn now to problems confronting public officials who must oversee housing funds and establish priorities.

Local and state housing officials and policymakers who provide public funds for housing development, including new HOME funds, must establish criteria for funding community-based organizations, and alternative forms of housing tenure. The following questions and concerns provide insight for decision makers who must weigh at times the competing variables of organizational needs, community desires, and resident needs.

How Will Tenants Be Chosen?

It is necessary to design programs that do not skim off the "better" tenants and leave the rest behind. "Better" tenants are two-parent households with incomes at the upper end of the target group and people or families who would succeed almost anywhere. This does not mean that such tenants should be excluded but that a balance must be struck between families needing little assistance and those needing much and various assistance. For programs to be successful, they must include very low income families as well as single-parent households, large family households, and families with a history of welfare dependency. Successfully serving these needy segments of society will greatly enhance both the community-based organization and the nonprofit housing movement as a whole.

There is another important consideration when deciding on a specific municipal package of housing programs. Should community-based organizations that are engaged in housing development market their units only to local residents (neighborhood preference), or should there be a policy of open occupancy (open access)? If the housing is for locals only, low-income residents who live outside the targeted area and racial minorities can be excluded from the selection process.

Which Nonprofits Should Be Funded?

Regarding operational support for a CBO, financing should be available that is flexible and based on the needs of the neighborhood and the organization.

A common misconception by government officials is that nonprofits can do housing much more cheaply than for-profits and therefore do not require additional operational funds beyond the subsidy for development. They should look to nonprofits not only for short-term benefits but for the quality of services and the long-run savings they can provide. Enough funds should be given to support the nonprofit's ability to manage the property after it is developed.

A second important criterion deals with capacity and accountability. Local governments must decide whether to target their funding to large nonprofits, small nonprofits, or newly emerging nonprofits. There needs to be a balance of all types. Larger nonprofits usually offer greater financial stability, larger staffs, and a proven record of success, yet they may have moved beyond their neighborhood base or become less attuned to the community. Smaller groups and newly emerging ones, while having less impressive track records, may be more community based and sensitive to neighborhood needs.

A third criterion has to do with effective and long-term retention of public subsidies. Public officials should give priority to nonprofits that exhibit an organizational commitment to models of housing that preserve public subsidies and preserve affordability in perpetuity.

What Happens to "Leftover" Tenants and Neighborhoods?

Many neighborhoods with dire housing problems but without a strong CBO may be completely left out if we depend solely upon nonprofits to produce affordable housing. This leaves many low-income neighborhoods out in the cold.

Given the scarcity of funding for nonprofit organizations and nonmarket models of housing, most tenants will remain in the private, for-profit housing market. Thus, it is important that tenants not benefiting from the few local and state government programs be protected. Tenants must have greater protection from market forces while they search for affordable housing alternatives.

Even in rental units developed and managed by nonprofits, residents must be equally protected as private rental tenants. The fact that the CBO is nonprofit and has roots in the community doesn't mean that abuses won't occur. The staff may be undertrained, too small, too much into the "bottom line," or it may have forgotten the organization's original mission. All tenant protections must be applicable to all types of tenants.

Landlord-tenant legislation must guarantee the rights necessary to live in secure, safe, and affordable housing. This includes such laws as just-cause eviction (eviction only for specific reasons), rent control (rent increases balancing landlords' right to make a profit and tenants' right to decent affordable housing), repair and deduct (right of tenant to spend rent money when a serious violation is not remedied by landlord), rent receivership (replacement of the landlord by a court-appointed person mandated to manage a troubled property), antidemolition (defining terms of demolition and requiring one-to-one replacement), antidisplacement (prohibiting condominium or cooperative conversion, demolition, or other means of displacing a renter without ensuring the tenant comparable affordable housing), and privacy protections (right to control access to the dwelling unit).

It is essential that local and state governments not turn their backs on private tenants while creating new affordable housing programs. For if additional protections for tenants are not enacted, then the gains by CBOs and other third sector housing groups will be neutralized and the current housing crisis will remain the same or intensify.

MAKING TENANTS WINNERS

When all is said and done, the number of housing units rehabilitated and constructed over the next few decades will not alleviate the problems encountered by the third of the nation that lives in private rental housing, most of whom have low incomes. The solution to decent affordable housing in this country requires a two-pronged approach: better protections for tenants, and more nonprofit housing. They go hand in hand.

Housing advocates, community organizers, land trust staff, CBO managers, and public officials must not get so caught up in putting in place new programs and new models of tenure that they forget the wants and needs of the people they serve. Tenants become winners, first, by being protected against the worst abuses of the existing system and, second, by having an alternative nonprofit housing system designed to accommodate their real wants and needs. Nonprofits should assist tenant organizers in securing better tenant protections. Tenant organizers should work with nonprofits in designing better housing models. This two-prong approach requires cooperation between both branches of the affordable housing movement.

A united front among advocates, nonprofit developers, tenants, and residents can help to shape public policy with elected officials and policymakers. We cannot afford to leave decision making to private market forces and persons seeking short-term housing solutions.

A comprehensive approach to solving the housing problems of low-income tenants requires a vision, commitment, and funds. This chapter attempts to provide direction for the development of a shared vision and a shared commitment to its implementation. We must then mobilize our forces, facts, and friends in order for the funds to follow.

NOTES

1. "Court Weighs Tax Rates on Affordable Housing," *The Star-Ledger* (Newark, N.J.), 6 November 1990, p. 13.
2. Constance Perin, *Everything in Its Place*, p. 56. Princeton: Princeton University Press, 1977.
3. *Tenants' Manual on the Law*, p. 1. New Brunswick, N.J.: Urban Legal Clinic, Rutgers Law School, October 1976.
4. *Village of Euclid, Ohio v. Ambler Realty Co.*, Supreme Court of the United States, 1926. 272 US 365, 47 S Ct. 114, 71 L Ed. 303.
5. Woody Widrow, "What's in the Cards? Past, Present, and Future: Candid Views from the Players," *Shelterforce* 12, no. 4 (March/April 1990): 6.
6. *Tenant Notes*, p. 2. Texas Tenants' Union, 1986.
7. Proposed new lease of Regents Park in Hyde Park with the Clinton Company as managing agent of 5020 and 5050 South Lake Shore Drive, Chicago, 1982.
8. "Slow but Steady Revival after Downturn in Texas." *New York Times*, 9 December 1990, p. 30.
9. Alan Mallach, "Re-shaping the American Dream: Expanding Homeownership Opportunities," *Shelterforce* 12, no. 5 (May/June 1990): 15.
10. Bill Black, "Limited Equity Co-ops: Pros and Cons of Buying," *Shelterforce* 6 (February 1983): 8.

11. Mallach, "Re-shaping the American Dream," p. 15.

12. Jacqueline Leavitt, "The Single Family House: Does It Belong in a Woman's Housing Agenda?" *Shelterforce* 12, no. 1 (July/August/September 1989): 8.

13. Ibid., p. 9.

14. Black, "Limited Equity Co-ops," p. 10.

15. National Congress for Community Economic Development, *Changing the Odds*, p. 1. Washington, D.C., December 1991.

16. Avis C. Vidal, "A Community-Based Approach to Affordable Housing," p. 3. *Commentator*, November 1990.

17. Mallach, "Re-shaping the American Dream," p. 18.

18. W. Dennis Keating, "The Emergence of Community Development Corporations—Their Impact on Housing and Neighborhoods," *Shelterforce* 11, no. 5 (February/March/April 1989): 11.

19. "For me, the greatest change has been coming from being a tenant advocate to being a landlord. We've got to operate it [the cooperative] just like the tightest landlord in town. It's a business." Robert Simon, president of Benning Heights Cooperative (474 units) in Washington, D.C. Quoted by Bill Black, "Limited Equity Co-ops. Part 2: Congratulations, You're the Landlord," *Shelterforce* 6 (August 1983): 7.

20. Urban Planning Aid was a federally funded nonprofit advocacy planning organization located in Boston that provided technical and organizing assistance to community and labor groups in eastern Massachusetts from the mid-1960s to the late 1970s.

21. Housing and Community Research Group, *Community Housing Development Corporations: The Empty Promise*, p. 39. Boston: Urban Planning Aid, 1973.

22. Black, "Limited Equity Co-ops. Part 2," p. 19.

PART TWO

Third Sector Housing in Action: Policies, Programs, and Plans

6 Building the Progressive City: Third Sector Housing in Burlington

JOHN EMMEUS DAVIS

Two months after Ronald Reagan assumed office as the fortieth president of the United States, Bernie Sanders was elected the thirty-second mayor of Burlington, Vermont. Both men remained in office for eight years. When Reagan stepped down in 1989, his policies and programs were continued by his vice-president, who was elevated to the presidency by the same conservative coalition that had supported Reagan. Sanders stepped down in 1989 after serving four two-year terms as mayor. His policies and programs were continued by Peter Clavelle, who had served as Sanders's director of community and economic development. Clavelle was carried into office on the shoulders of Burlington's "Progressive Coalition," the same third-party movement that had supported Sanders.

There is considerable irony in the fact that the decade of the "Reagan revolution" in Washington was also the decade of "Sanderista" rule in Burlington. These two political movements had little in common. Their leaders, Reagan and Sanders, shared even less. Indeed, it would have been difficult to find two elected officials anywhere in the United States during the 1980s who were further apart in background, ideology, and political agenda.

The man elected president was a middle-class midwesterner of Irish descent whose entire career, first in the movies and then in politics, had been heavily bankrolled and carefully scripted by men of wealth and power. Ronald Reagan was the most conservative politician to occupy the White House in fifty years, a person whose entire political philosophy was built around the single idea that private individuals and private markets could solve nearly every problem of poverty, unemployment, and injustice if government would just stop meddling in matters that were not its proper concern. Reagan's domestic agenda, accordingly, was dominated by a simple bias: get government out of the way of the private sector, and let a rising tide of capitalist prosperity lift all boats.

The man elected Burlington's mayor grew up in a working-class Jewish household in Brooklyn, New York. Bernie Sanders wrote his own scripts, first as a documentary filmmaker and later as a political maverick operating outside the traditional two-party structure of American politics. He helped to found Vermont's Liberty-Union Party soon after moving to the state in 1968. During the 1970s, he ran unsuccessfully for statewide office four times, never receiving more than 6 percent of the vote. In 1981, he challenged the five-term Democratic mayor of Burlington. Running as an independent, Sanders mounted an aggressive campaign stridently attacking the city's wealthiest individuals, interests, and institutions. He was given little money and little chance of success. Against all odds, he won—by ten votes.

A self-avowed socialist, Sanders's conception of the role and responsibilities of government was a radical rebuke to the right-wing Republican elected president only a few months earlier. The market, in Sanders's eyes, was the underlying *cause* of many of the problems faced by Burlington's people, not an untapped solution. Only an activist municipal government could solve these problems, intervening on behalf of lower-income neighborhoods and working-class people to curb the market and correct the harm that market forces often inflicted on vulnerable populations.

Nowhere was the need for municipal activism more apparent, believed Sanders and his supporters, than in housing. As Reagan was confidently extolling the virtues of unfettered markets, Burlington's own market in land and housing was stampeding out of control. Speculative pressures had been building for several years: a revitalized central business district, with the prospect of luxury redevelopment on the downtown waterfront; a burgeoning student population at the University of Vermont, with no accompanying expansion of on-campus housing; and a robust regional economy that was attracting thousands of newcomers to the area every year. By the early 1980s, average housing prices in Burlington for both rental and owner-occupied housing were rising at a rate roughly *twice* that of average household incomes (CEDO, 1986; Mallach, 1988). Lower-income renters were being displaced as rental property rapidly and repeatedly changed hands from one investor to another. Lower-cost housing was being lost through conversion and demolition. New housing was being built at a rate unmatched since the 1950s, but most of these units were pricey condos overlooking Lake Champlain, the city's western border. Few were affordable for Burlington's less affluent residents.

As the private sector was busily exacerbating Burlington's housing problems—and brusquely excusing itself from any special responsibility for addressing them—the public sector was displaying a more dramatic abdication. Reagan had pledged to get government "off the backs" of the people. When it came to housing, he delivered on that promise with a vengence. Federal support for public housing was cut. Support for the rehabilitation and construction of private housing was cut. Rental assistance was cut. Even the flagship of Richard Nixon's New Federalism, the Community Development Block Grant (CDBG) program was cut. So little federal funding remained by Reagan's second term that most cities the size of Burlington were doing little more for affordable housing than hanging on with broken fingers to a crumbling stock of public housing, a threatened stock of federally assisted private housing, and a dwindling pool of CDBG dollars for housing rehabilitation. In short, when the federal government got out of the housing business, so did most of America's smaller cities.[1]

Burlington never joined this municipal rush for the exits. Admittedly, the burning theater of Reagan's domestic policy was not the most desirable stage from which to launch an innovative housing program, but the Sanders administration was determined to play neither passive victim nor active accomplice to the federal retrenchment that was underway. Something better was expected by those who had voted for Sanders's brand of municipal activism; something better was needed for those who were being excluded or extruded from Burlington's overheated market. The difficulty faced by the "Sanderistas," however, was that most of the federal programs used by previous mayors to construct or rehabilitate affordable housing were being gutted by a hostile president and a compliant Congress. The Sanderistas had to try something different, something new.

TOWARD A PROGRESSIVE HOUSING POLICY

Sanders's first term was a season of siege.[2] A combined Democratic and Republican majority on the city council impeded nearly every initiative, every budget, and every appointment of the new administration. The incoming mayor was not even permitted to hire a secretary for his own office without a major confrontation with the city council. By the time of his first reelection, however, Sanders's base of political support in the community and on the council had grown broad enough to break through the intransigence of his political opponents. Control of the city council remained with the Democrats and Republicans, but enough members of Sanders's Progressive Coalition had been added to the council to sustain a mayoral veto.[3] By 1983, Sanders finally possessed enough power to begin enacting some of his own policies and programs. Affordable housing was near the top of the Progressive agenda.

Within the Sanders administration—and the Clavelle administration that followed—housing policy was largely a creature of the Community and Economic Development Office (CEDO). This municipal agency was created soon after Sanders's 1983 reelection to give an activist mayor—forced to operate within the structural constraints of a weak mayor, strong city council, commission form of government—the ability to function proactively in shaping the city's growth and development. CEDO was assigned general responsibility for economic development, community development, and housing. It was also given the politically lucrative task of administering and distributing the City's annual allocation of Community Development Block Grant funds.[4]

Prominent in CEDO's founding mission was the explicit charge "to develop, coordinate, and administer a comprehensive program to address the City's housing needs" (Burlington City Council, 1983). This mission was eventually translated by CEDO staff into three easily understood and frequently repeated goals: *protection* of the vulnerable, *production* of new affordable housing, and *preservation* of affordable housing already in existence.

The first of these goals sought to press into service the powers of municipal government on behalf of residents most at risk in a speculative, inflationary housing market. As later described by CEDO in the City's *1988 Annual Report*: "The housing situations of the poor, the disabled, and the elderly are often precarious. The needs of these populations are great; their resources are few. Their bargaining position in a competitive, high-priced housing market is extremely weak. The municipality must make the shelter of its most vulnerable citizens more secure."

Secondly, and most traditionally, CEDO embraced the goal of promoting the production of new housing. "Development," after all, was part of the name of this new municipal agency. It was expected that CEDO staff would take the lead in identifying and assembling sites, acquiring and packaging funds, and facilitating the construction of residential units affordable for lower-income residents—those with annual incomes below 80 percent of median.

Finally, there was early recognition within CEDO that preservation was as necessary as protection and production, especially in a city where 53 percent of the housing stock had been built before 1939. Striving to protect and house the city's low-income residents without striving simultaneously to preserve the low-cost housing they occupied was like working to save an endangered species while acquiescing in the destruction of its only habitat.

Problems of housing preservation were, in fact, some of the most pressing that the city faced: housing was being lost in inner-city neighborhoods through deterioration and deferred maintenance; housing was being lost in the neighborhoods surrounding the central business district, the University of Vermont, and Champlain College through demolition or conversion to nonresidential uses; affordable apartments were being lost in every neighborhood through luxury renovation or condominium conversion; and the clock was ticking on the city's largest federally subsidized housing project, Northgate Apartments, a 336-unit rental complex constructed nearly twenty years before under the HUD 221(d) (3) program. Unless something was done before 1989 to "save" Northgate, there was a high probability that the project's current (or future) owners would elect to prepay the mortgage, terminate the rent stabilization agreement with HUD, and displace most of the project's eleven hundred lower-income tenants—a community larger than most Vermont towns.

There was nothing unusual or especially "progressive" about any of these housing goals. Many cities have pursued similar ends, although few have pursued them as aggressively, comprehensively, and successfully as Burlington. What was special about protection, production, and preservation at the hands of the Sanderistas, however, was the decision to pursue these goals through a dual-track strategy of *empowering* those without residential property and *decommodifying* residential property itself. Their housing policy was, in effect, two separate policies: a policy of "tenants' rights" focused primarily on the goal of protection, and a policy of "third sector housing" focused primarily on production and preservation.

Only the policy of third sector housing is discussed in detail here. A few words should be said, however, about the administration's political efforts on behalf of tenants' rights. After all, empowering persons without property was the administration's first policy—and a seedbed for the second.

The idea of enlisting municipal government in the cause of tenants' rights predated the creation of CEDO. For that matter, it predated the election of Bernie Sanders. Neighborhood activists and tenant organizers had repeatedly petitioned the Democratic machine in City Hall throughout the 1970s to play a larger role in protecting tenants against soaring rents, deteriorating apartments, and displacement. That such entreaties had fallen on deaf ears was undoubtedly a factor in Sanders's surprising victory in 1981. Acknowledging that political debt, while seeking also to deliver on a prominent campaign promise, the new administration called for a special election two months after Sanders took office. Burlington's voters were asked to approve a "fair housing commission," a measure deemed by supporters and opponents alike to be little more than a stalking horse for rent control. It was defeated, three to one.

Despite this early setback, the protection of tenants' rights remained in the forefront of the administration's legislative priorities. It was kept there by the administration's close ties to the state's small but feisty tenants' movement, Vermont Tenants, Inc. (VTI), headquartered in Burlington, and by the administration's recruitment of key staff from the ranks of protenant housing activists and former legal aid attorneys. The most radical proposals put forward by the Sanders and Clavelle administrations, the Progressive Coalition, and VTI were defeated: an antispeculation tax on the sale of rental property was approved as a charter change by Burlington's voters but later rejected by the Vermont legislature (1986); apartment registration was amended out of existence by the city council (1987); and just-cause eviction was voted down by Burlington's electorate (1989). Progressives were more successful in winning approval for protenant initiatives ensuring fair access, promoting health and safety, and preventing displacement. The most significant of these legislative victories were:

- *Ensuring Fair Access*. Anti-discrimination Ordinance (enacted 1984); Security Deposits Ordinance (enacted 1986)
- *Promoting Health and Safety*. Overhaul of Minimum Housing Code (amended 1985); Apartment Inspection Fee Ordinance (enacted 1987)
- *Preventing Displacement*. Condominium Conversion Ordinance (enacted 1987); Housing Replacement Ordinance (enacted 1989)

Not included in this list but equally important from the point of view of protecting tenants was the administration's revitalization of the Burlington Housing Authority (BHA). Prior to 1984, the BHA was controlled by political appointees of the previous administration. Buildings were deteriorating, waiting lists were out of date, and tenants were not heard by the

BHA board. As Sanders's appointees to the BHA board gradually pushed aside the holdovers from the past, the BHA began to turn around. A talented new director was hired in 1985. That same year, a multimillion dollar modernization program was begun that aimed at rehabilitating all of the authority's older units by 1993. Senior BHA staff were replaced. Waiting lists were revamped. Tenants were added to the BHA board.

The turnaround of the BHA was pivotal to the overall success of the Progressives' program, for the BHA straddled the line between protecting vulnerable populations and decommodifying valuable property. Progress toward improving conditions for the 347 families in public housing had to be ensured before less traditional measures could be pursued. In effect, the administration had to secure this weakened flank in the ranks of its own constituency before it could march off in new directions. Equally important, the BHA was the local custodian for what remained of the federal Section 8 program. This meant that the BHA was in a position to withhold certificates and vouchers from the third sector housing that CEDO's nonprofit partners began to produce in 1984 or to use such subsidies in support of their efforts. By reforming the BHA, the Sanders administration both improved tenants' lives and enlisted the BHA in its push to remove housing from the speculative market.[5]

CEDO promoted this second policy on a parallel track with the first. The commitment to tenant protection and empowerment remained intact, but after 1984 an increasing amount of CEDO's time and resources were dedicated to the creation of an expanding pool of privately owned, perpetually affordable housing. This third sector housing policy had two programmatic components: (1) municipal support for *alternative models of housing tenure* that could lock in place any public subsidies put into affordable housing, while locking in place affordability itself; and (2) municipal support for a *network of nonprofit organizations* that would work in concert with CEDO to establish these alternative models of tenure, while constructing, rehabilitating, and managing an expanding stock of permanently affordable housing.

The two components, in practice, were often indistinguishable; one frequently led to the other. Promoting a new form of tenure sometimes brought into existence a new nonprofit organization. Thus CEDO's efforts to establish a legal, financial, and organizational foundation for price-restricted models of homeownership led to the formation of the Burlington Community Land Trust (BCLT) in 1984 and the Champlain Valley Mutual Housing Federation in 1990. The BCLT became an aggressive developer of affordable housing. The Champlain Valley Mutual Housing Federation became the primary source of training and support for the region's independently incorporated housing cooperatives—and the manager for all of the reserves built up by these cooperatives.

Conversely, sometimes promoting a new organization has inadvertently introduced a new form of tenure. CEDO's three-year support for a consortium of nonprofit organizations, gathered together to prevent the loss of Northgate Apartments, resulted not only in the successful acquisition and rehabilitation of this threatened project but in the creation of a tenant-controlled structure for owning and managing this property unlike any seen in Vermont before.[6]

At other times perpetual affordability has been achieved not by a new form of tenure but by the nonprofit status of a project's developer and owner. Thus, during the same year that CEDO helped to create the Burlington Community Land Trust, CEDO staff joined with municipal officials from neighboring towns to establish another nonprofit, the Lake Champlain Housing Development Corporation. CEDO has also supported Cathedral Square, Inc. (established in 1978) in developing affordable rental housing for the elderly and the Committee on Temporary Shelter (established in 1982) in developing emergency shelters and permanent single-room-occupancy (SRO) housing for the homeless. In each of these cases, the form of tenure is a rather traditional landlord-tenant relationship, but nonprofit ownership protects the long-term affordability of any units produced.[7]

In summary, while the Sanders administration was struggling to enact a series of measures within the city code for the protection of tenants, it was also working to establish new models and new organizations outside of City Hall for the production of housing with lasting affordability. These nonmarket models of tenure eventually included a citywide community land trust, limited equity condominiums, nonprofit and tenant-managed rentals, and a growing number of limited equity cooperatives tied together in a federated structure. Nonprofit organizations for the production and management of affordable housing eventually included the Burlington Community Land Trust, the Lake Champlain Housing Development Corporation, the Committee on Temporary Shelter, Northgate Housing, Inc., and CEDO support for the ongoing development activities of a preexisting nonprofit, Cathedral Square, Inc. By the end of 1992, nearly eight hundred units of privately owned, perpetually affordable housing had been created by CEDO's nonprofit partners through either the construction of new housing or the rehabilitation of old.

WHY THIRD SECTOR HOUSING?

Why did the Sanders administration decide to adopt a third sector housing policy? What were the strategic considerations behind a policy of directing municipal resources toward new housing models and new housing organizations created expressly for the purpose of decommodifying a growing percentage of Burlington's privately owned housing?

Some of the realities and concerns that formed the backdrop for this third sector housing policy have been mentioned before:

- Because federal funds for housing were drying up, new ways had to be found of doing more with less. It was clear that whatever was done for affordable housing would have to be accomplished using local powers, local resources, and local institutions to a greater degree than before. Little support—and even less leadership—could be expected from HUD.
- Because local plans for developing Burlington's waterfront were gearing up, new ways had to be found of investing in lower-income neighborhoods without displacing lower-income residents. It was clear that public and private investment in the central business district during the 1970s had already put considerable pressure on the residential areas surrounding it. Speculative pressures would only increase with the planned redevelopment of the downtown waterfront. Whatever was done to improve these inner-city neighborhoods would have to be accomplished without further fueling an overheated housing market.
- Because federal protections for the renters at Northgate were running out, new ways had to be found to produce affordable housing that avoided mistakes of the past. It was clear that even a twenty-year rent restriction was inadequate protection for scarce subsidies and vulnerable tenants. As long as privately owned housing could eventually return to the private market, affordability could not be assurred.

The administration's decision to pursue a policy of third sector housing was a conscious product of these practical considerations. There were political considerations as well. One of the main reasons for promoting new forms of price-restricted housing was the impossibility of achieving the same result via more conventional means. The crushing defeat of rent control by Burlington's voters in 1981 and the watering down of every protenant ordinance proposed to the city council in the years thereafter demonstrated the futility of looking primarily to the municipality's police power to stabilize local housing costs. Similarly, any hope of expanding the public ownership of housing was out of the question. The BHA of the early 1980s was a stagnant mess, and any other form of municipal ownership would have required approval from the same electorate that had soundly rejected the administration's bid to regulate rents. Prevented from following familiar paths pioneered by progressives of the past, the Sanders administration was forced to go in a different direction.

A politically more acceptable path than public control or public ownership was the prospect of decommodifying residential property by means of private contracts and private ownership. What a hostile Democratic and Republican majority on the city council would *never* accept, and what a majority of the electorate seemed *reluctant* to accept if enforced by Progressives in City Hall, became palatable and praiseworthy when pursued by private charities—that is, nonprofit housing development organizations with a 501(c) (3) status. Even better, one of these CEDO-sponsored organizations, the Burlington Community Land Trust, held out the irresistible promise of homeownership for all. True, there were contractual limits on the amount of appreciation that these homeowners could realize on the resale of their homes, but lifelong tenants were being offered a piece of the American Dream. So politically difficult was it for Democrats and Republicans to oppose such a lofty ideal that, despite their early opposition, they were soon jockeying for position on the BCLT bandwagon. By the 1989 election, the Democratic candidate for mayor was even suggesting that the BCLT had originally been a Democratic idea.[8]

Nonprofit control over private housing became a means of appeasing not only critics on the right but allies on the left. CEDO had established a home improvement program in 1983 that had begun directing hundreds of thousands of dollars in low-interest loans into the city's oldest and poorest neighborhoods. Some of these neighborhoods were among those most at risk from speculation and gentrification as the central business district continued to prosper and as plans for the downtown waterfront began to mature. Concerns were voiced by Vermont Tenants, Inc., and by newly elected Progressives to the city council that public investment in and around these inner-city neighborhoods would add to displacement pressures their constituents were already experiencing.[9] CEDO's support for a citywide community land trust and for other nonspeculative models of housing was a programmatic response to such concerns, a way of investing in lower-income neighborhoods without displacing lower-income people. By 1988, most of CEDO's home improvement dollars were going into units controlled by the BCLT, Lake Champlain Housing Development Corporation, or some other housing nonprofit.

The existence of political constraints and the pursuit of political acceptability are not the entire explanation for this third sector housing policy, however. There was also a quest for continuity. Half of Burlington's city council is elected every year. A mayoral election is held every other year. In 1981, when Bernie Sanders was first elected, his margin of victory was minuscule. No one expected the Progressives to hold onto City Hall very long. Just the opposite: there was an ever-present apprehension among Sanders's supporters and staff that each year might be their last. Consequently, an unusual amount of attention was devoted to searching for municipal initiatives that might permanently alter the social landscape—initiatives that might out-live the Progressives' temporary hold over City Hall.

This was especially true in the case of affordable housing, the issue around which many of Burlington's most contentious political battles were being waged. No other issue drew the line between the Progressives and their Democratic and Republican opponents more clearly. On no other issue did it seem more certain that the ouster of Progressives from City Hall would result in a dramatic reversal in municipal policy. CEDO staff argued from the beginning, therefore, that a nonprofit infrastructure should be established *outside* City Hall—*independent* of City Hall. Only in this way, it was believed, could whatever gains that were made in decommodifying residential property be protected against inevitable changes in the political wind.

INSTITUTIONALIZING PERPETUAL AFFORDABILITY

As it turned out, Progressives remained in office throughout the decade and into the next. This meant not only that perpetual affordability became rooted in the purposes and programs of a network of nonprofit organizations established outside municipal government but that the same principle was gradually woven into the policies, programs, and plans of the municipality itself.[10]

The City's support for perpetual affordability had its Burlington beginnings in the city council's 1983 decision to appropriate $200,000 for the start-up of a citywide community land trust. Few who voted for this original appropriation fully understood what a land trust was, let alone fully endorsed the decommodification of private property that lurked beneath the surface of this unfamiliar housing model. Even those on the council and within the Sanders administration who did understand and did endorse what was being proposed were hardly prepared to reorient *all* of the city's housing efforts toward long-term affordability. The Burlington Community Land Trust was conceived as one initiative among many being considered for the protection of the city's tenants, the preservation of the city's housing, and the production of more affordable housing.[11]

By the time the BCLT was firmly underway, however, the principle of perpetual affordability had begun to influence more and more of CEDO's thinking about affordable housing. A CEDO report that was adopted as an interim policy in September of 1984 recommended a complete review of all municipal land and housing programs with an eye toward linking these programs more closely with the BCLT. Listed prominently among the benefits of such a policy were the "retention of public subsidies," "development without displacement," and "rent stabilization without rent control." The report was quite explicit in describing the wider implications of this new approach to affordable housing (CEDO, 1984: 4): "By permanently removing land from the marketplace and placing a ceiling on the resale price of housing, a CLT . . . can control housing costs. Such measures 'decommodify' land and housing, assuring long-term accessibility and affordability for persons of modest means."

References to perpetual affordability soon began appearing with great regularity in documents and reports issued by CEDO. The most influential of these was the *Report and Recommendations of the Affordable Housing Task Force* (CEDO, 1986), a publication that eventually became a virtual blueprint for most of CEDO's subsequent housing efforts. The Affordable Housing Task Force was a committee of tenant advocates, public officials, and private developers appointed by the city council in June 1985 to explore ways of addressing Burlington's housing problems. Aside from the remarkable range of the twenty-five recommendations made by this committee for expanding and maintaining the supply of affordable housing, its final report is notable for the frequency with which perpetual affordability is mentioned. Thus the BCLT is praised for "creating a permanent stock of affordable housing for our community" (p. 12); the City is urged to support "cooperative housing, especially limited equity cooperative housing"

(p. 19) and to ensure the "perpetual affordability" of any housing created through municipal grants of lands or funds (pp. 19, 20); CEDO is urged to utilize "a model such as a land trust, limited equity cooperative, or mutual housing program which assures perpetual affordability" to save the city's threatened stock of federally subsidized housing (p. 23).

The *Report and Recommendations* made it clear that the notion of perpetually affordable housing had entered, by 1986, the mainstream of Burlington's ongoing housing debate; various models for making such housing a reality had moreover become favored contenders for municipal support. By 1988, these models had become such a mainstay of the City's policies and programs that CEDO added the "decommodification of housing" to the operational goals of its mission statement, declaring that "housing that is made affordable today, using sizeable public or private subsidies, will only remain affordable if limits are placed on the profits that property owners may remove from their increasingly valuable commodity."

The final stage in this multiyear process of incorporating perpetual affordability into the institutional fabric of Burlington's municipal policy was to make perpetual affordability, limited equity housing, and nonprofit development an explicit part of both the City's municipal plan and the City's Comprehensive Housing Affordability Strategy (CHAS). On May 3, 1991, the Burlington Planning Commission adopted a revised Municipal Development Plan that included among its housing policies the declaration that "the City of Burlington will . . . support housing models, organizations, and programs that insure perpetual affordability." There are no less than nine references in the plan to the need for municipal support for such "models, organizations, and programs."[12] Similarly, the City's first CHAS, submitted to HUD on January 10, 1992, included "perpetual affordability" among the five operating principles guiding Burlington's 1992–1996 plan for affordable housing:[13] "The municipality should target its scarce resources toward organizations, projects, and models of tenure that ensure long-term retention of public subsidies and long-term affordability for any housing that is assisted using public dollars" (CEDO, 1992: 69).

This spreading *conceptual* commitment to perpetual affordability was accompanied by an expanding *programmatic* commitment. The institutionalization of perpetual affordability in Burlington's policies and plans, in other words, was accompanied by the institutionalization of perpetual affordability in the municipality's grant making, loan making, and laws. Such programmatic support included the following: (1) existing municipal resources were redirected, (2) new resources were developed, (3) new ordinances were enacted, and (4) housing professionals employed by CEDO or under contract to CEDO were used to supplement the staff of CEDO's nonprofit partners in expanding the number of privately owned, perpetually affordable units under their control.

Redirecting Existing Resources

Burlington's commitment to perpetual affordability began in 1983 when the new city treasurer discovered a surplus in the general fund. The Sanders administration invested part of that surplus to establish a community land trust, instead of supporting some other worthy project. This was the first of many such trade-offs that forced municipal officials to decide whether to direct limited resources already on hand into *housing* in general—and into housing with *permanent affordability* in particular. These were not easy choices, since Reagan's budgetary ax had spared few domestic programs. Housing, in the early 1980s, was not the only unmet need in Burlington.

Nevertheless, the Sanders administration made an early decision to commit a large portion of the discretionary funds at its disposal to affordable housing. Roughly half of the City's annual allocation of Community Development Block Grant (CDBG) funds went to affordable housing from 1984 to 1992 (see Table 6-1). Equally significant was the later decision to distribute a growing percentage of these housing funds to nonprofit organizations operating outside City government; a nonprofit infrastructure for the development of perpetually affordable housing was thus created and sustained. Prior to 1986, for example, nearly 84 percent of the CDBG funds distributed by the City for affordable housing went to CEDO's own Home Improvement Program (HIP), a low-interest revolving loan fund for residential rehabilitation. From 1986 on, CDBG funds for housing were increasingly redirected away from HIP and toward CEDO's nonprofit partners. Even those funds that remained in CEDO's hands for HIP and for other housing initiatives were increasingly reserved for the nonprofits. This programmatic bias was made explicit in May 1988, when the "Applicant Qualifications" section of HIP's policy manual was amended to read that "HIP places top priority on making loans to nonprofit organizations which are dedicated to providing perpetually affordable housing."

Although CDBG is the most significant example of municipal resources being redirected toward what the 1991 municipal plan referred to as "models, organizations, and programs that insure perpetual affordability," there were others. A vacant fire station was conveyed for a dollar to the

Table 6-1. Community Development Block Grant (CDBG) Support for Nonprofit Housing: City of Burlington, FY1984–FY1992

CDBG Year (Fiscal Year)	*Total CDBG*	*CDBG for Housing*	*% of Total CDBG*	*CDBG for CEDO Housing (HIP)*	*% of CDBG Housing for CEDO*	*CDBG for Nonprofit Housing*	*% of CDBG Housing for Nonprofits*
CDBG 1983 (FY'84)	$778,000	NA	NA	NA	NA	NA	NA
CDBG 1984 (FY'85)	788,000	501,589	64	$451,944	90	$49,645	10
CDBG 1985 (FY'86)	798,000	394,855	49	300,000	76	94,855*	24
CDBG 1986 (FY'87)	684,000	249,000	36	175,000	70	74,000	30
CDBG 1987 (FY'88)	688,000	368,700	54	57,340	16	311,360	84
CDBG 1988 (FY'89)	658,000	343,400	52	87,500	25	255,900	75
CDBG 1989 (FY'90)	685,000	337,400	49	100,000	30	237,400	70
CDBG 1990 (FY'91)	678,000	278,400	41	100,000	36	178,400	64
CDBG 1991 (FY'92)	767,000	313,800	41	115,000	37	198,800	63

NA, not available.

*Includes $60,300 for the Burlington Housing Authority.

BCLT in 1986 for use as an emergency shelter for homeless families. The BHA directed Section 8 certificates and vouchers to the BCLT, Lake Champlain Housing Development Corporation (LCHDC), and other nonprofits. And CEDO, after obtaining a $3.5 million Housing Development Action Grant (HoDAG) for the *for-profit* developer of a 148-unit project in 1984, applied for two HoDAGs for *nonprofit* developers in 1986: one for a 50-unit housing cooperative to be owned by the BCLT; another for an 80-unit rental project to be owned by LCHDC. The latter project was eventually awarded a $2.9 million HoDAG and was completed in 1989.

Developing New Resources

The City also developed *new* sources of funding for third sector housing. In 1987, the Burlington Employees Retirement System (BERS) was persuaded by the mayor and city treasurer to establish a $1 million line of credit for the BCLT. These funds helped the BCLT to bring thirty units of housing, including fourteen single-family homes, into its system of perpetual affordability. In 1992 BERS gave preliminary approval to a second $1 million investment in economic development and affordable housing—one not targeted specifically to the BCLT—to be made through the purchase of community development certificates of deposit from a local bank.

Other favorable financing for the City's nonprofit partners was secured by more indirect means. In 1988, CEDO organized and bankrolled a statewide conference on the federal Community Reinvestment Act. This conference spawned a new nonprofit organization, the Vermont Community Reinvestment Association (VCRA). During the next few years, VCRA mounted formal challenges against the Bank of Boston in its bid to acquire the Bank of Vermont and against Vermont Federal Bank in its application to transfer its downtown headquarters from Burlington to an affluent suburb nearby.[14] Although both challenges were eventually rejected by federal regulators, community reinvestment became a public issue in Vermont for the first time. With VCRA and CEDO working to keep this issue alive, local lenders became unusually forthcoming in financially supporting nonprofit housing.

Bank support for the nonmarket models and nonprofit organizations of Burlington's expanding third sector cannot be attributed solely to outside pressure, however. At least four other factors were at work. First of all, the nonprofit projects that the banks were being asked to finance were getting better all the time, as the nonprofits gained experience developing affordable housing. Unlike those of many for-profit developers, moreover, the projects planned by the nonprofits were neither postponed nor bankrupted by the downturn in the New England economy at the decade's end. Second, the banks' investment in Low Income Housing Tax Credits made some of these nonprofit projects more lucrative than they would otherwise have been (see n. 10). Third, the City announced in 1991 that it would, in the future, place its own accounts with institutions that not only offered the best depository services at the best rates, but demonstrated the best performance in meeting community credit needs. Finally, there was the Community Banking Council. First convened in 1989 by CEDO and the Bank of Vermont, the Community Banking Council brought municipal officials, bankers, and nonprofits together every other month for the next four years to discuss community reinvestment. One result of these ongoing discussions was increased bank involvement in neighborhoods and projects given high priority by CEDO and its nonprofit partners.

The most significant step that the City has taken in institutionalizing its support for third sector housing occurred in 1989 when Burlington's voters approved a property tax increase of one cent on every one hundred dollars of valuation to capitalize the City's housing trust fund. This municipal fund had been created the year before to provide project subsidies for affordable housing and operational support for nonprofit housing organizations. The ordinance establishing the Burlington Housing Trust Fund was quite explicit in describing the kind of housing to be supported: "Priority in all disbursements intended for use in acquiring, constructing, rehabilitating, or financing housing units shall be given . . . to projects that guarantee the perpetual affordability of these units for very low, low, or moderate income households." When the city's residents voted in 1989 to raise their own taxes, therefore, they not only directly guaranteed long-term municipal support for nonprofit organizations like the BCLT and LCHDC that had been working so hard to address Burlington's housing problems but indirectly endorsed the principle of long-term affordability that lay at the heart of these organizations' housing efforts—and at the heart of the trust fund itself.

Regulatory Support

Other provisions have been incorporated into the City's code of ordinances that favor nonprofit developers and the private, nonmarket housing they produce. Such regulatory support comes in two different forms: projects and organizations that promote perpetually affordable housing have been granted *privileges* denied to others or they have been granted *exemptions* from conditions or fees required of others.

Examples of the first are found in Burlington's condominium conversion ordinance and in its inclusionary zoning ordinance. Enacted in 1987, the condominium conversion ordinance gives tenants in any building slated for conversion to condominium ownership 120 days to purchase their building from the current owner. Should they be unwilling or unable to accomplish this difficult feat, the City or a "designated housing agency" is granted the first right to purchase the building on the tenants' behalf. A "designated housing agency," according to the ordinance, is "a public entity or a 501(c)(3) tax-exempt, nonprofit corporation whose purpose is creating or preserving housing for low or moderate income persons." The city council eventually approved the BCLT, LCHDC, Cathedral Square, Inc., and the Burlington Housing Authority as "designated housing agencies."

A similar preemptive right to purchase residential property is granted these same "designated housing agencies" by the City's inclusionary zoning ordinance enacted in 1990. For 120 days after building permits are issued for any residential project with five or more units, these agencies are given an exclusive option to purchase all of the project's "inclusionary units" at a below-market price.[15] Should these units not be acquired by a "designated housing agency," they must still "remain affordable for a period of no less than ninety-nine years, commencing from the date of initial occupancy." In short, the ordinance mandates perpetual affordability, regardless of who purchases an inclusionary unit.

Regulatory support for third sector housing is also embodied in several key exemptions. Perpetually affordable rental housing is exempt from the annual "apartment inspection fee" collected from landlords for the support of Burlington's minimum housing inspection program.[16] Limited equity cooperatives and other forms of perpetually affordable housing are permitted waivers from the City's strict requirements for on-site parking. Affordable elderly housing is not subject to the same restrictions on density and coverage that govern other projects. And, as of 1992, impact fees on new residential development are reduced for housing that rents or sells at an affordable price. A 50 percent waiver of impact fees "for that portion of a residential project that meets the dual test of initial affordability and continuing affordability" is granted for projects serving households earning less than 75 percent of median income. A 100 percent waiver of impact fees is granted for perpetually affordable projects serving households earning less than 50 percent of median.[17]

Staff Support

Less obvious but no less important to the development of private, nonmarket housing has been the professional support provided by CEDO staff in supplementing the underpaid and overextended staff of the nonprofit sector, especially during the early stages of organizational or project development. Such support, it should be noted, has gone beyond the kind of clean-hands coaching from the sidelines that characterizes much of the "technical assistance" traditionally offered to neighborhood organizations by municipal officials. CEDO staff have often been on the field with their nonprofit partners, at the center of play, putting the administration's own political and financial fortunes on the line.

Organizational support has been paramount. Thus CEDO's first housing director was the principal organizer and de facto director for the Burlington Community Land Trust during its first year of existence. CEDO's second housing director was instrumental in founding the Lake Champlain Housing Development Corporation. CEDO's third housing director helped to write the Vermont Cooperative Housing Ownership Act and to found the Champlain Valley Mutual Housing Federation.[18] All three played key roles in "saving" Northgate Apartments: first in building the capacity of the Northgate Tenants Association; then in convening the Northgate Task Force and covering the early costs of Northgate Nonprofit; and finally in participating in the creation of Northgate Housing, Inc., the managing co–general partner of the limited partnership that eventually purchased Northgate on behalf of its current residents.

Project support has been equally important. CEDO employs a housing rehabilitation specialist and a housing development specialist, each of whom has sometimes functioned as a de facto member of a nonprofit project's development team.[19] CEDO staff have written rehabilitation specifications and overseen the quality of finished work for a number of projects undertaken by the nonprofits. On some occasions, CEDO staff have put together the early pro formas and financial packages that made a project possible. On other occasions, CEDO staff have played more of a trouble-shooting role, helping the nonprofits to work their way around unexpected obstacles in the development process. More recently, CEDO staff have themselves initiated several projects, securing site control and shepherding them through the early phases of the municipality's own planning and permit process before turning them over to a nonprofit owner.[20]

At times CEDO has also employed an independent contractor to provide full-time professional support for a nonprofit organization, someone who serves as a virtual member of an organization's own staff for a period of one or more years. For example, a tenant organizer for the Northgate project was funded by CEDO from 1987 to 1989 to ensure active tenant participation in the planning and development of the nonprofit buyout of this expiring use project. Similarly, a specialist in cooperative housing was employed by CEDO from 1989 to 1991, under a joint arrangement with the City of Winooski and the BCLT, to provide assistance to the first limited equity housing cooperatives being developed in Burlington and Winooski. This private contractor went on to become the founding director for the Champlain Valley Mutual Housing Federation.

THE PROGRESSIVE RECORD: 1984–1992

What was accomplished during these years of concentrated support for private, nonmarket housing and for the nonprofit sponsors of such housing? The outcomes can be considered under five headings: productivity, capacity, security, mobility, and constituency.

Productivity

From the end of 1984, the year in which CEDO began heavily investing in the establishment of a nonprofit infrastructure, to the end of 1992, approximately 800 units of housing were brought under some form of private price restriction through either the construction of new units or the acquisition and rehabilitation of existing units. All of these units will remain perpetually affordable. An additional 148 units—constructed, owned, and managed by a for-profit developer using a Housing Development Action Grant—were created with CEDO's assistance outside of the decommodified domain of the nonprofits. Since the tenants of this project have an option to buy out the developer after twenty years (or sooner, if he decides to sell) and since the entire $3.5 million HoDAG provided by the City can be claimed by the tenants if they organize themselves into a limited equity cooperative, all of these units may eventually become part of Burlington's expanding stock of third sector housing.

In sum, a respectable quantity of privately owned, perpetually affordable housing was created during a period of sharp cutbacks in federal aid. Adding these new units of third sector housing produced since the mid-1980s to the preexisting stock of public housing, HUD 202 housing, and project-based Section 8 housing produced in the 1960s and 1970s, Burlington possessed approximately 1,600 units of nonmarket housing by the end of 1992. A little more than 10 percent of the city's entire stock of housing had been brought under some form of multiyear price control.[21]

Capacity

The second accomplishment of Burlington's third sector housing policy was the creation of a nonprofit infrastructure capable of acquiring, rehabilitating, constructing, and managing both single-unit and multiunit housing. Whether initially established by CEDO, partially sustained by CEDO, or intensively supported on a project-by-project basis by resources and policies emanating from CEDO, six different nonprofit organizations were brought to a point in their own development such that each possessed the professional staff, internal systems, and operational experience to carry out major housing projects. Three of these nonprofits—the Burlington Community Land Trust, Lake Champlain Housing Development Corporation, and Cathedral Square, Inc.—possessed the mission, motivation, and means to develop additional units of affordable housing on an annual basis. Only one of the city's six housing nonprofits, Cathedral Square, already existed when the Progressives took over City Hall.

Supplementing the newly created capacity of these private, nonprofit corporations was the revitalized capacity of the Burlington Housing Authority, a municipal corporation that was transformed from crippled infirmity to vigorous health. Besides providing better housing for its own tenants, the BHA entered the 1990s providing maintenance services for the BCLT; management advice for Northgate Housing, Inc.; board leadership for LCHDC; and rental subsidies for the BCLT, LCHDC, Northgate, and the Committee on Temporary Shelter (COTS).

Security

The third accomplishment was to enhance the residential security of many who have been precariously housed. Despite the failures of rent control, an antispeculation tax, and just-cause eviction, significant progress was made during the 1980s in stabilizing rental costs and in reducing the speculative pressures that were causing tenant displacement. The existing stock of affordable rental housing was protected by the enactment of strict controls on conversion and demolition, the enhanced enforcement of minimum housing codes, the revitalization of the BHA, and the successful buyout of Northgate Apartments. At the same time, hundreds of new units were added to the affordable rental stock in and around Burlington by nonprofit organizations and for-profit developers taking advantage of the last few crumbs of federal support for affordable housing. A 1990 agreement between the City and the University of Vermont, moreover, imposed strict limits on the future growth in student enrollment, while committing UVM to construct new, on-campus housing for 544 students by 1995 (see n. 21). The combined effect of these measures, when magnified by an end-of-the-decade downturn in New England's economy, was greater security for Burlington's tenants. By the 1990s, rents had begun to moderate and the rental vacancy rate had crept above 5 percent for the first time in nearly two decades.[22]

Security of tenure was increased, as well, through new models of limited equity homeownership that enabled lower-income tenants for the first time to enjoy many of the rights reserved only for those who own their homes. These innovative models became, with CEDO's support, an influential part of the city's housing scene.[23]

Finally, CEDO's efforts helped to increase the residential security of the city's lower-income homeowners and the city's homeless. Low-interest rehabilitation loans, free paint, and a reverse equity program for the payment of taxes and insurance helped lower-income homeowners to maintain, and retain, their housing. The creation of three emergency shelters, a transitional housing program, and ninety-five units of permanent SRO housing provided basic accommodations for the homeless. Although these efforts neither solved the problem of homelessness nor saved the home of every person of modest means whose income or age had made homeownership a precarious proposition, progress was made on both fronts.

Mobility

A somewhat serendipitous outcome of enhancing the security and protecting the affordability of every rung on Burlington's housing tenure ladder was the opening up of new opportunities for upward mobility from one rung to another. As missing rungs at the bottom of the tenure ladder were replaced, homeless families and homeless individuals found it easier to make their way into secure tenancy. As a pool of price-stabilized rental housing was developed by nonprofit organizations, tenants moved out of some of the worst for-profit rentals and into the best of the nonprofit rentals. As new rungs of limited equity housing were introduced into the yawning gap between for-profit rentals and market-priced homeownership, lower-income households gained a firm foothold on homeownership, leaving tenancy behind. In short, the *lateral* mobility made possible by stabilizing the city's rental market was matched by new opportunities for *vertical* mobility made possible by rebuilding the city's housing tenure ladder.[24]

Constituency

Finally, in building a broad-based consensus for affordable housing in general, and for third sector housing in particular, Burlington's Progressives accomplished, during the late 1980s and early 1990s, the political equivalent of a double somersault on a very high wire. They retained the allegiance of lower-income tenants while winning the acquiescience of moderate-income homeowners for a well-publicized policy of directing most of the City's scarce resources for affordable housing toward a handful of nonprofit organizations promoting unusual models of tenure.

These nonprofits, in turn, helped to broaden the base of popular support for precisely the sort of municipal activism being championed by the Progressives. Each of these organizations has members, beneficiaries, contributors, and staff numbering in the hundreds, a vocal constituency for affordable housing. Drawing on such support, neither the Sanders nor the Clavelle administration was ever alone, from about 1984 onward, when going before the city council or the city's voters with a new housing initiative. It was this constituency, organized outside of City Hall, that helped to win such electoral victories as a condominium conversion ordinance and a one-cent tax increase for the housing trust fund. It was this constituency that helped to win such legislative victories as inclusionary zoning.[25] And it was this constituency that continued the fight for affordable housing—and for perpetual affordability—when the Progressives lost their grip on City Hall at last.

BUILDING THIRD SECTOR HOUSING: CONTROVERSY AND CONFLICT

Behind this record of accomplishment, a record summarized in Table 6-2, lay a ten-year political and ideological struggle between two very different approaches to housing development: on the one side, supporters of an activist administration who regarded the private market as a run-amok source of misery and mayhem that should be closely regulated; on the other, allies of private capital—developers, landlords, business owners, bankers, and realtors—who regarded that market as a self-regulating source of prosperity and profit that should be left alone. Between these two extremes, Burlington's politicians and voters were forced to say again and again just how far they were willing to go in using the municipality's powers and resources to modify the market character of privately owned housing.

Although the supporters of perpetual affordability won many of these contests, the Progressives were frequently forced into political compromises that weakened this general commitment. They were sometimes forced to surrender the principle altogether. In 1990, for example, the Clavelle administration won city council approval for a ninety-nine-year affordability period for any units created under inclusionary zoning. The year before, the same administration had to accept a very modest ten-year affordability restriction on any "replacement units" created under the housing preservation and replacement ordinance. Another example: beginning in 1986, CEDO's Home Improvement Program targeted most of its resources to the price-restricted housing of nonprofit developers, but it still made available a small number of low-interest loans and a large number of free cans of paint to low-income homeowners without restricting the future price of their homes.[26]

Some of the most rancorous housing battles in Burlington—and some of the most concessionary compromises—had less to do with who the agent of development should be or what the duration of affordability should be than with whether development should occur at all. Factions within a particular neighborhood sometimes resisted a proposed housing project because they feared that the "wrong" type of people would live there, or they opposed construction of any sort on local lands that had long been vacant. Other factions within the city opposed development on general principle because of its impact on the environment, city services, or the quality of life. Caught in the cross fire of such sentiments, nonprofit developers, and the unfamiliar models of housing tenure promoted by them, sometimes became convenient targets for attacks that were rooted in a deeper bias against a particular class of people or a particular use of land.

CEDO, too, became a frequent target: sometimes because of its backing for unpopular projects like SRO housing for the homeless but more often because of its relative autonomy within Burlington's commission form of government. CEDO was the only major department, aside from administrative offices like the treasurer, clerk, and city attorney, without a commission appointed by the city council; it was the only major department accountable directly to the mayor. Its independence was further reinforced by its receiving nearly all of its funding from state and federal sources, not from municipal revenues controlled directly by the city council. The result was an activist, innovative, and politicized department doing research and development directly for the mayor, a result that never sat well with any of Burlington's opposition parties, whether Democrat, Republican, or Green. Indeed, about the only issue on which all of them agreed was that CEDO was "out of control" and "unaccountable to the people." By the early 1990s, CEDO was continually under attack, facing closer scrutiny by the city council and repeated calls by opposition parties for a commission to oversee its activities.

Other kinds of conflict posed a more direct threat to Burlington's hard-won consensus around third sector housing, for they emerged not out of fault lines in the political landscape surrounding the policy but out of stresses internal to the policy itself. The most common of these "internal" conflicts occurred between the municipality and its nonprofit partners. There were occasions when the municipality's housing officials became frustrated with the cautious and crawling pace of nonprofit development and pressured the nonprofits to do *more*. On other occasions, the municipality's political leaders became frightened by neighborhood resistance to a proposed development and pressured the nonprofits to do *less*. Such tensions became inevitable and unavoidable once the decision was made to rely upon a network of independent organizations, established outside municipal government, for the delivery of most housing services. As much as

Table 6-2. Burlington Housing Highlights, 1983–1992

	Protection of the Vulnerable	*Preservation of Affordable Housing*	*Production of Affordable Housing*
1983		Home Improvement Loan Program	
1984	Anti-discrimination Ordinance	Burlington Community Land Trust	Burlington Community Land Trust
1985	Accessibility Grants Program	Lake Champlain Housing Development Corporation	Lake Champlain Housing Development Corporation
	Overhaul of Minimum Housing Code	Overhaul of Minimum Housing Code	Howe Meadow linkage project (40 units)
1986	Security Deposits Ordinance	Antispeculation tax (passed by city; rejected by state)	Fairmount Place demolition project (40 units)
		Northgate task force	
1987	Reverse Equity Program for Elderly	BERS $1 million credit line for BCLT	BERS $1 million credit line for BCLT
	Condominium Conversion Ordinance	Condominium Conversion Ordinance	South Meadow HoDAG (148 units)
		Modernization program for BHA housing	
		Apartment Inspection Fee Ordinance	
1988	Firehouse family shelter	Vermont Cooperative Housing Ownership Act	Firehouse family shelter (5 units)
	Just-cause eviction referendum (defeated by Burlington voters)	Burlington Housing Trust Fund	Burlington Housing Trust Fund
1989	Rehabilitation of Wilson SRO	Rehabilitation of Wilson SRO (22 units)	Salmon Run HoDAG (80 units)
	Housing Replacement Ordinance	Acquisition of Northgate (336 units)	Heineberg Senior Housing (80 units)
	Accessibility requirements added to building code	Tax levy for Housing Trust Fund	Tax levy for Housing Trust Fund
		Housing Replacement Ordinance	Mini-Act 250: housing linkage

	Protection of the Vulnerable	Preservation of Affordable Housing	Production of Affordable Housing
1990	St. John's Hall SRO Transitional housing program Group housing zoning amendment	Energy conservation bond ($11 million) Champlain Valley Mutual Housing Federation	St. John's Hall SRO (21 units) Transitional housing program (9 units) Inclusionary Zoning Ordinance City/UVM agreement on student housing (544 new on-campus beds by 1995)
1991		Completion of $7 million Northgate rehabilitation First limited equity co-ops	Wood Street inclusionary project (7 units) Employer-assisted 10-cent housing program
1992	Sarah Cole SRO Vermont Security Deposits Statute	Rehabilitation of YWCA apartments $2 million Rehabilitation Loan Pool	Sarah Cole SRO (12 units) Impact Fee Ordinance Flynn Avenue Co-op (28 units)

these organizations might have depended upon City Hall for operational and project support, they were not always or automatically going to do the City's bidding.[27]

There were also tensions among the nonprofits themselves. Multiple nonprofits may share a similar commitment to perpetual affordability, but they must still jockey for position and advantage in acquiring preferred properties, in securing scarce funding, and in ensuring their own survival. Competition increased as public funding for affordable housing continued to decline and as the nonprofits' need for ever-more-elusive operational funding continued to grow. CEDO found itself more and more in the uncomfortable position of being forced to choose one nonprofit over another or being forced to act as a third party referee between two (or more) of its nonprofit partners.[28]

Finally, despite the Progressives' best efforts to harmonize the separate halves of their housing policy, there existed from the very beginning a degree of tension between the strategy of empowering tenants and the strategy of decommodifying property. Nonprofit housing developers are not always the best landlords. They may know more about producing affordable housing than they know about managing it. They may lack the resources to fully rehabilitate rundown units purchased at a bargain to prevent the displacement of low-income tenants. They may be so focused on the long-term goal of converting their rental holdings to limited equity homeownership that they ignore the short-term necessity of operating rental housing in an effective, efficient manner. Whatever the reason, Burlington's nonprofit housing in the beginning was not always as well managed as its occupants might have wished. Confrontations between local advocates for tenants rights and local providers of nonmarket housing became an occasional feature of the city's housing scene.

Even when nonprofit developers could be counted among the best landlords, they were sometimes accused of skimming off the best tenants: those with a little more money, a little more education, and a lot more tolerance for the interminable meetings that are often a part of third sector housing. There was some truth to this charge. Many of the units being developed by Burlington's nonprofit organizations, "perpetually affordable" though they may be, were unaffordable and inaccessible for people with the lowest incomes and the greatest need. On the other hand, the accusation of skimming ignored the fact that both the BCLT and LCHDC, after 1989, devoted part of their development efforts to permanent SRO housing for the homeless. The BCLT, in addition, played a leading role in developing an emergency shelter for homeless families, transitional housing for mother-led families, a downtown service center for homeless individuals, and a new facility for the Chittenden County Emergency Food Shelf. It is worth remembering, as well, that the Committee on Temporary Shelter *always* focused on the poorest of the poor and that Northgate Housing, Inc., saved the home of *every* tenant who was in residence at the time of its successful buy-out of Northgate's 336 apartments.

In the end, these conflicts and controversies do less to overshadow the many accomplishments of Burlington's progressive housing policy than they do to highlight the many obstacles an activist municipal government confronted, and managed mostly to overcome, in comprehensively addressing a clear crisis in affordable housing. The most formidable obstacle confronting the City of Burlington, on the other hand, was circumvented more than it was ever overcome. Rooted neither in conflicts surrounding third sector housing nor in stresses internal to the policy itself, the greatest impediment to the City's progressive housing policy remained the decade-long indifference of a national administration dedicated to doing less, not more, for affordable housing. Every housing accomplishment of both the Sanders and the Clavelle administrations must be seen against the harsh backdrop of this dwindling federal commitment. Whatever was done for affordable housing during the years of Progressive rule was accomplished *despite* a shrinking pool of federal funds.[29]

The election of Bill Clinton raised hopes that this federal drought might finally be coming to an end. If so, Burlington was well prepared. Unlike most U.S. cities, Burlington's capacity for effectively and efficiently utilizing public dollars had been heightened during the 1980s, rather than diminished. CEDO had developed the systems, the partners, and the personnel to administer any new housing program that Washington might devise. The Burlington Housing Authority, after renewing itself and revitalizing all of its older units, was ready for new challenges. A handful of nonprofit organizations were developing and managing hundreds of units of perpetually affordable rental and owner-occupied housing and were beginning to tackle the redevelopment of some of the city's worst inner-city blocks. In short, after years of private effort and public support an organizational infrastructure was firmly in place that was capable of responding immediately and productively to whatever additional resources for affordable housing might be forthcoming from the new administration in Washington.

But on April 5, 1993, Burlington got a new administration of its own.

Just as twelve years of Republican rule were being brought to an end in Washington, twelve years of Progressive rule were brought abruptly to an end in Burlington. Peter Clavelle was defeated for reelection to a third term as mayor and replaced by a conservative Republican who had campaigned on the theme that local government needed to get "back to basics": fire, police, schools, and streets.[30]

Conspicuously missing from this very short list was any mention of a municipal role in promoting affordable housing. It seemed likely that City Hall's past policy of aggressive support for nonmarket housing and nonprofit development was about to change. The expansion and survival of Burlington's third sector would be determined, during the next few years, not by activists inside city government but by those inside the nonprofit organizations, limited equity cooperatives, and land trust homes that an activist government had helped to create. The future was now in their hands.

NOTES

Acknowledgments: Critical comments were offered on earlier drafts of this chapter by Tim McKenzie, Brenda Torpy, Erhard Mahnke, Kirby White, and Tom Dillon. Their assistance is gratefully acknowledged. Any errors of fact, emphasis, or interpretation that remain are the responsibility of the author alone. Unintended distortion is always a risk whenever a chronicler of past events was also a participant in them (see n. 18).

1. Burlington's population of 37,712 in 1980 occupied 13,763 units of housing. By 1990, the city's population of 39,127 was housed in 15,480 units. This housing was 60 percent rental and 40 percent owner occupied, percentages that have remained fairly constant over two decades.

2. The origins, constituencies, issues, and struggles of Burlington's Progressive movement are examined in greater detail by Clavel (1986), Soifer (1988), Guma (1989), Conroy (1990), Rosdil (1991), and Wimpey (1992).

3. During the entire period under discussion, 1981–1993, Progressive allies of the Sanders and Clavelle administrations never held more than six seats on Burlington's thirteen-member city council.

4. Prior to 1983, federal CDBG funds were distributed locally by the Burlington Planning Department and the Burlington Planning Commission, both dominated by political cronies of the previous Democratic regime. By convincing HUD to make Burlington an entitlement city, with its own allocation of CDBG funds, and by assigning these funds to an executive office accountable directly to the mayor, the

Sanders administration increased its ability to set the City's development agenda and reduced the Democrats' ability to block that agenda.

5. The importance of having a well-run, sympathetic, and supportive housing authority backing the Progressives' efforts to establish a permanent pool of privately owned, price-restricted housing is underscored by Allen David Heskin's (1991) account of a ten-year struggle to establish limited equity cooperatives in a Los Angeles neighborhood. In the latter case, the housing authority's own incompetence was combined with suspicion and hostility toward the co-op model, making the housing authority more of a hinderance than a helper in this grassroots effort to develop third sector housing for lower-income people. In Burlington, from 1985 onward, the opposite was true.

6. The successful multiyear struggle to "save" Northgate, the nation's first tenant-led buy-out of an "expiring use" project under the 1987 federal Preservation Act, is described in more detail in Torpy (1988), Wallace (1991), and Achtenberg (1992).

7. Although the landlord-tenant relationship is a traditional one, the guarantees of long-term affordability are not. Affordability is ensured not only by the nonprofit status of the owner, but by loan conditions imposed by the City, deed covenants imposed by the Vermont Housing and Conservation Board, or grant conditions imposed by federal rules. On several projects, affordability controls have been further enhanced by giving the BCLT the land under these projects or a first option to purchase them.

8. In reality, Democrats on and off the city council were vigorous opponents of the BCLT during its early years. One year after the BCLT was founded, for example, CEDO negotiated a linkage agreement with a private developer that would have added forty newly constructed single-family houses to the BCLT. Prominent Democrats immediately attacked this plan. With these Democratic leaders stirring the caldron, an angry citizen's group arose within the area where the planned BCLT housing was to be built. This group named itself HALT, Homeowners against the Land Trust. In the end, the forty houses were built, but the opposition was successful in limiting to six the number of houses that became part of the BCLT.

9. In 1985, the cost of ignoring these speculative pressures on affordable housing was made painfully clear to every tenant organizer and housing activist in northern Vermont. Two publicly subsidized housing projects on the outskirts of Burlington, Thorn Hill Apartments and Indian Brook Apartments, were converted to market-rate rentals and condominiums, displacing 142 lower-income households. The unsuccessful but widely publicized fight to prevent the loss of these affordable units convinced many activists that new models of nonspeculative housing had to be found.

10. Although the focus here is on *municipal* policy, it is important to note that perpetual affordability also became a key aspect of *state* policy during the late 1980s, at least insofar as that policy was embodied in programs and priorities of the

Vermont Housing and Conservation Board, the Vermont Housing Finance Agency, and Housing Vermont. The most expensive and most successful housing projects undertaken by CEDO's nonprofit partners would simply not have been possible without the financial backing of these three statewide organizations. Vermont has been especially far-sighted in its use of Low Income Housing Tax Credits, directing most of these credits (via Housing Vermont) toward projects with nonprofit partners committed to preserving affordability long after the tax benefits are depleted. More information on Vermont's commitment to perpetual affordability can be found in Harmon (1992) and Libby (1990).

11. One of Sanders's closest political allies, Terry Bouricius, had invited representatives from the Institute for Community Economics to meet Sanders in January 1982. The seeds for a community land trust (CLT) in Burlington were planted in this early meeting. It was not until the fall of 1983, however, that Progressives were able to bring a proposal for CLT funding before the city council. Most of the public debate surrounding this proposal emphasized the homeownership aspects of this housing model, not its potential for "decommodifying" private property. A different debate went on within the administration and the Progressive Coalition. It focused on two issues: whether a CLT should concentrate on new construction on the waterfront or on rehabilitation in existing neighborhoods, and whether a CLT should be one housing program among many or the centerpiece for all of CEDO's housing efforts.

12. Although the political lead in making perpetual affordability the cornerstone of the City's policies and programs was clearly taken by CEDO, it should be noted that the Planning Department was equally committed to this principle after 1986. A new planning director, Mark Eldridge, was hired that year. Under Eldridge, Burlington's Planning Department was just as likely as CEDO to propose innovative ways of promoting and preserving the affordability of newly constructed housing.

13. The other four "operational principles" in Burlington's 1992 Comprehensive Housing Affordability Strategy were "municipal activism," "redistribution of benefits and burdens," "balance of stability and mobility," and "nonprofit partnership."

14. During the challenge against the Bank of Boston, Mayor Sanders, the city attorney, and CEDO attempted to enter the legal fray on the side of VCRA. They were prevented from doing so by a negative vote from the Democratic-Republican majority on city council. The administration was successful in winning approval from the council only for a resolution creating a Community Banking Council.

15. The percentage of inclusionary units required in any given project runs from 10 percent to 25 percent, depending upon the sales price of the market units and the location of the project. The price of these inclusionary units is set at 65 percent of median for rental projects and 75 percent of median for sales projects. Also included is a density bonus of 15 percent to 25 percent.

16. The revenues raised by this fee also pay for staffing the City's Housing Board of Review, a municipal commission that, among other duties, ensures that landlords return tenants' security deposits. Another portion of this fee has been used to support a landlord-tenant resource center.

17. From 1989 to 1990, CEDO convened and staffed the Regulatory Review Task Force, a committee of public officials, private developers, and affordable housing advocates appointed by the city council to evaluate the impact of municipal regulations and fees on the development of new housing. Among the fifty-six findings and suggestions of this task force in its final report was the recommendation that "City Council should consider deferring or waiving all impact fees for affordable housing" (CEDO, 1990: 10). Two years later, a CEDO-sponsored ordinance implementing this recommendation was enacted by the city council.

18. CEDO had three different housing directors during the period 1983–1993: Brenda Torpy (1983–1985); Amy Wright (1985–1987); and John Davis (1987–1993). Despite such turnover, CEDO's third sector housing policy remained remarkably consistent for over a decade. This was due to four factors: overlapping terms of service allowed all three housing directors to work closely together in putting this policy in place; a succession of Progressive city councillors with a special interest in third sector housing helped to keep this policy on track; both of CEDO's directors, Peter Clavelle and Michael Monte, had backed the policy from the very beginning; and the same person presided over this policy during the entire period, first as CEDO's director and then as mayor. Clavelle's particular contribution was recognized in 1992 when *Shelterforce* named him "one of the country's best elected officials when it comes to securing decent housing for all" (1992: 9).

19. CEDO staff who have played such key supporting roles for the nonprofits have been Amy Wright, Jeffery Glassberg, Tom Dillon, and Richard Moffi. (Moffi also served as acting housing director in CEDO during Davis's one-year absence, 1992–1993.)

20. Sometimes, of course, projects being developed by CEDO's nonprofit partners have needed technical support that cannot be provided by CEDO staff, especially when a project's initial feasibility was being evaluated. CEDO has often helped to defray these predevelopment costs. At other times it was not the feasibility of a new housing *project* that was in question but the feasibility of a new housing *model*. Prior to the BCLT's incorporation in 1984, for example, CEDO hired a private attorney to research the authority under Vermont law for this unusual housing model. Similarly, prior to the development of Vermont's first limited equity cooperatives, CEDO joined with other co-op advocates to help push a cooperative housing enabling act through the state legislature (in 1988) and then to assist in the preparation and dissemination of model documents for the formation of cooperative housing corporations (in 1989).

21. Despite their focus on third sector housing, both the Sanders and Clavelle administrations devoted significant resources to producing and preserving units

of housing that were neither owned by nonprofits nor perpetually encumbered by price controls. These units are part of the Progressive record, even if somewhat removed from the epicenter of Progressive policy. Included in this count are approximately 450 units of housing rehabilitated with grants and loans from CEDO's Home Improvement Program; 77 modestly priced units constructed by private developers under a CEDO-negotiated linkage agreement and a HUD demonstration program; and 544 dormitory beds planned for construction by 1995 under a 1990 agreement between the University of Vermont (UVM) and the City. The last was the result of nine years of municipal pressure on UVM, which culminated in the City's refusal to issue planning or building permits for new university facilities until UVM committed to the construction of additional on-campus housing.

22. The 1990–1992 recession introduced a spate of new problems, however: vacant buildings, bank foreclosures, and deferred maintenance. Throughout the 1980s, much of the City's housing policy was premised on coping with problems of speculative *reinvestment*. The 1990s opened with the specter of *disinvestment* hanging over Burlington's older neighborhoods. By the end of 1992, this changing economic climate had caused three shifts in City policy: priority was being given to the rehabilitation of existing housing over the construction of new housing; the minimum housing inspection program was being overhauled (once again); and reductions in impact fees were being offered to the developers of affordable housing.

23. Although any form of homeownership customarily ensures far more security than any form of tenancy, security of tenure is also a priority of Burlington's nonprofit landlords. All subscribe to the principle that eviction should be for "just cause" only, a principle that the city's for-profit landlords would have been forced to adopt if a just-cause eviction charter change had been approved by Burlington's voters in 1988. It wasn't, so they didn't.

24. This aspect of Burlington's housing program received national recognition in 1991 as one of twenty-five outstanding "Innovations in State and Local Government," an awards program of the Ford Foundation and Harvard's JFK School of Government. CEDO's comprehensive and creative commitment to "rebuilding the housing tenure ladder" was chosen as a finalist out of nineteen hundred state and local programs reviewed by the Innovations staff. Earlier, one of CEDO's principal partners in rebuilding the tenure ladder received *international* recognition for its innovative approach to affordable housing. In 1987, the Burlington Community Land Trust received a "Special Merit Award" from the United Nations International Year of Shelter for creating "a new kind of partnership in the fight against poverty . . . that links needy families, the private sector, and government."

25. Inclusionary zoning is a good example of the political effectiveness of the nonprofit network. This measure was brought to the city council in 1985 as an ordinance and in 1987 as a recommendation of the Affordable Housing Task Force. It

was voted down both times. Three years later, it was enacted into law. What had changed? In 1990, when for-profit developers asserted they could not build housing with a mandatory affordability component, nonprofit developers challenged their conclusions. Having neutralized the "expert witnesses" for the opposition, the nonprofits helped to create the political space for a liberal Democrat and two liberal Republicans to vote with Progressive members of the city council.

26. With the advent of HOME in 1992, another exception was made. CEDO used its first $500,000 in HOME funds to create a $2 million loan pool for the rehabilitation of multiunit housing. (The balance of these funds was provided by the Vermont Housing Finance Agency.) These low-interest loans were made available not only to nonprofit developers promising long-term affordability but to for-profit developers willing to abide by HOME's affordability restrictions and willing to invest in distressed areas targeted by CEDO.

27. Other sources of tension between City Hall and its nonprofit partners were impact fees on new housing and property taxes on existing, price-restricted housing. The nonprofits argued that the City should not give subsidies for affordable housing with one hand and take them back with the other. The issue of impact fees was addressed in 1992 (see n. 17). The issue of property taxes remained unresolved.

28. The principal source of tension among CEDO's nonprofit partners has been the competition for *operating* funds. Having helped to create a diverse network of nonprofit housing organizations, CEDO has had to find new ways of helping to *sustain* this network over time. This quest has met only limited success. Even when combining CDBG, HOME, and the City's housing trust fund, CEDO has never had many resources to direct toward the general operations of its nonprofit partners. Barring a new federal housing program or dramatic changes in the rules governing CDBG and HOME, this is a problem that will only grow worse.

29. It should be pointed out, however, that CEDO was unusually aggressive and remarkably successful in going after whatever federal dollars remained. When it came to larger projects like Northgate Apartments and the Flynn Avenue Co-op, moreover, CEDO had a Washington ally in its quest for scarce federal funds: Senator Patrick Leahy. Without the help of Senator Leahy and his legislative aid, John Romano, Burlington would have been harmed far worse by cutbacks in federal housing assistance than it was.

30. How much this message of minimalist government might have contributed to Clavelle's defeat is difficult to say. After all, Clavelle won four out of six of Burlington's wards in the 1993 election, and the Progressive Coalition retained six out of thirteen seats on the city council. The key issue in the 1993 campaign, moreover, was a wildly unpopular "domestic partners" measure supported by Clavelle and enacted by the city council a month before the election. This issue was successfully exploited by Clavelle's opponent who as a member of the city council had voted against the "domestic partners" measure.

REFERENCES

Achtenberg, Emily P. *Preserving Expiring Use Restriction Projects*. Boston: Citizens' Housing and Planning Association, July 1992.

Burlington City Council. "Resolution Creating the Community and Economic Development Office." May 23, 1983.

Clavel, Pierre. *The Progressive City*. New Brunswick, N.J.: Rutgers University Press, 1986.

Community and Economic Development Office, City of Burlington (CEDO), "The Burlington Community Land Trust as a Private Complement to Public Land and Housing Programs." 1984.

———. *Report and Recommendations of the Affordable Housing Task Force*. Burlington, Vt.: Community and Economic Development Office, 1986.

———. "Final Recommendations of the Regulatory Review Task Force," July 1990.

———. *Comprehensive Housing Affordability Strategy, FY 1992–FY 1996*. January 1992.

Conroy, W. J. *Challenging the Boundaries of Reform: Socialism in Burlington*. Philadelphia: Temple University Press, 1990.

Guma, Greg. *The People's Republic: Vermont and the Sanders Revolution*. Shelburne, Vt.: New England Press, 1989.

Harmon, R. Natasha. *Affordable Housing: The Vermont Model*. Amherst: Center for Rural Massachusetts, University of Massachusetts, 1992.

Heskin, Allan David. *The Struggle for Community*. Boulder, Colo.: Westview, 1991.

Libby, James. "Vermont's Housing and Conservation Trust Fund: A Unique Approach." *Clearinghouse Review*, February 1990.

Mallach, Alan. "Inclusionary Zoning in Burlington, Vermont: Laying the Groundwork for an Inclusionary Zoning Ordinance." Report prepared for the City of Burlington, Community and Economic Development Office, August 1988.

Rosdil, Donald. "The Context of Radical Populism in U.S. Cities: A Comparative Analysis." *Journal of Urban Affairs* 13, no. 1 (1991): 77–96.

Shelterforce. "Best Elected Officials: Peter Clavelle, Mayor of Burlington, Vermont." 14, no. 2 (1992): 8–9.

Soifer, Steven. "Electoral Politics and Social Change: The Case of Burlington, Vermont." Ph.D. diss., Brandeis University, 1988.

Torpy, Brenda. "Saving Northgate: A Model of Cooperation." *Shelterforce* 11, no. 3 (1988): 13–14.

Wallace, James E. "Who Benefits from Preservation: The People Behind the Numbers." *Housing Policy Debate* 2, no. 2 (1991): 219–244.

Wimpey, Ted. "City Politics and a Winning Housing Agenda." *Shelterforce* 14, no. 2 (1992): 10–11, 21.

7

Boston in the 1980s: Toward a Social Housing Policy

CHUCK COLLINS AND KIRBY WHITE

Under Mayor Raymond Flynn, first elected in 1983, the City of Boston developed one of the most progressive approaches to housing to be found among major American cities. It cannot be said that this approach involved a complete commitment to a fully articulated "social housing" policy, yet the essential features of such a policy emerged in Boston in the 1980s. The Flynn administration moved decisively to mobilize new resources for the production of affordable housing. Many of those resources were channeled to nonprofit, community-based organizations. And the City adopted a policy requiring the affordability of municipally assisted housing to be preserved for the long term.

The process through which this policy developed was complicated. New practices evolved as different city agencies charged with administering different programs sought to deal with changing market conditions and shifting neighborhood needs and demands. But these initiatives were not undertaken in isolation from broader policy considerations. Policy discussions were vigorous and thorough among city housing personnel, many of whom were progressive activists hired out of the third sector by the Flynn administration. Much of their discussion focused on the controversial issue of resale restrictions on municipally subsidized owner-occupied homes. The factors that shaped this discussion, as well as the resale policy that emerged from it, are the central concerns of this chapter.

BACKGROUND: THE KEVIN WHITE ADMINISTRATION, 1967–1983

During the sixteen years prior to Flynn's election, from 1967 to 1983, Kevin White was mayor of Boston. In the early years of the White administration, disinvestment and bank redlining, combined with suburban flight and population decline, had caused serious deterioration of inner-city neighborhoods, eroded tax revenues, and undermined the city's morale. During White's tenure, Boston also suffered sharp conflicts over school desegregation that set neighborhoods against each other and against City Hall.[1]

White was initially elected with strong neighborhood support. During his early years in office, he endorsed tenant protection and neighborhood revitalization. Neighborhood interests were promoted through a neighborhood-based governance structure that featured "little city halls" and a commitment to neighborhood planning councils. Community development funding was channeled through these little city halls in an effort to reverse neighborhood decline.

Other City efforts were less popular in the neighborhoods. During the late 1960s and early 1970s, Boston received billions of dollars in federal urban renewal and interstate highway funds. Neighborhood protests arose in response to City plans to demolish low-cost housing and displace thousands of low-income residents. In 1968, for instance, black and Latino residents of the South End occupied the offices of the Boston Redevelopment Authority to protest their impending displacement. A protracted "tent city" occupation on another redevelopment parcel continued for more than ten years, until the City agreed to construct mixed-income housing next to the Copley Place redevelopment site.

Neighborhood protests such as these led to the creation of some of the first community development corporations (CDCs) in the city. Most of these early CDCs were controlled by grassroots members, but each was unique in its focus and in its relationship to city government. Some functioned as extensions of the City's neighborhood revitalization efforts, administering community development funds for home repairs.

In the later 1970s, however, the White administration moved away from the kinds of neighborhood concerns represented by the CDCs and became increasingly involved in a dual effort to attract commercial development to the downtown area and upper-income residents to inner-city neighborhoods. Federal Urban Development Action Grants were targeted for downtown commercial development, including luxury hotels and shopping malls such as Copley Place and Lafayette Place. Neighborhood revitalization efforts were increasingly focused on retaining Boston's middle-class residents through tax rebates and grants and loans for home improvements—a policy of "paying people to stay in the city," as one neighborhood activist described it. The City also labored to attract middle- and upper-income people through programs designed to market Boston's neighborhoods to suburbanites. In 1979, the little city halls were closed.

These efforts were going forward at a time when Boston's real estate market was heating up. By 1980, real estate prices in some neighborhoods had doubled in a five-year period, yet the City's housing policies continued to provide incentives for downtown development and to subsidize home improvements for middle-class residents, as though the goal should still be to "prime the pump." These policies contributed to the increasing gentrification of Boston neighborhoods such as Jamaica Plain, the South End, and Back Bay and led to a citywide reduction in the supply of affordable housing.

The conversion of multifamily rental properties to condominiums removed thousands of units from Boston's rental housing stock. Rent levels increased throughout the city. Rent control, which had been introduced in 1969, was undermined in the late 1970s when the city council, without objection from the mayor, introduced vacancy decontrols while failing to provide adequate staffing and financial resources to the board administering the controls.

The City was also lax in dealing with tax-delinquent and municipally owned properties. It often failed to foreclose on tax-delinquent property in a timely manner. When it did foreclose, the property was auctioned off to the highest bidder with minimal regard for community concerns or low-income housing needs. Many of the vacant city schools in upscale neighborhoods were purchased for redevelopment as market-rate housing, while schools in lower-income communities sat vacant.

The City's growing neglect of tenants and lower-income neighborhoods led to a number of local organizing efforts. In the South End, the range of resident initiatives included efforts to stop displacement, efforts to ensure that lower-income residents would benefit from construction jobs, and efforts to redirect Urban Development Action Grant (UDAG) paybacks into neighborhood development. Other neighborhoods, such as the Fenway, Back Bay, Roxbury, and Jamaica Plain, underwent similar struggles over the disposition of City-owned properties, funding for neighborhood projects, and linkages with downtown development. By the time of the

1983 mayoral election, the problems of tenants and lower-income neighborhoods had become major political issues.

EARLY YEARS OF THE FLYNN ADMINISTRATION

In 1983, ten candidates competed in Boston's mayoral election. The leading vote-getters were the two candidates who most strongly supported neighborhood interests: Raymond Flynn, a city councilor from working-class Irish South Boston, and Mel King, a state representative who had played a principal role in many neighborhood struggles in the South End. The runoff election between these two men focused on neighborhood issues and helped to build momentum for change. Both candidates promised to be "neighborhood mayors" and to help the disenfranchised and neglected residents of the city. Debate centered on the question of which policies and programs would most effectively benefit these people and their neighborhoods. It was clear that either candidate would depart sharply from the policies of the White administration (interviews with Dreier [1991] and Kane).

When Flynn took office in January of 1984, the housing problems of lower-income Boston residents were severe and growing worse. The real estate market, which had been heating up during the later years of the White administration, was now one of the hottest in the country. It would remain so throughout most of the 1980s. Between 1974 and 1989, housing prices increased 81.1 percent, adjusted for inflation. During the same period, incomes rose only 3.2 percent, making Boston second only to Los Angeles in the disparity between housing prices and household incomes. Among the most vulnerable residents were those in rooming houses and other single-room-occupancy buildings that were being converted to upper-income housing. Thousands of people displaced from these buildings had no affordable housing options.

The new mayor confronted this disastrous situation at a time when the Reagan administration was slashing federal low-income housing programs. The Commonwealth of Massachusetts partially filled the resulting vacuum through its own housing programs, which included a rental assistance program similar to the federal Section 8 program, as well as programs subsidizing housing production. The state was also vigorous in its support for community-based organizations involved in producing affordable housing.

However, the total financial resources available to meet the growing need for affordable housing remained woefully inadequate.[2]

Also standing in the way of swift and comprehensive action by the Flynn administration was a cumbersome bureaucracy and an uncooperative city council. Within the bureaucracy, many departments or divisions had jurisdiction over planning, zoning, code enforcement, grants allocations, property disposition, and other housing-related matters. Within the city council, strong representatives of private real estate interests remained.

Not surprisingly, the new Flynn administration did not bring immediate benefits to the neighborhoods. Those hungry for change, including many housing activists, felt that Flynn should have moved more quickly to consolidate the City's housing bureaucracy, replace personnel from the White administration, and increase the flow of resources to nonprofit organizations.[3] They also objected to the fact that many of the White administration's twelfth-hour "sweetheart deals," giving property to for-profit developer friends and retiring administration staff, were allowed to stand (interviews with Johnson and Thall).[4]

Overall, however, Flynn's initial efforts were viewed positively by most local housing activists. The new mayor was perceived as having a personal commitment to stopping homelessness and increasing the supply of housing. He was perceived as sympathetic to the many community-based housing organizations that had been developing with the help of state funding, although it was also in Flynn's political interest to consolidate support for his administration among these community organizations, a number of which had supported Mel King in 1983. Flynn's support for a more progressive approach to housing was signaled as well by his appointment of housing activist and Tufts professor Peter Dreier as his assistant on housing.[5]

Flynn's first-term housing agenda focused on tenant protections, the development of resources for affordable housing production, and the restructuring of the city's housing bureaucracy. Those initiatives requiring city council support met with mixed success. Efforts to bolster legislative protections for tenants, such as rent control and restrictions on condominium conversions, encountered stiff opposition and litigation. A condominium conversion ordinance finally passed in 1986, too late to prevent the wave of conversions already underway.

Efforts to expand capacity and resources for affordable housing production were more successful. In all areas where it had powers and resources, the City emphasized production of affordable housing and supported community-based nonprofit organizations as the primary vehicle for increased production. To generate more resources for these efforts, Flynn's transition team had recommended strengthening the City's linkage program and making use of vacant municipal property for affordable housing. The new administration moved with speed on both recommendations.

The linkage program charged impact fees to the developers of downtown commercial property and dedicated this revenue to the Neighborhood Housing Trust. The program had been established late in 1983, when it had become clear that the new mayor would be prolinkage. Some supporters of linkage had obviously hoped that enacting this measure would prevent the imposition of higher fees under a new administration, but in April of 1986 the Flynn administration raised the linkage contribution from $5 to $6 per square foot for projects with more than 100,000 square feet and accelerated payments by reducing the payment period from twelve years to seven. Between 1983 and 1990, impact fees totalling $46.1 million were collected. To date, 84 percent of this amount has been allocated to community-based nonprofit organizations developing and preserving affordable housing.[6]

Moving to address the issues around vacant property, the City began to accelerate the foreclosure of tax-delinquent properties in 1984, with particular attention to vacant lots and abandoned buildings that posed a threat to neighborhood health and safety. At the same time, citizen action organizations such as Massachusetts Fair Share, ACORN, and the Boston Affordable Housing Alliance were exposing abuses in the City's process of auctioning City-owned properties and, in late 1984, demanded that the auctions be halted. In response, the mayor formed the Property Disposition Work Group, composed of department heads and staff from a number of City agencies. In 1986, based on the work group's conclusions, the City instituted new procedures and priorities for foreclosing on tax-delinquent properties and replaced the auction process with a request-for-proposal process that promoted affordable housing development (interviews with Kane, Dreier [1991], and Thall).

These measures greatly expanded the opportunities for an already growing nonprofit housing sector in Boston. They also raised important questions about the long-term disposition of affordable housing produced with the help of municipal resources. If municipal property, linkage fees, and other City resources were to be used to reduce the cost of housing to an affordable level, what steps should be taken to preserve the benefits of this municipal investment? What steps should be taken to preserve affordability for the long term?

FACTORS PROMPTING A LONG-TERM AFFORDABILITY POLICY

Late in 1985, serious policy discussions began on the question of how best to preserve the long-term affordability of housing subsidized by the City. A number of factors moved the City to address this question and shaped the extensive discussions that ensued. The most obvious factor was the local real estate market boom. Any housing not sheltered from this market by restrictions on rents and resale prices would not continue to be affordable. Other important factors included (1) local problems created by federal housing policy, past and present; (2) support for long-term affordability among professionals in the nonprofit housing sector, a number of whom were being hired by the City; (3) increasing disposition of municipal property for affordable housing; and (4) controversies around proposed restrictions on the resale prices of owner-occupied homes assisted with public funds.

Effects of Federal Policies

By middecade, the Reagan administration's cutbacks in the Housing and Urban Development budget severely affected affordable housing development. In addition, the Tax Reform Act of 1986 eliminated most of the tax advantages for owners of rental property, which had played an important part in the financing of many affordable rental housing projects. The Low Income Housing Tax Credit program established by the new law would result in far fewer units. As a result of these drastic reductions in federal resources, there was increased incentive to maximize the public benefits from the resources that remained by preserving the affordability of subsidized units for as long as possible.

A further incentive for truly *long-term* affordability requirements was provided by Boston's "expiring use crisis." The continued affordability of more than nine thousand units of rental housing subsidized through past federal and state programs was threatened by the impending expiration of twenty-year affordability requirements imposed by these programs (Clay, 1989; Kane interview). Released from the obligation to manage their projects as affordable housing, the owners of "expiring use" projects would be free to sell or convert their properties to more profitable uses in the city's booming real estate market. Boston stood to lose thousands of units of affordable housing at a time when resources were not available to replace them. To the extent that these existing affordable units could be saved or that new housing could be built using scarce public resources, there was a newfound concern for ensuring continued affordability.

Support for Long-Term Affordability in the Nonprofit Sector

By the late 1970s, it had become evident in certain neighborhoods that the affordability of subsidized projects would be short-lived if measures were not taken to preserve it against the effects of a rapidly appreciating market. Housing activists associated with a growing number of organizations, including CDCs and low-income housing advocacy organizations, came to believe that stronger resale controls should be placed on affordable housing projects. In some cases, they established such controls on their own projects.

Although some CDCs did not support such controls, particularly in the case of owner-occupied homes, those working in neighborhoods that had gone through severe gentrification and displacement, such as Allston-Brighton, Fenway, and Jamaica Plain, were concerned with the overall impact of rising real estate values and the resulting loss of community stability. For these CDCs, resale restrictions seemed not only reasonable but necessary (interviews with Black and Thall).[7]

The Fenway Community Development Corporation, founded in 1973, was among the first organizations in the city to institute provisions to protect long-term affordability. In the early 1980s, it developed the forty-six-unit Fensgate Cooperative, one of the higher-profile limited equity cooperatives in the city. The CDC also created a land trust subsidiary to hold land under the co-op to ensure continued affordability (Thall interview).

Several other Boston area CDCs were also involved in developing limited equity housing cooperatives, and some developed single-family homes that were sold with deed restrictions to limit resale prices and preserve affordability. Through such efforts, these organizations gained considerable sophistication in the design of resale formulas and legal mechanisms for implementing them.

In 1981, the Boston nonprofits involved in developing limited equity co-ops came together to form the Cooperative Housing Task Force as a means of advocating for cooperatives and sharing information. The task force played a significant role in heightening the visibility and credibility of the concept of "permanent affordability" (interviews with Thall and Goddard).[8] As the 1980s progressed, two other citywide nonprofit organizations also played significant roles in this respect: the Boston Community Loan Fund and the Boston Citywide Land Trust, both organized in 1984–1985.

The Boston Community Loan Fund was formed, primarily by people drawn from neighborhood organizations and the religious community, to channel low-interest loans from socially concerned investors into affordable housing projects. In the course of extensive discussions of possible lending criteria, the organizers of the fund agreed that they wanted to support housing projects that preserved affordability for the long term. BCLF was the first funding source in the city to clearly establish "long-term affordability" as a threshold criterion for access to funds.

The Boston Citywide Land Trust (BCLT) was organized by a coalition of CDCs and neighborhood activists to provide a unified structure for the purpose of preserving long-term affordability and negotiating with the City over the disposition of municipally owned property. Initially, the organizers envisioned the land trust playing a significant land-banking role, assembling parcels for development several years before local CDCs would break ground. The BCLT was also to own and lease land under a number of projects developed by CDCs throughout the city. As debate over housing policy developed in the Flynn administration, BCLT members lobbied the City to target limited resources to community land trusts and other organizations committed to permanent affordability. The BCLT was not destined to play a role quite as central to the City's programs as its organizers had envisioned for it; however, it had an impact as one of the organizations that took the lead in advocating longer and more effective resale controls, thereby allowing the city to consider such controls without having to "get out in front" on the issue (interviews with Johnson and Black).

The experience of the nonprofit sector also affected policy debate in the Flynn administration in another way. Between 1984 and 1987, dozens of housing activists who had been working with nonprofit organizations were hired by the City, many of them in the Public Facilities Department, where much of the debate regarding the preservation of affordability was centered. The presence of these people within the Flynn administration was an indication not only of the administration's sympathy with third sector housing efforts but of its willingness to allow housing policy to be shaped by experience and views developed within the third sector. Some of these people, such as Rebecca Black, previously executive director of the Allston-Brighton Community Development Corporation, were directly involved in framing proposals for long-term affordability requirements.[9]

Increasing Commitment of Municipal Property for Affordable Housing

The possibility of hundreds of parcels of municipal land being transferred to private development organizations gave particular urgency to the efforts to establish a comprehensive resale policy. In the summer of 1987, as Flynn was running for his second term, he announced the "747 Program," involving 747 vacant lots acquired by the City through tax foreclosure and identified as appropriate for housing. A number of abandoned buildings were also being committed to this purpose. City staff now began to prepare requests for proposals with a willingness to sell properties for as little as one dollar for worthy affordable housing projects. There was a clear need for a consistent policy regarding long-term affordability for the many projects that resulted (interviews with Black and Goddard).

Emphasis on Homeownership Projects

Some of this city land would be used for rental and limited equity co-op projects, but much of it would be committed to affordable homeownership projects. One reason for the emphasis on homeownership was the reduction in resources for affordable rental housing caused by federal cutbacks and changes in the tax law. Another reason was that homeownership projects were more popular at the neighborhood level and less controversial than siting low-income rental housing. It was believed that homeownership also contributed to neighborhood stability and increased tax revenue. The word coming up from neighborhood councils, community-based nonprofits, and other citizen organizations was "homeownership" (interviews with Dreier [1992], Johnson, and Black).[10]

While there was relatively little disagreement regarding provisions to preserve the affordability of rental and co-op units, owner-occupied units were another matter. Provisions that would limit the equity of homeowners in single-family houses and condominiums raised a more complicated and controversial set of questions. The pressure to provide municipally assisted homeownership opportunities forced the City to address these questions.

POLICY DEBATE ON RESALE RESTRICTIONS

As early as 1984, program staff at the Public Facilities Department (PFD) and the Boston Redevelopment Authority (BRA) had begun to utilize deed restrictions and second mortgages, on a project-by-project basis, to control resale prices on some municipally subsidized properties. PFD was responsible for allocating federal and state housing funds, disposing of public property for housing, and implementing most of the City's housing programs.[11] At the beginning of 1986, PFD's approach to resale provisions on the projects it supported ranged from no restrictions at all, to provisions for subsidy recapture, to the use of restrictive covenants limiting resale prices for relatively short periods of time.

Resale restrictions were also a concern for the Boston Redevelopment Authority, the City's planning and zoning authority—an agency with an independent board that includes mayoral appointees. Together with PFD, the BRA staffed the Neighborhood Housing Trust, which allocated linkage funds. The BRA negotiated with developers over affordable housing set-asides and used its powers of eminent domain to facilitate the creation of affordable housing. The BRA had the authority to establish or approve resale provisions for all the affordable housing created through these programs.

Both the BRA and PFD recognized the need for agreement on the design and application of resale restrictions and understood that the lack of consistency among existing resale policies threatened their enforceability (interviews with Dreier [1992], Goddard, Black, and Flashman).[12] Beginning in 1985, policy staff from both agencies conducted research and convened ad hoc meetings to discuss various aspects of the design and implementation of resale policies. The process did not involve public hearings or formal public input, but many staff people had first-hand experience with nonprofit housing development and with organizations such as the Cooperative Housing Task Force, the Boston Community Loan Fund, and the Boston Citywide Land Trust. Staff also conducted interviews with a number of organizations that were already using resale restrictions on owner-occupied homes.[13]

Research and discussion regarding policy options continued until early 1988, when both PFD and BRA adopted policies requiring relatively strong resale restrictions on all projects receiving significant assistance through their programs. In the case of the Public Facilities Department, the process culminated dramatically on February 5, 1988, when Lisa Chapnick, PFD's director, convened a meeting of her senior staff to discuss proposed resale restrictions. In this forum, Chapnick heard summations from both staff who opposed resale restrictions on owner-occupied homes and those who supported the proposed restrictions. Following the debate, Chapnick approved the proposed policy (interviews with Black and Goddard).

The PFD policy provides for a fifty-year deed restriction on all owner-occupied homes that are developed with significant PFD support in the form of land, buildings, or financial resources. The restriction requires continued owner occupancy and gives PFD an option to repurchase the home at a price that is allowed to increase beyond the original purchase price by only 5 percent per year, plus a maximum of 1 percent per year for improvements made by the owner. (The option does not need to be exercised directly unless it is necessary to prevent the sale of the home at a higher price.) The restriction remains effective for the full fifty-year period, regardless of the number of times the property is resold in that time. The BRA adopted the same resale formula, although specific requirements and enforcement provisions differed somewhat from those of PFD.

The debate that culminated in the adoption of this policy involved a number of difficult issues. The following outline identifies those that received the greatest attention (interviews with Black and Goddard).

To Restrict or Not to Restrict

- Should restrictions be placed on owner-occupied homes, or only on rental properties?
- Should the City limit the resale prices of subsidized units or only establish "recapture provisions" requiring the repayment of subsidies upon resale at market prices?
- Should projects receiving smaller subsidies be exempted from restrictions?

Design of Resale Restrictions

- What legal mechanism should be used to establish and enforce resale restrictions—deed restrictions or ground leases?
- To what extent should resale prices be limited? How much equity should owners be allowed to accumulate?

- What factors should determine resale prices? What kind of resale formula should be adopted?
- How long should restrictions be maintained?

Legal, Financial, Administration Issues

- How would a municipal resale policy interact with the policies of lenders and other funding sources?
- How would resale-restricted units be assessed and taxed by the City's assessment office?
- How should restrictions be administered and monitored? Should the City create a compliance program of its own or contract with other organizations to monitor the restrictions?

We will not attempt to discuss all of these issues. We will highlight, however, the main questions addressed in Boston that must be addressed by *any* municipality considering resale restrictions.

To Restrict or Not to Restrict

As in the nonprofit sector, there were different perspectives within PFD and the BRA as to whether the resale of owner-occupied homes should be restricted at all. The basic argument of those who supported such restrictions was outlined in a memo prepared by PFD staffers Rebecca Black, Sherry Flashman, and Nelson Merced in November 1986.

> In a time of scarce public resources, it is critical that Boston maximize the use of its public property and below-market financing to create and maintain affordable housing for present and future low to moderate income residents of the city. . . . The overriding perspective of these recommendations is that public resources should be used first and foremost to provide affordable shelter to those unable to purchase on the private market, promoting security, stability, and control of residents over their living environment; that the use of housing as an investment opportunity should not take precedence over the public purpose of creating long term affordable housing opportunities.

Although this memo expressed the dominant point of view within the policy arms of PFD and the BRA, this perspective was not shared by all. The subject of resale restrictions on owner-occupied homes stirred strong feelings about the social and economic role of homeownership. Opposition to restrictions was particularly strong among some staff members from minority communities. In their view, resale restrictions had a disproportionate impact on low-income minority households, denying them the opportunity so widely enjoyed by other Americans, particularly in the 1980s—the opportunity to build wealth through the appreciating market value of their homes. Other arguments against restrictions included the following:

- Resale controls require a level of intervention that people do not associate with homeownership, undermining the feeling that "this property is all mine."
- Such restrictions can discourage or prohibit upward and lateral mobility in the housing market. Because the return for limited equity owners may not keep pace with housing prices, they may be unable to purchase other homes if they wish to move.
- Homeowners with resale restrictions on their property may have less incentive to reinvest in their property and maintain it over time.
- Such restrictions require the creation of relatively complicated legal arrangements and potentially burdensome bureaucratic procedures for enforcement.

Proponents of resale restrictions addressed these points by arguing that the proposed resale policy struck a fair balance between individual benefit and the protection of public resources and would not discourage individual economic advancement. Individuals could still build reasonable equity, they argued, and would not necessarily be discouraged from reinvesting in their property. They saw the restrictions as promoting owner occupancy and neighborhood stability and thus as discouraging rapid mobility, while still allowing those who moved to take with them what they had invested. The tasks involved in establishing and monitoring the restrictions were acknowledged to be substantial, but they were seen as quite manageable and well worth the effort (interview with Black).

It should be noted that, given the limited availability of subsidies, there was relatively broad agreement that the City should *at least* provide for the recapture of subsidies at the time of resale. Much of the debate therefore took place between those who favored a policy that *only* recaptured the subsidy and those who favored going beyond subsidy recapture to limit the resale price itself. The latter group prevailed, arguing that, in a market where housing prices were increasing faster than incomes, a policy that merely recycled the original subsidies would not sustain the original level of affordability when homes were resold.[14]

Design of Restrictions

Among the most complicated issues to be addressed were those relating to the design of the restrictions themselves, their duration, and the legal mechanism to be used to establish them. A number of possible resale formulas, each using a different method of determining the resale price, were explored. Some of these formulas would have established the resale price through a detailed accounting of the owner's actual investment in the property, but these were rejected in favor of a simpler approach that is less burdensome to administer.

Regarding the mechanism used to establish the resale restrictions, a basic choice had to be made between using deed restrictions and using a ground lease. In the latter case, the land would be owned by a land trust, or possibly by the City itself. Resale restrictions on the home would be written into the ground lease issued to the homeowner and could be enforced perpetually rather than for a fixed period of time such as fifty years. Several PFD staff advocated using a ground lease to ensure long-term compliance with use and resale restrictions. They recognized three advantages of the ground lease over deed restrictions: (1) stronger long-term enforceability because of the separation of ownership, (2) more consistent monitoring by a third party, and (3) an opportunity for resident participation through membership in a community land trust and representation on a land trust board.[15]

However, several factors prevented the acceptance of this approach at the time of these policy discussions. Many staff remained skeptical of a model that was still relatively untested and that might involve turning over long-term control of affordable housing to a third party (interviews with Black and Flashman). They also feared it would be difficult to finance housing on leased land. These barriers have since been reduced. In fact, the City is now working with a community organization in using ground leases to preserve the affordability of housing developed in the Dudley neighborhood of Roxbury (see below). Between 1985 and 1988, however, policy staff focused on developing a more familiar device that would leave long-term control in the hands of the City: a fifty-year deed restriction.[16]

Legal, Financial, and Administrative Issues

As the essential features of the proposed deed restrictions were being developed, PFD and BRA staff began to address the various legal, financial, and administrative issues that the restrictions would entail.

One of their first concerns was to coordinate the new policy with the policies of private lenders and state programs, making sure that the City's resale restrictions would be acceptable to these important sources of project funding. Staff from the BRA and PFD were successful in working with staff from the state's Executive Office of Communities and Development, the Massachusetts Housing Partnership, and the Massachusetts Housing Finance Agency to clear the way for the City's restrictions to be used with other state housing programs.

City staff also met with local banks, including Shawmut and Bank of Boston, as well as with private secondary market institutions such as Fannie Mae, to review the proposed restrictions. The City had already agreed that the restrictions could be released in the event of foreclosure, but other issues remained. Fannie Mae, for instance, was concerned about the effect of resale restrictions on property maintenance and reinvestment. Such concerns were mitigated, however, by the fact that the City's subsidies were deep enough to reduce the debt financing needed to a relatively safe level. In the end, the City was successful in gaining lender acceptance of the restrictions.

PFD and BRA staff were also successful in negotiating an agreement with the City's tax assessment personnel regarding the valuation of resale-restricted property. It was agreed that assessments would be based on the price determined by the resale formula rather than on the "fair market value" of the property (interviews with Black and Goddard).

Finally, issues needed to be resolved around the monitoring and administration of resale restrictions. Originally, the BRA and PFD planned to develop a cooperative interagency program to oversee compliance with the City's restrictions. BRA and PFD staff also explored the possibility of contracting monitoring tasks out to a third party, such as the Boston Citywide Land Trust. A debate ensued about the best way to monitor resale-restricted housing, replete with stories of nonprofit corruption and City corruption. No conclusion was reached. Each agency went on to perform its own monitoring tasks separately (interviews with Goddard and Dreier, 1991). How effective such monitoring will be over the long term remains to be seen.[17]

APPLICATIONS OF BOSTON'S RESALE POLICY

Since the formal adoption of resale restriction policies by PFD and BRA in 1988, changing economic conditions have reduced the amount of affordable housing produced through the programs of these agencies. Nevertheless, the policies have been applied to a substantial number of housing units. Particularly significant is the application of the policy to *all* projects using City-owned land, whether sponsored by for-profit developers, nonprofit housing organizations, or individuals.

PFD Programs

The 747 Program. This program, which designated 747 City-owned vacant lots for the planned development of 1,311 affordable housing units had helped to precipitate the development of a uniform resale policy. While fewer units have been developed than originally hoped—350 units as of 1992, with projects involving another 380 units on the drawing board—all of these units are bound by the PFD's new resale policy (interview with Black).

The Resident Development Program. More than one hundred resale-restricted, owner-occupied homes have been developed through the Resident Development Program, established to help first-time homebuyers acquire and renovate housing owned by the City as the result of tax foreclosure. All units transferred by the City through this program are subject to the resale policy. To date, more than twenty of these units have been resold. The City monitors the transfers to ensure that the homes are conveyed at prices permitted by the deed restrictions.

Grant and Loan Programs. The City offers a range of grants and loans to support affordable housing development (most development subsidies are actually provided as deferred loans secured by second mortgages to allow subsidy recapture if necessary). These funds are drawn from a variety of sources, including the federal Community Development Block Grant program, municipal appropriations, and linkage fees dedicated to the Neighborhood Trust Fund (administered jointly by PFD and BRA). Funds are allocated for predevelopment and technical assistance for nonprofit organizations, home improvement grants and loans, and development subsidies. PFD's resale policy applies to all housing projects receiving substantial assistance. Where assistance from the City has not been considered "substantial," the requirement of resale restrictions has sometimes been waived (interview with Dreier [1991]).

BRA Programs

The Boston Redevelopment Authority is less involved in providing direct subsidies for housing production. Through its zoning and eminent domain powers, however, the BRA plays a significant role in negotiating with private developers for affordable housing production. BRA's resale restriction policy has generally been applied to any affordable units generated through its regulatory actions (interview with Dreier [1992]).

Affordable Housing Set-asides. Set-asides of affordable units are negotiated on a case-by-case basis with residential developers, who have the choice of either constructing affordable units or contributing cash to the Neighborhood Trust Fund. As a result, hundreds of units of affordable housing have been either integrated into mixed-income housing developments or constructed on separate locations, mostly as condominiums. The BRA has imposed resale restrictions on most of these condominiums.

Eminent Domain. In some instances, the BRA has used its eminent domain powers to take property for use as affordable housing. In such cases, it has entered into regulatory agreements with private developers, requiring them to construct affordable housing. The state statute authorizing this use of eminent domain requires that such agreements guarantee a long-term public benefit. The BRA has interpreted this to mean that the affordability of housing developed by this means must be preserved for as long as possible.

Dudley Street Neighborhood Initiative. One of the most striking examples of the BRA's commitment to long-term affordability is its support for the Dudley Street Neighborhood Initiative (DSNI). Through intensive community organizing efforts, DSNI developed a comprehensive, community-controlled redevelopment plan for the badly neglected Dudley Street area of Roxbury and Dorchester. The BRA and PFD have supported DSNI and its land trust subsidiary, Dudley Neighbors Incorporated (DNI), by providing land, grant funding, and staff support.[18]

The City agreed to make available fifteen acres of vacant, municipally owned land in the Dudley Triangle, a central section of the area where the redevelopment plan called for construction of more than 350 units of housing. The BRA, in an unprecedented action, delegated to DNI the use of its eminent domain powers to take privately owned vacant parcels in the triangle to consolidate land for redevelopment. DNI will retain title to all of the land and, through its ground leases, will permanently preserve the affordability of the housing. Both DSNI and the City have insisted that there be long-term resale restrictions on all of these units.[19]

CONCLUSION: TOWARD A SOCIAL HOUSING POLICY

The resale policy formally adopted by the BRA and PFD is not etched solidly in stone. Nor does it reflect a complete municipal commitment to social housing. Nevertheless, the adoption of this policy was an important step, for it shifted significantly the political framework within which any further discussion of the issue must take place. Whereas the burden of proof once rested (and still rests in many cities) with those who argue in *favor* of imposing long-term restrictions on resale prices, in Boston the burden now rests with those who would argue *against* such restrictions.

Without a formal resale policy, it is likely that PFD and BRA staff would have discontinued the practice of imposing resale restrictions once Boston's overheated real estate market had begun to cool. This has not happened. The rigorous research and detailed debate that preceded the adoption of this policy have established it as more than a temporary response to a particular market situation. The existence of this policy, moreover, has strengthened the hand of those within the PFD and BRA who believe it is important to perpetuate affordability regardless of current market conditions.

Despite such support within the housing bureaucracy, however, the policy could still be undermined by a number of factors. These include changes in personnel and continuing dissent within the bureaucracy, a lack of broad understanding of the policy throughout City government, a lack of broad support outside of City government, potentially insufficient capacity to enforce the policy, and the absence of a truly comprehensive social housing strategy to define the continuing need for resale restrictions.

Within the housing bureaucracy, some policy staff who opposed the adoption of resale restrictions continue to oppose the policy, and several key staff who participated in the decision to adopt the policy have moved out of PFD.[20] In addition, staff who are negotiating agreements with private developers in what is currently a buyer's market have come under increasing pressure to waive resale restrictions because of their potential effect on the marketing of homes.

The base of support for the resale policy remains quite narrow. Understanding of the policy has generally been limited to PFD and BRA staff and to housing professionals in the nonprofit sector. PFD and BRA staff believe that the mayor was not aware of the development of the resale policy as such, though he has been very supportive of community-based nonprofit organizations as developers of affordable housing. Nor is it likely that the city council is aware of the particulars of the policy, which has no statutory basis. Outside of City Hall, support for the policy is not unanimous. The leaders of many nonprofits and limited equity coops are committed to the principle of long-term affordability, and the Dudley Street Neighborhood Initiative has built significant grassroots support for the principle as a means of neighborhood preservation. But understanding and support for these unusual restrictions on privately owned housing are not yet widespread, and the restrictions are still opposed by some, particularly by those who favor unrestricted homeownership as a means of economic advancement for low-income minority households.

The policy may also be threatened by a lack of municipal administrative capacity to monitor and enforce resale restrictions. It is not clear that sufficient resources are being committed to monitoring and enforcement. A failure to ensure compliance with resale restrictions, unit by unit, would not only allow the immediate loss of some affordable units but would tend to discredit the policy of imposing such restrictions. If restrictions on existing units cannot be enforced, it will be difficult to defend the idea that the same kind of restrictions should be placed on newly subsidized units.

Boston's resale policy might have been made more secure, commanding broader support and a greater commitment of resources, if it had been possible to establish the policy as part of a more comprehensive social housing strategy aimed at building, over time, a large pool of privately owned, permanently affordable housing. Under the Flynn administration, support for community-based nonprofit housing efforts has indeed been strong, but the broader emphasis has been on nonprofit *production* rather than nonprofit *stewardship*. Some of the staff within PFD and BRA would have liked to support a more comprehensive social housing strategy, but in the debate over resale restrictions they were forced to emphasize the immediate goal of preventing owners of subsidized housing from profiting at public expense. The policy that was adopted was therefore seen by many, in the words of one housing administrator, as an "antispeculation policy"—an effort to curb the excesses of the marketplace rather than as a true alternative to market-rate housing. In a market where speculative pressures have subsided, a policy perceived mainly as an antispeculation measure is vulnerable.

Of course, to have expected any major American city to adopt a "comprehensive social housing strategy" in the 1980s is probably unrealistic. A progressive resale policy such as that developed in Boston would be politically vulnerable in any large American city, if for no other reason than that it is ahead of its time. On the other hand, *because* it is ahead of its time, it is significant. Boston does not offer a complete blueprint for other cities, but it has pointed the way toward a more effective municipal policy. Boston's policies and programs, moreover, have had a significant effect on state and federal policy.

Boston housing staff have interacted with staff from the Massachusetts Housing Partnership, the Massachusetts Housing Finance Agency, the Massachusetts Government Land Bank, and the Executive Office of Communities and Development to explain the rationale for the strong resale policy and remove programmatic barriers to housing with resale restrictions. And, in 1988, Boston-based nonprofits, housing co-ops, and housing advocates joined City Hall in successfully lobbying for the creation of the state-administered Housing Innovations Fund to support limited equity cooperatives and single-room-occupancy housing with long-term affordability provisions.

At the federal level, Boston's policies and programs contributed to the design of the "community-based housing supply" bill, sponsored in 1989 and 1990 by Representative Joseph Kennedy. This bill, supporting the development of permanently affordable housing by community-based organizations, strongly influenced the design of the HOME program, established through Title II of the National Affordable Housing Act of 1990. The 1990 act specifically required all HOME-assisted projects to be affordable for the "remaining useful life of the property." Although this requirement was weakened in the HOME regulations issued by HUD—and further weakened by the Housing and Community Development Act of 1992, amending the National Affordable Housing Act—it remains an important legislative precedent, with a lineage reaching back to Boston's efforts to preserve the affordability of publicly assisted, privately owned housing. One day,

Boston's innovative policy of long-term affordability may be buttressed by broader trends in national policy. If so, they will be trends that Boston itself helped to initiate.

NOTES

1. Discussion of the White administration is based on Lukas (1985), Boston Urban Study Group (1984); Lupo et al. (1971), King (1981), Dreier and Keating (1990), and on interviews by Chuck Collins with Peter Dreier, Boston Redevelopment Authority, in Boston on 13 November 1991; Rolf Goetze, Boston Redevelopment Authority, in Boston on 16 April 1991; Arthur Johnson, attorney, in Boston on 20 January 1992; and Michael Kane, Boston Affordable Housing Alliance, in Boston on 16 February and 9 April 1992.

2. The failure of public housing to provide an adequate alternative for low-income people was notable. Flynn was saddled with a Boston Housing Authority that had been placed in receivership by Judge Arthur Garrity in 1981 after years of mismanagement and vacancy problems.

3. In 1983 the Citizens Housing and Planning Association's Task Force on Boston Reorganization published recommendations to the transition team, including one that the City's housing agencies be consolidated.

4. Collins interviewed Max Thall, Local Initiatives Support Corporation (former director, Fenway Community Development Corporation), in Boston on 9 December 1991.

5. Peter Dreier had been active in a number of housing organizations in the state, such as the Massachusetts Tenants Organization. He had written extensively about tenant organizing and national housing policy issues. He was also an active member of the Institute for Policy Studies Working Group on Housing, which had proposed a national housing policy modeled on Canadian and Western European social housing programs. In 1986 Dreier became housing director for the Boston Redevelopment Authority.

6. Discussion of Flynn's first-term accomplishments is based on Dreier and Keating (1990), Dober (1991); and Collins's interviews with Dreier (13 November 1991) and with Monica Friar, former staff member, Linkage Study Commission, in Boston (18 August 1992).

7. Collins interviewed Rebecca Black, Public Facilities Department, in Boston on 5 April and 12 November 1991.

8. Collins interviewed Deborah Goddard, Public Facilities Department, in Boston on 12 March 1992.

9. Rebecca Black joined the Public Facilities Department (PFD) in 1986. In her previous role as director of the Allston-Brighton Community Development Corporation, she had overseen the subsidized conversion of a municipally owned school

building into low- and moderate-income condominium units, which were sold without resale restrictions. Units put back on the market as little as two years later were no longer affordable to the CDC's lower-income constituency. This experience deeply affected Black, as similar experiences affected many other Boston housing activists in the 1980s. Her first assignment within PFD was to design a resale policy for municipally owned properties and projects receiving City grants. Others who came to PFD from the nonprofit sector included Nikki Flionis and Janet Van Zandt, strong advocates for permanent affordability who had been active in the formation of the Boston Citywide Land Trust, and Nelson Merced, a former community organizer from the Dudley Street neighborhood.

10. Collins interviewed Peter Dreier again in Boston on 4 February 1992.

11. In 1985, the Neighborhood Development and Employment Agency was merged into the Public Facilities Department, giving one department control over property disposition, Community Development Block Grant allocations, and neighborhood planning. This action helped to streamline the process of assisting neighborhood developers and set the stage for comprehensive policy discussions regarding resale restrictions on the projects assisted through the unified process.

12. Collins interviewed Sherry Flashman, Public Facilities Department, in Boston on 15 September 1992.

13. In 1985, Peter Dreier asked several BRA staff, including Beth Marcus, Anne Wilson, Barry Berman, and Jerry Rubin (who later worked at PFD), to begin researching a number of issues related to a resale policy for resident-owned homes. Beth Marcus had recently graduated from MIT's Department of Urban Studies and Planning and had written her thesis on resale policies for limited equity housing. In pursuing this task, these BRA staff people worked closely with PFD policy staff, including Sherry Flashman, Rebecca Black, and Nelson Merced.

14. PFD does hold a second mortgage on subsidized properties as a means of recapturing the subsidy in the event that PFD decides at some point to release the resale restrictions and allow a home to be resold for a higher price. Additional information on the issue of price restrictions versus subsidy recapture can be found in Chapter Three.

15. Representatives of the Boston Citywide Land Trust suggested that the BCLT function as the steward for all vacant City lands and that property be turned over to the BCLT prior to development to promote community participation in the planning and development process. Because City staff viewed land use planning as the responsibility of the public sector, these proposals were not seriously considered. Staff were also concerned about the long-term viability of the BCLT and uncertain as to how this centralized citywide organization might relate to neighborhood-based organizations.

16. The BRA hired an attorney, John Achatz, who was a founder of the Cooperative Housing Task Force, to prepare draft legal documents for PFD and the BRA and to assist in negotiations with other agencies and institutions.

17. PFD monitoring functions were originally performed by one person but are now more widely distributed. It is difficult to judge how thoroughly PFD's deed restrictions are being enforced under this system, particularly in the case of owner-occupancy requirements, which require continuous monitoring. BRA is primarily concerned with monitoring agreements with developers, possibly at the expense of monitoring compliance by owners of individual units.

18. DNI has a nine-member board with three members appointed by the city and six appointed by DSNI.

19. Additional information on the history, plans, and accomplishments of DNI and DSNI can be found in Medoff and Sklar (forthcoming).

20. Advocates for long-term resale restrictions who have left PFD include Rebecca Black, Nelson Merced, and David Treisch. Peter Dreier has left his position as housing director for the BRA.

REFERENCES

Boston Urban Study Group. *Who Rules Boston: A Citizen's Guide to Reclaiming the City*. Boston: Institute for Democratic Socialism, 1984.

Bratt, Rachel. *Rebuilding a Low-Income Housing Policy*. Philadelphia: Temple University Press, 1989a.

Bratt, Rachel. "Nonprofit Housing Development: Boston." Medford, Mass.: Tufts University, 1989b.

Clay, Phil. *Housing at Risk*. Cambridge: MIT, 1989.

Committee on Planning, Development and Housing, Boston City Council. "Expanding Housing Development in Boston." Report. February 1983.

Committee on Housing, Boston City Council. "Recommendations to the Boston City Council from the Committee on Housing." Report. 1984.

Dober, Patrick. *House of Cards: Absentee-owned Condominiums and Neighborhood Instability*. Boston: Boston Redevelopment Authority, 1991.

Downie, Leonard. *Mortgage on America: The Real Cost of Real Estate Speculation*. New York: Praeger, 1974.

Dreier, Peter, and Dennis W. Keating. "The Limits of Localism: Progressive Housing Policies in Boston, 1984–1989." *Urban Affairs Quarterly* 26, no. 2 (1990): 191–216.

Goetze, Rolf. *Understanding Neighborhood Change*. Cambridge, Mass.: Ballinger Publishing, 1979.

Goodman, Robert. *After the Planners*. New York: Simon and Shuster, 1971.

King, Mel. *Chain of Change: Struggles for Black Community Development*. Boston: South End Press, 1981.

Levine, Hillel, and Lawrence Harmon. *Death of an American Jewish Community: A Tragedy of Good Intentions*. Boston: Free Press, 1991.

Lukas, Anthony J. *Common Ground*. New York: Vintage Books, 1985.
Lupo, Alan, Frank Colcord, and Edmond P. Fowler. *Rites of Way: The Politics of Transportation in Boston and the U.S. City*. Boston: Little, Brown, 1971.
Medoff, Peter, and Holly Sklar. *Breaking Ground: The Dudley Street Neighborhood Initiative*. Forthcoming.
Metropolitan Area Planning Council. *Inclusionary Housing and Linkage Programs in Metropolitan Boston*. Boston, 1986.
Office of Mayor, City of Boston. "Protecting Our Homes, Rebuilding Our Neighborhoods: A Housing Program for Boston." Report. 1984.

8 The Legacy of *Mt. Laurel*: Maintaining Affordability in New Jersey's Inclusionary Developments

ALAN MALLACH

The 1983 *Mount Laurel II* decision by the New Jersey Supreme Court[1] broke new ground in many areas linked to the provision of low- and moderate-income housing, not least of which was the first judicial enshrinement of the principles of inclusionary development into law. Building on the principles set forth in the first *Mount Laurel* decision in 1975, in which it had ordered New Jersey's towns to meet their fair share of regional lower-income housing needs,[2] the court now set out a detailed strategy to ensure that the obligation would indeed be met. Central to that strategy was inclusionary zoning, described as a "mandatory set-aside" of lower-income housing in developments otherwise built for the marketplace; the court noted with some emphasis that it was an "inclusionary device that municipalities must use if they cannot otherwise meet their fair share obligations."[3]

More specifically, the court, recognizing that massive public subsidies could no longer be counted on to provide lower-income housing, invited municipalities to place the burden on developers building in their communities by making the provision of affordable housing a condition of development approval. The court did not set forth explicit guidelines for inclusionary development. Although the first projects varied widely with respect to both the percentage of lower-income housing and the income mix within that percentage, a consensus soon emerged that a "normal" inclusionary development would set aside 20 percent of its units as lower-income housing,[4] equally divided between moderate-income households (those earning 50 to 80 percent of the area median income) and low-income households (those earning under 50 percent of the area median.[5] Initiated when the development boom of the 1980s had just begun, the inclusionary strategy proved to be a highly effective tool to create lower-income housing units. A study conducted early in 1988, or only five years after the court decision, found that some 2,100 lower-income units in inclusionary developments had already been completed and were occupied, and that another 2,100 were under construction and 3,000 were approved and ready for construction.[6] By 1992, nearly 7,000 low- and moderate-income families in New Jersey occupied units in inclusionary developments.[7]

Having adopted an inclusionary strategy as a means of creating lower-income housing, the court found that it would have to address affordability controls on that housing as well; noting that "the problem of keeping lower income units available for lower income people over time can be a difficult one,"[8] the court added that there appeared to be two ways in which the problem could be addressed. After suggesting without much conviction that units might somehow be built inexpensively enough to be and remain affordable without external controls, the court concluded: "The other . . . approach for dealing with the re-sale or re-rent problem is for the municipality to require that re-sale or re-rent prices be kept at lower income levels."[9] In one blow the court held that affordability controls be tied to future inclusionary development and that their establishment and enforcement would henceforth be the duty of the municipality in which the development was located. Whatever ideological arguments might have been brought to bear on the subject were rendered academic; the issue was no longer whether extended affordability should be preserved, with controls to ensure that happened, but how such controls should be established and maintained.

At the time the New Jersey Supreme Court acted, the history of affordability controls in inclusionary development was limited, and reflected more haphazard improvisation than a coherent strategy to create and maintain an affordable housing stock. Many programs, particularly in California, had been enacted in the face of strong opposition from the real estate industry and offered little real assurance that the lower-income housing created with such effort would remain available to those for whom it was intended for more than a symbolic period, if at all. Even a cursory study of these programs found numerous cases in which units were quickly lost to the lower-income stock on resale, either deliberately or through a host of avoidable regulatory and administrative errors and oversights.[10]

It was apparent to those trying to make the *Mount Laurel* doctrine work in New Jersey from 1983 onward that the experience available elsewhere was of little value. As a result, through a process of trial and error—the outcome of which was accelerated by the aggressive management of post–*Mount Laurel* cases by the courts—each of the many issues raised by the adoption of affordability controls was investigated and addressed essentially anew. It would be hard to argue that all have been resolved, but over the past nine years a body of procedures and practices has emerged; it adds up to a workable system by which lower-income housing can indeed remain affordable and available to lower-income families over an extended period without undue burden on any of the parties involved in the transaction. This system has been codified, although not without significant compromises, in rules adopted by the New Jersey Council on Affordable Housing (COAH), a state agency established in 1985 by the legislature to manage the *Mount Laurel* process and to remove the process in large part from the jurisdiction of the courts.[11]

The crucial issues in the framing of affordability controls were those affecting housing offered for sale. Not only does the issue of extended affordability pose more complex questions when applied to ownership than to rental housing,[12] but it was soon clear that the lion's share of the units to be built under inclusionary programs would be offered for sale. The 1988 study cited above found that 86 percent of all lower-income units built or planned in inclusionary developments in New Jersey were to be owner occupied, most often as limited equity condominiums.[13]

It seemed clear from the beginning that any system of affordability controls applied to housing offered for sale would have to incorporate three elements: determination of the sales price on resale, selection of qualified buyers, and creation of a suitable entity to set prices and select buyers. Over time, as practical experience accumulated, two more elements also came to be seen as important: finding ways to ensure that units would not inadvertently be lost from the affordable stock, and addressing the problem of windfalls at the end of the price control period. In the following pages I examine each issue, addressing both the nature of the problem posed by the issue and the manner in which it has been resolved.

THE MANAGEMENT OF AFFORDABILITY CONTROLS

Although opinions differed on who should manage affordability controls, it was not difficult to see that some clearly defined and visible body had to take the responsibility. This was more obvious to those who were already familiar with subsidized housing and the elaborate systems established in such housing to ensure that benefits were made available only to qualified families than to those approaching the issue from the private market, many of whom initially believed that the controls could be self-executing. Early suggestions that affordability controls could be more or less automatically enforced by title companies at closing were soon abandoned as both placing an undue burden on the lower-income seller and creating dangerous opportunities for abuse.

The responsibility for creating the body was most often assumed, albeit grudgingly, by local government. Although many municipalities sought to have the developers of inclusionary housing projects handle the initial sale of newly created lower-income units, a step not without pitfalls,[14] it was nonetheless apparent that developers, who rarely had any long-term ties to their projects, could not be expected to assume a similar responsibility for ensuring long-term affordability. A small number of municipalities entered into contracts with existing nonprofit housing organizations to administer the controls or created new nonprofit entities.[15] Other municipalities created local public agencies, often named affordable housing boards or commissions, to handle this responsibility. More recently, in a step following from both the reluctance of some municipalities to carry out these responsibilities and the sheer inefficiency inherent in having dozens of separate agencies administer controls for small numbers of units, the New Jersey Department of Community Affairs established an Affordable Housing Management Service, which has become involved in both the initial marketing and resale management of a substantial part of New Jersey's inclusionary housing stock.[16]

One effective solution emerged from the resolution of lengthy exclusionary zoning litigation in Bedminster Township, an affluent northern New Jersey suburb. This was the creation for this and related purposes of a new entity named the Bedminster Hills Housing Corporation (BHHC). It was governed by a board on which the township, the developer,[17] a lender, and the New Jersey Department of the Public Advocate[18] were initially represented. As lower-income housing has been built in Bedminster over the past seven years, the board has been expanded to accommodate representatives of the families living in that housing and the number of developer representatives has been reduced. While atypical in its complex structure, the BHHC was typical of other municipalities, though ahead of most, in the nature of the issues it had to address.

Entities such as the BHHC, whether municipal agencies or private corporations, were charged with three fundamental duties:

- to determine the appropriate sale price for resale;
- to select qualified buyers on resale; and
- to manage resale transactions.

Since the issues raised by the first duty—setting resale prices—are particularly numerous and complex, that topic is treated separately. The other duties are addressed in this section, with illustrations drawn from the experience of the BHHC, with which I have been associated for many years.[19]

It was soon apparent that a fourth duty was implicit in the first three; that is, to prevent the inadvertent loss of units from the affordable housing stock. This was an important concern. Many earlier programs had not made adequate provisions to address the situation in which no qualified buyer was found within a set period after the owner indicated an intention to sell.[20] In those programs, particularly in California, a lapse of the affordability controls would enable the owner to sell the unit at market price.[21] That problem was easily addressed; all New Jersey resale control covenants provide that if no qualified buyer is found and the unit must be sold to a family of higher income, the transaction nevertheless takes place at the controlled price and the controls remain in effect. At the next resale transaction, the unit can return to the ranks of lower-income housing. Thus the affordable housing stock cannot be diminished through the inadvertent oversight of the body responsible for managing the resale controls.[22]

As the above discussion suggests, an early decision was made to handle the resale requirements through a deed restriction or covenant rather than through community land trusts or other more overtly social or community-oriented strategies. This decision reflects both the lack of the social infrastructure for such strategies in most parts of New Jersey and the generally conservative nature of most of the key actors involved—municipal officials and developers. It is important to remember that for most of those involved in carrying out the *Mount Laurel* mandate at the local level, the issues were and remain narrowly defined. Their objective was to provide, either willingly or reluctantly, a certain amount of housing within the *Mount Laurel* parameters; this objective was rarely, if ever, part of a larger progressive agenda at the local level for social change or housing reform. In that context, a deed restriction was not only the least obtrusive means of imposing affordability controls but the one that bore the greatest resemblance, and did the least visible violence to, customary real estate practices.

The threshold task of the entity administering affordability controls was to select qualified buyers for units available on resale. In the typical resale control covenant, the seller gives the entity an exclusive right to refer prospective buyers to his or her unit for a set period, typically ninety days. The power inherent in this right relinquished by the seller imposes an obligation to use it effectively; the entity must find qualified buyers quickly in order to ensure the continued use of the unit for lower-income housing and also to keep faith with the seller, who has relinquished the right to find a buyer for the unit.

The only way in which qualified buyers can be selected effectively and without undue delay is by creating waiting lists of prequalified buyers. Through advertising and other marketing methods, the BHHC creates pools of prospective buyers and then carefully sorts them by income level and household size. In contrast to communities that allow a unit to go to a family of any size meeting the income qualifications—so that a single person or a couple could end up in a two- or three-bedroom unit—the BHHC gives priority to the largest family for which the unit is suitable. Families in each pool are ranked in priority order before specific units are available. When a unit becomes available, the highest-ranking families meeting the income and household size requirements for that unit are identified and referred in sequence to the unit offered.

From that point on, the BHHC monitors the transaction to make sure that the referral leads as often as possible to a closing, something which is considerably more important—as well as more difficult—than it might seem. Obtaining a mortgage is a difficult hurdle that many would-be moderate-income buyers, and a large majority of low-income buyers find difficult if not impossible to overcome. The barriers imposed by poor credit ratings and ceilings on other debt are compounded by the helplessness of the typical low-income wage earner confronted with the seemingly arbitrary bureaucracy of the typical lender.

The BHHC counsels prospective buyers to help them not only improve their objective position with lenders by clearing up credit report problems or restructuring existing debt but also to improve their understanding of the process so that they can effectively present themselves and their circumstances to a lender. The BHHC was able to reduce the lender rejection rate for prospective low-income buyers, which initially approached 90 percent, to slightly more than 50 percent. The fact that, even with the BHHC's support, half of the would-be buyers—all of whom had been screened to ensure that they had enough income to carry the unit they were seeking to buy—could not qualify for mortgages reflects the extent to which homeownership, at least in its more conventional forms, is poorly adapted to the needs of much of the low-income population.[23]

Providing these services is not inexpensive. Many municipalities—particularly those on which lower-income housing has been imposed by court decree—are reluctant to support their administering entities at an effective level. The BHHC, which currently administers controls for 516 limited equity condominium units (as well as for 106 rental units), handles approximately fifty resale transactions per year, reflecting a 10 percent annual turnover rate. This volume of resales, along with a variety of related but lesser tasks, is managed by one full-time manager with part-time clerical support on a total operating budget of approximately $60,000 per year.

Three different approaches to funding these costs have been used. In some cases, the municipality requires the developer to deposit a per unit payment in a fund to cover the cost of future resale transactions; this practice has triggered objections that are not unreasonable from developers.[24] In other cases, the administering entity charges a fee for each transaction, which is added to the—often already burdensome—closing costs. Finally, a few municipalities have paid for the costs of the entity from general municipal funds.

The BHHC is not dependent, however, on the unpredictable generosity of developers or of Bedminster Township. Under the terms of the resale control covenant, as will be discussed below, appreciation of the unit's selling price is determined by a formula. Once the amount of the appreciation has been established and the unit sold, the BHHC and the seller divide the appreciation, the BHHC receiving 20 percent as "resale recapture" and the seller retaining 80 percent. By mid-1991, the BHHC was receiving an average of $1,600 per resale, and its resale recapture proceeds significantly exceeded its operating requirements.

As a result of this surplus, the BHHC Board voted in 1990 to begin using its resources to assist homeowners who, as a result of temporary hardship, had fallen seriously behind in mortgage payments or homeowners' association dues and were at risk of losing their unit. One such loan has been made under this program; in addition, the board has used its surplus to purchase the lien of a unit going into foreclosure in order to ensure that the unit would not be lost to the lower-income stock. The resale recapture provision not only gives the BHHC a measure of financial security that would be absent if it were dependent on annual appropriations or on developer largesse but provides it with a vehicle to expand its mission into other areas of benefit to its client population.[25]

SETTING RESALE PRICE FORMULAS

A crucial element in determining whether inclusionary units remain affordable and continue to provide a source of housing for lower-income families is the resale price. It is clear that some method is needed to ensure that the resale price is within the means of a lower-income buyer and that, at the same time, it fairly reflects the legitimate interests of the seller. Generally an appreciation formula is incorporated into the covenant by which the resale price is determined by adjusting the initial purchase price for inflation as well as for the cost of improvements made by the seller.

Precisely what is meant by "remaining affordable" is subject to various interpretations. A stringent standard would be that the unit should remain affordable over time to a household with an income no greater—at least relative to the median—than the family for whom it was initially affordable; that is, if the unit was initially affordable to a household earning 64 percent of the median, it should remain affordable to households earning no more than 64 percent of the regional median income.[26]

The New Jersey process is based on a less stringent, but not unreasonable, standard—namely, that the unit should remain affordable to a household *in the same income class* as that for whom it was initially affordable. Thus, if a unit was initially affordable to a moderate-income household—earning from 50 to 80 percent of median—it should remain affordable to a moderate-income household. It need not, however, remain affordable to a household at precisely the same income level as the initial buyer. Unfortunately, even a seemingly well-designed formula, as discussed below, may not ensure the preservation of affordability even by this more lenient standard.

The issue of adjustment for inflation raises both technical and more fundamental questions. The threshold problem is to define what represents a fair return to the seller. While it is readily accepted that the seller should not be entitled to sell at market value and reap a windfall by virtue of the below-market price for which he bought the unit, it is nonetheless widely held that the seller should be entitled to appreciation on his purchase price equal to the rate of inflation, however measured, from the date of purchase to the date of sale. This assumption is incorporated into the rules of the Council on Affordable Housing.[27]

That premise is questionable. The purchaserof a home on the open market is not guaranteed a minimum return; although during the mid-1980s house prices appreciated at far more than the underlying inflation rate, since 1988 house prices have not only not appreciated but, in large parts of New Jersey, have dropped. This is not to suggest that the resale price on price-controlled units should drop with declines in the market price; since the lower-income buyer of a unit subject to resale controls is being denied windfall opportunities available in the market, it is not unreasonable to shield him from some of the downside risks incurred by the market buyer. It does suggest, however, that his entitlement to appreciation equal to the rate of inflation should be given some scrutiny rather than accepted at face value.

I would suggest that the seller has a claim to a reasonable return on the equity investment, along with the amortized principal up to the date of sale, rather than appreciation based on the total price of the unit. If this premise is accepted, it follows that the appreciation that a resale price formula should offer, as a percentage of total selling price, can be far less than the total inflationary change in the price of the unit. Assuming a down payment of 10 percent or less and closing costs of about 5 percent of the price of the unit, the total equity investment of the buyer of a limited equity condominium in New Jersey is rarely more than 15 percent of the purchase price, and often less. With a 15 percent equity investment and minimal amortization of principal during the initial years, an annual rate of increase of 4 percent in the purchase price translates into a return on the buyer's investment of nearly 27 percent. It is hard to make a compelling case that such a return is dictated by simple fairness.

This issue is far more than an abstract question, because the greater the return offered the seller, the greater the risk that the unit will no longer remain affordable to the households for whom it is intended. In theory, if the price of a unit rises at the same level as the regional median income, the unit should be affordable on resale to a household at the same income, relative to the median, as on initial sale. In reality, that is far from certain. Changes in mortgage interest rates, property tax rates, and condominium association fees can lead to drastic changes in the affordability relationship between household income and sales price. A unit purchased initially with an 8½ percent mortgage will not be affordable to a household at the same income on resale if the new buyer can obtain a mortgage only at 10½ percent. Sharp increases in association fees, in particular, are commonplace during the first few years of condominium operations because developers have a compelling interest in setting the initial fees lower than realistic experience would dictate.[28]

If a cushion is to be created to allow for increases in the components of the carrying cost without reducing the affordability of the unit relative to the median income, the seller's appreciation must be set below, perhaps significantly below, the inflationary change in incomes or prices over time. Some New Jersey formulas, although not the one used in Bedminster, set the appreciation at a percentage of inflation—often 75 percent.

Another and better approach would be to craft a formula in which the return to the seller would be determined by working backward from a resale price that would, even with changes in carrying costs, ensure that the unit remained affordable at the same income level relative to the median. The formula could build in a minimum return to the seller, which might be the inflationary change applied not to the selling price but to the initial equity investment plus principal amortization. Such a formula would be more complex, but not to any undue degree, both to frame and to administer; it might well represent the best balance available between remaining true to the overriding goal of maintaining the affordability of the unit over time and ensuring fairness to the seller.[29]

I have assumed that the index used to set the appreciation permitted the seller is that of the increase in the median income for the region in which the unit is located. That index is to be preferred because it is the area median household income, after all, that defines the affordability of the unit. These data are published annually in New Jersey by the Council on Affordable Housing; in other states, however, this information may not be readily available.

Where it is not available, alternatives exist but may lead to unanticipated problems. Many California programs have permitted the initial purchase price to rise on resale on the basis of the change in the consumer price index (CPI) during the holding period. While prices and incomes have tended, on a long-term basis, to parallel one another, there are often marked short-term discrepancies, particularly during highly inflationary periods. Table 8-1, which shows the relationship between price and income change from 1973 through 1984, vividly points out the risks of using the CPI as an index. A unit first sold at the end of 1978 and resold at the end of 1981

Table 8-1. Comparative Trends in Year-by-Year Increase in U.S. Consumer Price Index and U.S. Median Household Income, 1973–1984

	Annual Increase: CPI	*Annual Increase: Median Income*
1973	6.2%	8.4%
1974	11.0	6.5
1975	9.1	5.4
1976	5.8	7.5
1977	6.5	7.0
1978	7.7	11.0
1979	11.3	9.3
1980	13.5	7.6
1981	10.4	7.7
1982	6.1	5.8
1983	3.2	4.2
1984	4.3	6.6

Source: Bureau of Labor Statistics, U.S. Bureau of the Census, *Current Population Reports.* Washington, D.C., 1974–1985.

would have had a resale price 40 percent higher than the initial price, if the increase in the unit's price had been based on the (compounded) increase in CPI 1979–1981; during the same period, however, household incomes rose by only 27 percent.[30]

Finally, whether the seller should recapture the value of improvements made to the unit should be briefly addressed. While it can be argued, once again, that fairness dictates that the seller recoup the value of any permanent improvements made while he lived in the unit, the resulting increase in the price of the unit inevitably affects—perhaps severely—the unit's affordability. Furthermore, if the improvement is something that serves the owner's whim rather than resulting in an improvement likely to benefit future owners, it is questionable whether it is appropriate to penalize future generations of homebuyers to reward the owner making the improvement.

Various measures have been adopted to anticipate this problem. In some cases, the deed restriction defines what improvements are reimbursed, limiting them to those that render the unit capable of accommodating a larger family or more accessible to the physically disabled.[31] In other cases, it may provide that improvements can be reimbursed in the selling price only if the owner has received prior approval from the entity administering the affordability controls. It should be noted, however, that in most New Jersey inclusionary developments, including those managed by the BHHC, the lower-income units are condominium apartments in which the scope of permitted improvements is extremely limited. As a result, despite the potential problems raised by this issue, it has tended to remain rather more a theoretical than an immediate concern.

THE DURATION OF AFFORDABILITY, OR PREVENTING WINDFALLS

Affordability under New Jersey procedures is rarely forever. Rules adopted by the Council on Affordable Housing set the minimum duration of controls on newly constructed units not in urban centers at twenty years and those on units in urban centers as short as ten years.[32] While some communities have set longer control periods—the units managed by the BHHC are controlled for forty years—most find it more comfortable to accept the council's minimums as their maximums. In any event, nearly all lapse sooner or later.

The fact that controls lapse means that, in the absence of explicit provisions to the contrary, the buyer in possession at the time that the controls expire gains a windfall as a direct result of the removal of the unit from the affordable housing stock. It would be hard to argue that the owner of the unit has "earned" the windfall, which as Table 8-2 shows, is likely to be substantial.

The magnitude of the windfall is a product of two factors: the disparity between the initial selling price of the unit and its initial market value, had it not been subsidized to be affordable to a low- or moderate-income buyer; and the potential disparity between the formula appreciation permitted on resale of the controlled unit and the appreciation of housing in the private market during the same period.

As the table shows, even where the market rate of appreciation is no greater in percentage terms than the rate permitted by the resale controls, the disparity between the selling price and the market value alone, extended over thirty years, is enough to create a substantial windfall. Where that disparity is augmented by a further disparity in the rate of appreciation, the magnitude of the windfall increases dramatically.

If controls are to be time limited, as the Council on Affordable Housing staunchly holds, the only solution to this problem is to embody provisions

Table 8-2. Potential Windfall Profits on Expiration of Thirty-Year Affordability Controls

	Initial Price	*Rate of Appreciation*	*Price after 30 Yr.*	*Windfall*
Market rate of appreciation = rate of appreciation permitted on controlled unit				
Market value	$80,000	4%/YR.	$259,470	
Affordable purchase price	40,000	4/YR.	129,730	$129,740
Market rate of appreciation 50% more than rate of appreciation permitted on controlled unit				
Market value	$80,000	6%/YR.	$459,475	
Affordable purchase price	40,000	4/YR.	129,730	$329,745

to recapture the windfall in the covenant establishing the resale controls. This solution, however, came into widespread use only a number of years after the first inclusionary developments had been constructed and left large numbers of units uncovered.[33] Although the council repeatedly rejected proposals to extend the minimum duration of resale controls, it finally adopted a rule in the fall of 1989 requiring recapture of windfall proceeds. Under the rule, unless the seller agrees to remain under the affordability controls, and renew them for another twenty years, he must pay the municipality 95 percent of the total "price differential"—that is, 95 percent of the disparity between the market price of the unit and the sales price as determined by the resale control covenant.[34] The proceeds of the windfall recapture must be taken by the municipality and dedicated to the creation, rehabilitation, or maintenance of low- and moderate-income housing.

The council rule effectively addresses the windfall problem. Recapture, however, is not a substitute for the continued existence of affordability controls. It is far from certain that the funds received by the municipality can or will be used to replace the lost unit. The cost of producing such units may have risen disproportionately, or the availability of land for new housing may have diminished. Finally, the political will, or judicial fiat, which created the unit initially may no longer prevail. Ironically, the statute creating the Council on Affordable Housing did not mandate its adoption of such a restrictive rule; the statute requires that "low and moderate income units remain affordable to low and moderate income households for an appropriate period of not less than six years."[35] Handed the opportunity to mandate truly extended affordability controls, the conservative membership of the council rejected it and only later mollified its critics by providing for the recapture of windfalls created by its initial failure to address this issue with appropriate seriousness.

CONCLUSION

Affordability controls have come to be accepted as a normal part of the New Jersey landscape, as a necessary concomitant of homeownership opportunities for low- and moderate-income families. The debate has changed from whether controls should exist to how they should be administered in order to balance the fairness to buyers and sellers against the overarching goal of a stable and long-term affordable housing stock.

Eight years after the first inclusionary units resulting from the *Mount Laurel* decision began to appear, it has become clear that the balance is achievable not through a complex process requiring sophisticated skills but through mechanisms that can be administered in a straightforward and cost-effective manner. The controls cannot be perfunctorily administered. While the minimal requirements of an affordability control system can perhaps be handled as little more than a clerical operation, proper management of such a system requires substantially more than the clerical processing of paperwork necessary for each resale transaction. The experience of the BHHC shows that effective management of the affordable housing stock requires at least as much sensitivity and attention to the needs of the human beings occupying, or seeking to occupy, those housing units. The test of a successful program lies in its ability to imbue its rules and procedures with that sensitivity and attention.

While resale controls can be considered a success, it cannot be said that the New Jersey experience, either with respect to inclusionary development generally or resale controls in particular, has led in most cases to a wider perspective on what John Davis has dubbed "forever housing" or to wider adoption of progressive housing policies or strategies. At least in part as a result of COAH's assiduous efforts to blunt political controversy by bureaucratizing the process, the creativity and initiative with which lower-income housing problems have been addressed in most communities subject to its jurisdiction have tended to diminish. Most towns have met their *Mount Laurel* obligations through a combination of inclusionary zoning, home improvement loans to lower-income homeowners, and in many cases transfer of up to half of their fair share to urban centers through regional contribution agreements.[36]

The landscape, however, is not devoid of promise. More than a few municipalities have built relationships with nonprofit development corporations, some preexisting and some created through local government initiative, going well beyond the management of resale controls. More than three thousand lower-income units have been built through the implementation of the *Mount Laurel* process by means other than inclusionary zoning; the majority of these have come about through the initiative of nonprofit developers. These developers have been able to benefit from the donation of municipal land, the creation of special zoning districts, and the establishment of municipal housing trust funds.

While these municipalities may be the exception, they are not isolated exceptions. Slowly and haltingly perhaps, the process of creating and maintaining a housing stock affordable to low- and moderate-income families, in suburban as well as urban communities, is beginning to take hold in New Jersey.

NOTES

1. *Southern Burlington County NAACP et al.* v. *Township of Mount Laurel*, 92 NJ 158 (1983).

2. The 1983 decision was preceded by *Southern Burlington County NAACP et al.* v. *Township of Mount Laurel*, 67 NJ 151 (1975), in which the township was ordered to rezone to accommodate its lower-income housing needs and those of its region. The 1983 decision, to which rulings in five other exclusionary zoning cases were added, arose from the appeal of the decision of the trial court after the first case had been remanded for decision in 1975.

3. 92 NJ at 267.

4. Although the court did not mandate 20 percent as a norm for inclusionary set-asides, it did cite that figure with approval in two separate places, at 268 and 279, thus making it clear that projects designating 20 percent of their units for low- and moderate-income housing would have no difficulty passing legal muster.

5. These definitions of *moderate income* and *low income* are those used by the court in *Mount Laurel* II and subsequently adopted in New Jersey in the arguably mislabeled Fair Housing Act, N.J.S.A.52:27D-301 et seq. (1985); they correspond to *low income* and *very low income* in Federal law. The term *lower income*, as used in New Jersey and in this article, refers to the sum of the low- and moderate-income ranges; i.e., all those earning between 0 and 80 percent of regional median income.

6. Martha Lamar, Alan Mallach, and John M. Payne, "*Mount Laurel* at Work: Affordable Housing in New Jersey, 1983–1988," *Rutgers Law Review* 41, no. 4 (1989): 1210.

7. A recent and still unreleased survey by the Council on Affordable Housing has found that as of early 1992, the *Mount Laurel* process has resulted in the creation of 13,827 completed and occupied units in New Jersey, including 10,123 new (6,764 through inclusionary development, 3,104 through other means, and 255 in urban areas funded through Regional Contribution Agreements) and 3,704 rehabilitated units. Conversation of the author with Douglas Opalski, Executive Director.

8. Note 3 supra, at 269.

9. Ibid.

10. See Alan Mallach, *Inclusionary Housing Programs: Policies and Practices* (New Brunswick, N.J.: Rutgers Center for Urban Policy Research, 1984), pp. 153–154.

11. The Council on Affordable Housing, a state body made up of nine members appointed by the governor, was created by the Fair Housing Act, note 5 supra. Although it has no power to compel municipalities to submit their plans for its approval, its power to grant substantive certification to those plans, thus freeing those municipalities from the legal sanctions established by the *Mount Laurel II* decision, has made many municipalities eager to conform to its standards and criteria for what constitutes an acceptable plan for the provision of low- and moderate-income housing.

12. More recently there has been a slight increase in the amount of rental housing being constructed, as private developers have discovered the benefits of the tax credits for building low-income rental housing created by the 1986 Tax Reform Act. Just the same, few developers active today in New Jersey have any serious interest in owning and maintaining rental housing on a long-term basis.

13. Lamar et al., "*Mount Laurel* at Work," p. 1212.

14. The pitfalls largely stem from the fact that the developer has a compelling financial motive to sell these units as quickly as possible in order to keep his carrying costs to a minimum. Under these circumstances, many developers cut corners with respect to the process of finding and qualifying lower-income buyers in order to sell their units expeditiously.

15. Local parochialism, in at least a few cases, prompted municipalities to create new entities even when an adjacent or at least nearby town already had in place a capable nonprofit that was willing to provide the services the municipality was seeking.

16. As the Bedminster experience has shown, it is difficult for an entity administering resale controls to offer services of the quality needed without, at a minimum, one full-time, well-qualified employee. That experience has also shown that in order to use such a person most effectively, the entity should be responsible for a pool of at least five hundred units, a number far in excess of what exists in most municipalities.

17. Under the resolution of the lawsuit, a single developer, who had been a party to the suit from the beginning, was charged with nearly full responsibility to

create the units that would make up Bedminster's fair share. Over the following seven years, the Hills Development Company built some three thousand units in the township, including more than six hundred low- and moderate-income units. This developer was alloted three of the initial eight seats on the board; a fourth went to a lender who was also a joint-venture partner in the first phase of the development.

18. The Department of the Public Advocate, created in 1974, is a New Jersey state agency that acts as a sort of statewide public interest law firm and ombudsman. It was an active party to the settlement of the Bedminster lawsuit, representing a number of low- and moderate-income plaintiffs in the matter. The Public Advocate was alloted two of the initial eight seats on the board.

19. The author acted as an expert witness on behalf of the low-income plaintiffs in the litigation and was subsequently appointed by the Public Advocate to one of its seats on the BHHC Board. He served as chair of the BHHC Board from 1989 through 1992.

20. This situation arises from the underlying structure of the resale control covenant, which provides the administering entity with an exclusive right to offer the unit for some period after the owner has notified the entity of intent to sell. The period was set at sixty days in most early California programs, but it is typically ninety days in New Jersey.

21. Mallach, *Inclusionary Housing Programs*, p. 152.

22. Another condition triggering a potential reversion of the unit to market price was foreclosure. Lenders making mortgages to buyers of lower-income units have insisted on language in the deed restrictions providing that controls would lapse in the event of foreclosure. The BHHC sought, with varying degrees of success, to work out agreements with lenders to be notified in the event an owner was seriously in arrears on mortgage payments; moreover, the BHHC required each buyer to provide it with a limited power of attorney through which it could compel an owner facing foreclosure to sell the unit to the BHHC, which, after satisfying the lender, would immediately sell the unit to another qualified buyer with the controls intact. During the nearly seven years since the first units were occupied, the BHHC has used this power only once.

23. The American mortgage system, in particular, with its stringent credit and earnings standards and its down payment requirements, blocks homeownership for many households that not only could afford to carry the unit, but in many cases are paying substantially more to rent the units they currently occupy.

24. *Mount Laurel* makes clear that the underlying obligation belongs to the municipality, though it permits government to pass at least some of the burden on to developers. The latter have argued, not without reasonable basis, that while a municipality may impose an obligation on them with respect to creating lower-income units, the obligation should cease once they have sold the units and are no longer involved in the development.

25. The agreement between Bedminster Township and the BHHC does provide,

however, that in the event the BHHC's revenues do not cover its operating costs, the township must make up the difference. No funds have ever been sought from the municipality, nor is the BHHC likely to seek such funds soon.

26. The question of what price level renders a unit affordable in the first place to a household with a given income is not a simple one; varying assumptions about the appropriate mortgage interest rate, the level of the down payment, the use of buy-downs, and other factors can result in substantial variability in the relationship between sales price and income.

27. N.J.A.C. (New Jersey Administrative Code) 5:92–12:13 provides that "The price of an owner-occupied housing unit . . . may increase annually based on the percentage increase in median income for each housing region." COAH rules further provide that a municipality has no responsibility to replace the unit should the application of this standard render the unit no longer affordable to a lower-income household on resale (N.J.A.C. 5:92–12.14). This overemphasis on the seller's interests at the potential expense of the buyer, and of the low-income population generally, is not atypical of the council.

28. This is a serious problem with respect to developer-driven lower-income housing. The determination of the initial selling price is a function of the annual carrying costs; that is, what sales price, given reasonable assumptions about taxes, mortgage interest rates, and association fees, will result in annual carrying costs representing 28 percent of the target income for which the unit is to be affordable. As a result, the lower the association fees are projected to be, the more money is left for mortgage payments and the higher the price the developer can charge for the unit. This creates a compelling incentive for the developer to underestimate association fees in the initial computation of the purchase price.

29. Even this minimum floor could result, under exceptional circumstances, in a relative loss of affordability, but it is not likely to be a problematic loss.

30. The BHHC, which adopted its resale price formula before COAH was established and before local median income data were regularly available, used an index based on the national median household income published annually by the Bureau of the Census and taken from the *Current Population Survey*. This is an acceptable index where more current, and more localized, data are not available.

31. COAH has adopted a rule that permits adjustments only for improvements that render the unit suitable for a larger household; it further provides that "in no event shall the maximum price of an improved housing unit exceed the limits of affordability for the larger household" (N.J.A.C. 5:92–12.16).

32. N.J.A.C. 5:92–12.1.

33. Some jurisdictions are addressing this problem by "retrofitting" recapture provisions, amending the deed restriction at the resale closing subsequent to the adoption of this rule.

34. The council chose to require recapture of 95 percent, rather than the entire windfall amount, on the theory that offering the seller some small benefit from the

windfall would serve to encourage the seller to maximize the selling price and thus the recapture amount (N.J.A.C. 5:92–12.7).

35. New Jersey Fair Housing Act, N.J.S.A.52:27D-301 et seq., Sec. 11(a)1.

36. Section 12 of the Fair Housing Act permits municipalities to transfer up to one-half of their fair share obligation to another municipality by making a cash payment to the latter municipality, a procedure known as a regional contribution agreement (RCA). As of early 1991, a total of twenty-eight RCAs had provided $61 million to sixteen separate urban jurisdictions. The RCAs were designed to underwrite the rehabilitation and, in a few cases, the construction of 3,130 units with an average price of $19,444.

9 Housing Trust Funds

MARY E. BROOKS

With more than seventy housing trust funds in cities, counties, and states throughout the country—twice as many as two years ago—it is now almost commonplace to include consideration of such a fund in any housing study. Cities and states all over the country—none of them immune to the 75 percent cuts in housing programs from the federal government over the last decade—are searching for ways to finance needed low-income housing.

While housing trust funds are simple in concept, they are tough to achieve, many taking several years of concerted work by a broad-based coalition to succeed. Housing trust funds are simply a way to generate revenue to support the production and preservation of low-income housing. They offer no magical solutions to many of the most difficult problems faced by producers of low-income housing. Even with funds from the best-run housing trust fund, low-income housing projects may face opposition, creative financial packaging is still required, and any number of issues—including the continued affordability of the units—must be resolved.

What makes housing trust funds interesting in the context of exploring the need to guarantee continued affordability of low-income units is that they are relatively new and most are concerned with addressing housing needs that have otherwise been ignored. The vast majority of these funds would not be in existence were it not for the efforts of housing advocates to get them passed. Thus, many components of these funds are "just exactly what we've been looking for!" They may include targeting to households with 50 percent or less of median income, they encourage participation by nonprofit development corporations, they discourage displacement, and they seek continued affordability in the units supported, among other worthy requirements.

It is nonetheless important to note at the outset that housing trust funds can incorporate any number of specific requirements, just as any other government housing program can. There is nothing peculiar to housing trust funds, nothing inherent in their design that makes them a better host to innovations. The fact that many housing trust funds have innovative components is most likely to the singular credit of the housing advocates that put the fund in place. They had the foresight, understanding, knowledge, and ability to put together a program that works the way they wanted it to.

Housing trust funds are but one way that local and state governments have taken charge of addressing their own housing problems—recognizing that they have resources to commit and that they can design programs to take advantage of unique opportunities and circumstances locally. While there is still—and always will be—an essential role for the federal government to play in providing adequate housing for low-income citizens, cities and states are taking on a larger role in shaping housing policy in this country. Housing trust funds have been a popular way for them to play this role.

DEFINING HOUSING TRUST FUNDS

Housing trust funds are the result of committing an on-going revenue source or several sources to a special fund restricted for use in providing needed low-income housing. They exist in cities, counties, and states of every size and with widely varying characteristics (see Table 9-1).

The Key Is the Revenue Source

Many believe today that we are technically fully capable of providing decent affordable housing for every American family and individual, yet we are unwilling to do so. While as a country we have the skills, knowledge, and experience to build and rehabilitate good homes, we are not compassionate or smart enough to commit the resources required to house all of us.

The primary objective of housing trust funds is to address this issue. They

Table 9-1. Housing Trust Funds in the United States

Cities

Ann Arbor, Michigan: Housing Trust Fund
Berkeley, California: Housing Trust Fund
Boston, Massachusetts: Neighborhood Housing Trust
Boston, Massachusetts: Workers Local 26 Housing Trust Fund
Boulder, Colorado: Community Housing Assistance Program
Burlington, Vermont: Housing Trust Fund
Cambridge, Massachusetts: Affordable Housing Trust
Chicago, Illinois: Low Income Housing Trust
Cleveland, Ohio: Housing Trust Fund
Dayton/Montgomery County, Ohio: Housing Trust Fund
Denver, Colorado: Housing Special Revenue Fund
Duluth, Minnesota: Housing Trust Fund
Hartford, Connecticut: Housing Preservation and Replacement Program
Knoxville, Tennessee: Housing Trust Fund
Los Angeles, California: Central City West Specific Plan—Housing
Menlo Park, California: Housing Reserve—BMR Program
Miami, Florida: Affordable Housing Fund
Modesto, California: Village One Plan
New York, New York: Battery Park City Housing New York Program
Palo Alto, California: The Housing Reserve
Phoenix, Arizona: Public Purpose Program
Pittsburgh, Pennsylvania: Community Development Investment Fund
Sacramento/Sacramento County, California: Housing Trust Fund
Salt Lake City, Utah: Housing Trust Fund
San Antonio, Texas: Housing Trust Fund
San Diego, California: Housing Trust Fund
San Francisco, California: Office Affordable Housing Production Program
San Francisco, California: Hotel Room Tax Trust Fund
Santa Monica, California: Housing Mitigation Fund
Seattle, Washington: Downtown Housing Bonus Program
Seattle, Washington: Growth-Related Housing Program
Toledo/Lucas County, Ohio: Housing Trust Fund
Washington, D.C.: Housing Production Trust Fund
West Hollywood, California: Affordable Housing Trust Fund

Counties

Dade County, Florida: Documentary Surtax Program
Fairfax County, Virginia: Housing Trust Fund
Howard County, Maryland: Housing Opportunity Fund
Jackson County, Missouri: Housing Resources Fund
King County, Washington: Housing Opportunity Fund

Table 9-1. Continued

Montgomery County, Maryland: Housing Initiative
St. Charles County, Missouri: Housing Resources Fund
St. Louis County, Missouri: Housing Resources Fund

States

Arizona: Housing Trust Fund
California: Housing Trust Fund
Delaware: Housing Development Fund
Florida: Housing Trust Fund
Georgia: Housing Trust Fund for the Homeless
Hawaii: Rental Housing Trust Fund
Idaho: Housing Trust Fund
Illinois: Affordable Housing Trust Fund
Indiana: Low Income Housing Trust Fund
Kansas: Housing Trust Fund
Kentucky: Housing Trust Fund
Kentucky: Affordable Housing Trust Fund
Maryland: Affordable Housing Trust Fund
Maine: Housing Opportunities for Maine Program
Michigan: Housing Trust Fund
Minnesota: Housing Trust Fund
Nebraska: Homeless Shelter Assistance Trust Fund
Nevada: Housing Trust Fund
New Jersey: Neighborhood Preservation Balanced Housing Program
North Carolina: Housing Trust Fund
Ohio: Low and Moderate Income Housing Trust Fund
Oregon: Low Income Rental Housing Fund
Oregon: Oregon Housing Fund
Rhode Island: Housing and Conservation Trust Fund
South Carolina: Housing Trust Fund
Tennessee: Housing Program Fund
Texas: Housing Trust Fund
Utah: Housing Development Restricted Account
Vermont: Housing and Conservation Trust Fund
Washington: Housing Trust Fund

Source: Housing Trust Fund Project, 1993.

are, at the simplest level, a mechanism for focusing revenues and making them available for low-income housing. The key to a housing trust fund is the ongoing nature of the revenue source. Housing trust funds are not simply funds created by a one-time appropriation of the city council or the state legislature. Instead, they receive money continuously from a "dedicated" source of revenue, which can range from a tax on real estate sales, to a fee paid by developers of office buildings, to interest on real estate escrow accounts, to repayments of government loans (see Table 9-2).

A city council or state legislature usually establishes a housing trust fund by ordinance, resolution, or legislation. The legislation dedicates a revenue source (often more than one source) and establishes the fund as a distinct entity that can receive and disburse funds. While a separate fund is established, with standard accounting and auditing protections, the housing trust fund itself is the program that enables these funds to be used to achieve established purposes, also set forth in the legislation. The legislation usually states how the fund is administered, who is eligible to apply for funds, what kinds of projects qualify, and overall program requirements.

Many funds have been started or supplemented by a one-time appropriation: a good way to get the fund under way and demonstrate its potential. But it is the dedicated, ongoing source of revenue that makes housing trust funds unique and insulates them from the vagaries of local or state budget processes. Trust funds are relatively permanent in that they are created by ordinance or legislation and can only be dismantled by an equivalent legislative action.

Administration of a Housing Trust Fund

Almost all housing trust funds are administered by city, county, or state departments or agencies. Although a few funds are established as separate nonprofit entities, even these are created through government action, often depend on city or county staff support, and usually have a board appointed by the mayor or another elected official. This close tie to government should come as no particular surprise when one realizes that the money to be spent is usually a public source of revenue.

Regardless, most housing trust funds have a rather innovative element in their administration. While city or state staff may do the day-to-day work of the housing trust fund, an appointed board of trustees or an advisory committee can have much of the responsibility for overseeing the fund, establishing policies, and making decisions about who receives funds. These

Table 9-2. Revenue Sources Committed to Existing Housing Trust Funds

Development ordinances, fees, or taxes

Linkage programs
Inclusionary zoning fees in lieu
Preservation ordinances fees in lieu
Condominium/cooperative conversion fees

Real estate or development activities

Real estate transfer or excise taxes or fees
Recording document tax or surcharge
Mortgage transfer tax
Penalty for failure to pay real estate transfer or excise tax
Sale or lease of city-owned property
Real estate property tax
Real estate tax increment funds
Hotel/motel tax
Windfall sales profit tax on city housing programs

Government programs

Loan repayments from government-funded programs, e.g., UDAG, CDBG, preservation programs
Bond programs, e.g., commitment of bond proceeds, interest earned from surplus or reserve accounts
Interest on application deposits for government programs
Public deposit insurance fund
Unclaimed property funds
Unclaimed rent overpayments
Program income, e.g., CDBG
Court settlements or fines for code violations

Market-based revenues

Interest from real estate escrow accounts
Interest from tenant security deposits
Interest from title insurer accounts
Voluntary state income tax check-off
Employer contract contributions per hour worked

Miscellaneous

Extraction revenues, e.g., petroleum overcharge funds, taxes from off-shore oil drillings

Sales tax

boards are usually created by the legislation or ordinance that creates the trust fund, and members of most advisory committees are appointed for specified terms by an elected official or body. Members typically represent a broad range of interests, including: elected officials, government agencies or deparments, financial institutions, private industry (real estate, building, management), for-profit developers, nonprofit developers, housing advocacy organizations, social service providers, unions, churches, public housing, and low-income neighborhoods, among others.

These boards are usually charged with creating their own bylaws, appointing officers, and developing meeting schedules. They are typically responsible for developing program guidelines and rules, developing applications for funds, assessing needs to be addressed, deciding which projects to fund, and reporting the activities and progress of the fund.

Program Guidelines for Housing Trust Funds

Most housing trust funds use a request for proposals process to award funds to eligible projects. Two to four times a year, the fund announces a request for proposals and makes a set amount of funds available to distribute. The fund evaluates proposals received and awards funds on a competitive basis to those that best meet its criteria. These funds are often used as first money in or last money out, meaning that they may provide the very first funds necessary to get the project underway or the last funds needed to complete the financial package. This type of gap financing is the most common use of housing trust funds.

A few funds commit their money to existing or new housing programs administered by the city or state itself, such as a rental housing preservation program. The program then uses trust fund money to further its existing work or grants the money to others that meet the program's requirements.

Funds are typically distributed according to requirements outlined in the enabling legislation and detailed in rules and regulations. Eligible applicants and eligible projects are specified. In addition, many funds outline criteria used for ranking applications or these that are given priority in evaluating applications.

Most funds provide grants or loans to nonprofit development organizations, private developers, local governments, or individuals. Some housing trust funds include housing authorities and other nonprofit organizations.

Housing trust funds typically support a broad range of eligible projects. The money usually can be used to support new construction, acquisition, rehabilitation, or other housing services for permanent housing. Some funds also support transitional or emergency housing facilities. Rental assistance, predevelopment funds, organizational support, and other services or facilities may be eligible for funding.

Funds Benefit Low-Income Households. Virtually all funds support only low- and moderate-income housing. One of their most exciting aspects—and often justification for their development—is that they attempt to address housing needs that no one else is addressing. Thus, for instance, housing trust funds shy away from providing low-interest mortgages for first-time homebuyers. Not that there isn't a need for such programs, but often a state housing finance agency or some other authority has already developed such a program and supports it through the issuance of bonds.

Most housing trust funds target their money to projects that serve low-income households (80 percent or less of median income), and some target very low income households (50 percent or less of median income). Three-quarters of the housing trust funds in the United States require that all of their funds benefit households with incomes at or below 80 percent of the median income for the area. And about one-fourth set aside some or all of their funds to benefit even lower-income households.

Nonprofit Development Organizations are Important Partners. The ability of nonprofit organizations to respond with feasible low-income housing projects is integral to the success of most housing trust funds. They often share the same concerns and goals the housing trust fund is pledged to address. Nonprofit development corporations are frequently the only development entities that attempt to provide housing for very low income households, work in neighborhoods others consider too risky, work with special populations in need of housing, or build in characteristics to help expand the supply of needed housing, such as multibedroom units, long-term affordability safeguards, related services, and other benefits.

Thus it stands to reason that housing trust funds would consider nonprofit development corporations their partners in making the funds successful. Some housing trust funds have seen it as integral to the achievement of their goals to help nonprofit organizations acquire the capability to create needed housing projects. They have done this in a variety of ways.

Very few housing trust funds make their funds available only to nonprofit development organizations. Some of them, however, give priority to nonprofit development organizations or otherwise make it more likely that such organizations will compete for funds. However, several housing trust funds have discovered that nonprofit organizations wishing to compete for available funds have a real need for technical assistance and capacity building. This may be the case in rural areas of a state or in a city where only a few nonprofits have dominated the development scene.

To address these circumstances, housing trust funds have provided organizational support to organizations that want to add another project to their portfolio or that want to enter the development field for the first time. This assistance can come through grants for operating budgets, consulting services, skills training, or staff development. Other housing trust funds offer funds for predevelopment costs, feasibility studies, site options, or short-term construction loans. Technical assistance has been another important tool enabling nonprofits to get past any number of steps in the development process.

HOUSING TRUST FUNDS AND CONTINUED AFFORDABILITY

Consistent with their attempt to address numerous issues affecting the supply of low-income housing that have too often been left out of housing programs, some funds have given attention to the need to ensure that units they support remain affordable to the intended beneficiary population. Housing trust funds are intended to provide a continuous source of funding to support low-income housing. As such, then, they are not specific mechanisms for guaranteeing the continued affordability of such units. If such guarantees exist within a specific housing trust fund, it is because this issue, along with any number of other objectives, was seen as a critical objective in establishing a housing trust fund.

At least half of existing housing trust funds have some form of continued affordability requirements (see Table 9-3). They generally fall into two broad categories: those that encourage or require some form of continued affordability within the projects funded, and those that employ some method as part of the conditions upon which funds are made available. In the former, it is left up to the applicant to devise and demonstrate a method to ensure affordability; in the latter, the fund itself incorporates such guarantees as part of the funding package.

Table 9-3. Housing Trust Funds with Continued Affordability Requirements

Locality	*Fund*
Ann Arbor, Michigan	Housing Trust Fund
Arizona	Housing Trust Fund
Berkeley, California	Housing Trust Fund
Boston, Massachusetts	Neighborhood Housing Trust
Burlington, Vermont	Housing Trust Fund
Cambridge, Massachusetts	Affordable Housing Trust
Dade County, Florida	Documentary Surtax Program
Delaware	Housing Development Fund
Florida	Housing Trust Fund (Partnership Program)
Hartford, Connecticut	Housing Preservation and Replacement Program
Indiana	Low Income Housing Trust Fund
Los Angeles, California	Central City West Trust Fund
King County, Washington	Housing Trust
Minnesota	Housing Trust Fund
New Jersey	Neighborhood Preservation Nonlapsing Revolving Fund
New York City, New York	Battery Park Housing, New York Program
North Carolina	Housing Trust Fund
Oregon	Housing Trust Fund
Palo Alto, California	The Housing Reserve BMR Program
San Antonio, Texas	Housing Trust Fund
San Diego, California	Housing Trust Fund
San Francisco, California	Hotel Room Tax Fund
San Francisco, California	Office Affordable Housing Production Program
Santa Monica, California	Housing Mitigation Fund
Seattle, Washington	Downtown Housing Bonus Program
Seattle, Washington	Growth Related Housing Program
Tennessee	Housing Program Fund
Texas	Housing Trust Fund
Utah	Housing Trust Fund
Washington	Housing Trust Fund

Requirements to Comply with Continued Affordability

Some housing trust funds use the objective of continued affordability as a criterion for reviewing projects seeking funds. They rarely specify how continued affordability is to be guaranteed but merely regard its demonstration favorably in evaluating competitive projects.

For example, the Delaware State Housing Authority has developed review criteria for its Housing Development Fund. Regulations state that a project must satisfy at least one of the following criteria:

- Households with very low, low, or moderate incomes inhabit units for a minimum of fifteen years.
- Project meets special housing needs not otherwise met.
- Neighborhoods with little housing currently for households with very low, low, or moderate incomes receive new housing opportunities.
- Substandard housing is rehabilitated to provide moderately priced units.
- A deteriorated neighborhood is revitalized.

Another set of housing trust funds gives priority to projects that demonstrate a commitment to continued affordability. The extent to which the applicant project guarantees continued affordabilty is used in ranking competitive projects.

For example, the Washington Department of Community Development uses the following criteria for ranking projects seeking funds from the Washington Housing Trust Fund:

- leveraging of other funds
- contributions to total project costs from recipients
- contributions to total project costs from local government
- encouragement of ownership, management, and other project-related responsibility opportunities
- strong probability of serving the original target group or income level for at least fifteen years
- demonstrated ability to implement the project
- service of greatest need
- service of persons and families with lowest incomes

Most housing trust funds with continued affordability requirement apply such requirements to funded projects for ten to twenty years. The instrument used to ensure continued affordability is not always specified within the ordinance or legislation. This method is a straightforward requirement that continued affordability must be promised in order for the project to be eligible for aid from the housing trust fund. For example, the ordinances establishing the Neighborhood Housing Trust of Boston, Massachusetts, require that the funds be used "to support units that will remain affordable for a minimum of fifteen years."

The North Carolina Housing Partnership uses the following criterion in determining eligibility to receive funds from the state's Housing Trust Fund: "For projects providing construction or rehabilitation of rental projects, contractual guarantees must exist to ensure that at least 20 percent of the units are occupied by eligible persons and families for a period of time not less than 10 years."

Continued Affordability Requirements Tied to the Funding Package

Often the requirement for continued affordability is enforced through loan documents signed by the housing trust fund and the recipient of funding. Affordability is ensured for at least as long as the loan is outstanding.

San Francisco's Office Affordable Housing Production Program offers a good example of a trust fund with continued affordability provisions. These provisions are, in fact, spelled out in the ordinance that established the fund:

> In San Francisco, the sponsor of the housing project must execute a promissory note payable to the City, secured by a deed of trust on the unit and a grant to the City of a right of first refusal to purchase the unit.
>
> The note is to be cancelled 20 years from the date of record and is to be in a designated amount plus the excess of the market value of the unit over the base price. The base amount is revised annually according to a formula.
>
> If the unit is sold to other than a low or moderate income household, the promissory note is due and payable to the City. If sold to a low and moderate income household, the City exchanges the original commitments for a new promissory note equal to the excess of the market value of the unit over the base price, plus simple interest at 5% per annum. The note extends for 20 years and the right of first refusal to purchase remains with the City.
>
> An owned unit can only be rented to a household of low or moderate income at the base rent. Violation of this restriction makes the promissory note immediately due and payable. The same requirements apply to a rental unit. A note must be executed and a deed of trust drawn with the City as sole beneficiary.
>
> Annual reports are required on the incomes of owners and tenants of the units, as well as prospective renters or purchasers.
>
> Failure to comply with these requirements permits the City to record a special assessment lien against the office development project for each housing unit required. Administrative and recording fees are charged, plus 1.5% per full month compounded monthly on all charges due. All monies collected are

placed into the City Wide Affordable Housing Fund and must be used solely to increase the supply of housing for low and moderate income persons.

Seattle's Density Housing Bonus Program requires that projects be committed to providing housing to serve a specific income range for twenty years. Developer obligations regarding the rents or sales prices and income levels are controlled by a developer agreement secured through a covenant or other legal mechanism approved by the City. In addition, rent levels, sales prices, incomes of new residents, and occupancy rates are reported annually. The program permits buyout options at the end of ten years. The option allows the rent or sales price to rise above the original level with a subsidy recapture that must be used for low-income housing production by the City. Conversions may also occur after ten years, with subsidy recapture provisions and the requirement that the units continue to serve households with incomes at or below 150 percent of the area median income for the remainder of the twenty-year commitment period. Converted rehabilitation projects must continue to provide 25 percent of units for households with incomes at or below 50 percent of the Standard Metropolitan Statistical Area (SMSA) median household income. All buyout options or conversions must be approved by the Department of Community Development.

San Diego's Housing Trust Fund provides another good example of continued affordability requirements. The ordinance establishing this fund reads in part:

> Whenever funds from the Trust Fund are used for the acquisition, construction or substantial rehabilitation of an affordable rental or cooperative unit, the Commission shall impose enforceable requirements on the owner of the housing unit that the unit remain affordable for the remaining life of the housing unit, assuming good faith efforts by the owner to maintain the housing unit and rehabilitate it as necessary. The remaining life of the housing unit shall be presumed to be a minimum of fifty-five years.
>
> Whenever funds from the Trust Fund are used for the acquisition, construction or substantial rehabilitation of ownership housing, the Commission shall impose enforceable resale restrictions on the owner toward the end of keeping the housing unit affordable for the longest feasible time, while maintaining an equitable balance between the interests of the owner and the interests of the Commission.
>
> For programs funded with funds from the Trust Fund which are not described above, the Commission shall develop appropriate mechanisms to ensure affordability which shall be described in the Program Plan.

> The affordability restriction requirements described in this section shall run with the land and the Commission shall develop appropriate procedures and documentation to enforce these requirements and shall record such documentation in the Office Records of the Recorder of San Diego County.

A few housing trust funds address the issue of continued affordability by granting the first right of purchase to the housing trust fund, the jurisdiction, or the jurisdiction's designee. In this way, affordability of the units is guaranteed for as long as the jurisdiction elects to do so.

Burlington, Vermont, has tied its inclusionary zoning ordinance to the local housing trust fund by granting the fund a preemptive option to purchase any affordable units that are created in the projects covered by the inclusionary housing ordinance. The fund may assign its option to any one of the City's four designated housing agencies: the Burlington Community Land Trust, the Cathedral Square corporation, the Burlington Housing Authority, or the Lake Champlain Housing Development Corporation. If the fund (or its designee) chooses not to exercise its option, the developer may rent or sell the affordable units at the required affordable price to any household earning less than the median income.

The Vermont Housing and Conservation Fund supports continued affordability in another important way. The fund was created to respond to problems caused by the pressure of development in the state. Two fears were paramount: that affordable housing would move hopelessly beyond the reach of most residents, and that substantial portions of naturally and agriculturally significant land would disappear. The Vermont fund gives priority to projects with perpetual affordability. It uses mortgages, covenants, and other legal instruments to enforce the continuing affordability of assisted projects.

Specific continued affordability requirements in selected housing trust funds are listed in Table 9-4.

CONCLUSION

Housing trust funds are generally too new for the true impact of their continued affordability efforts to be assessed. With only a few years of experience, it is impossible to tell if housing trust funds will be able to ensure that the units supported will indeed create a continuous supply of housing affordable to the intended beneficiaries.

Table 9-4. Continued Affordability Requirements in Selected Housing Trust Funds

Location	*Income Targeting*	*Continued Affordability Requirements*
CITY HOUSING TRUST FUNDS		
Ann Arbor, Michigan: Housing Trust Fund	Less than 80% median income; priority to less than 50%	Eligibility requirement: must have plan for long-term affordability of units Priority: projects addressing the perpetual affordability of units
Berkeley, California: Housing Trust Fund	40% of units less than 60% median income, or 25% of units less than 50% median income	Requirement: units must be affordable for the life of the project, except for funds awarded to the city for rental rehabilitation loans, where affordability must match term of the loan or no less than 15 years
Boston, Massachusetts: Neighborhood Housing Trust	Less than 80% of median income Review criteria: less than 50%	Requirement: units must remain affordable for minimum of 15 years Review criteria: no. of years beyond 15 and strength of enforcement mechanisms
Boulder, Colorado: Community Housing Assistance Program	30–60% median income	Requirement: units must remain affordable for minimum of 15 years Right of first refusal clause required in all agreements
Burlington, Vermont: Housing Trust Fund	Less than 100% median income Set-asides for low and very low income	Priority: projects that guarantee perpetual affordability or a term of affordability of 10–40 years with recapture provision
Cambridge, Massachusetts: Affordable Housing Trust	Less than 80% median income	Requirement: units conveyed with restrictions guaranteeing permanent availability
Cleveland, Ohio: Housing Trust Fund	Less than 60%, with 20% less than 50%, median income	Requirement: compliance with restrictions on rent levels and tenant income for 5 years

Table 9-4. Continued

Location	*Income Targeting*	*Continued Affordability Requirements*
Hartford, Connecticut: Housing Preservation and Replacement Program	Uses Section 8 low-income limits	Requirement: must remain rental housing for at least 10 years
Los Angeles, California: Central City West Specific Plan—Housing	Less than 80% median income, or 30% less than 50% median income	Requirement: deed restriction to retain affordability for the life of the units or for 30 years, whichever is greater; rents cannot exceed specified limits
New York, New York: Battery Park City Housing New York Program	Less than 175% median income Set-asides for 55% and 90% median income	Requirement: units subject to rent stabilization laws for a minimum of 15 years
Phoenix, Arizona: Public Purpose Program		Qualified subsidy period: 40 years
San Antonio, Texas: Housing Trust Fund	Less than 80% median income	Eligibility requirement: must remain affordable for the period of trust assistance or the useful life of the unit, as specified in the RFP and negotiated in the agreement
San Diego, California: Housing Trust Fund	Less than median income Set-asides for low and very low income	Requirement: rental units must remain affordable for the life of the unit, a minimum of 55 years; ownership units for the longest feasible time
San Francisco, California: Office Affordable Housing Production Program	Less than 120% median income	Requirement: promissory note executed for 20 years due if affordability violated
San Francisco, California: Hotel Room Tax Trust Fund		Requirement: rental units for low-income elderly and physically handicapped must remain affordable for 40 years

Location	Income Targeting	Continued Affordability Requirements
Seattle, Washington: Downtown Housing Bonus Program	Less than 150% median income Set-aside for rehabilitation projects	Requirement: units must remain affordable for 20 years
Seattle, Washington: Growth-related Housing Program	Less than 50% median income, with 50% for less than 30% median income	Requirement: units must remain affordable for a minimum of 20 years
Toledo, Ohio: Housing Trust Fund	Less than 80% median income, with 75% to less than 60% median income	Requirement: rental units must remain affordable for a minimum of 15 years; owners must remain in homeowner units for at least 5 years
Washington, D.C.: Housing Production Trust Fund	Less than 80% median income	Requirement: 20% of units must remain affordable for the term of assistance or 40 years, whichever is greater
COUNTY HOUSING TRUST FUNDS		
Dade County, Florida: Documentary Surcharge Program	Half of the funds targeted to less than 80% median income	Requirement: homeowners must occupy assisted homes for 2 years
Fairfax County, Virginia: Housing Trust Fund	Low and moderate income households with priority to less than 50% median income	Priority: projects adding to the permanent stock of low income housing
STATE HOUSING TRUST FUNDS		
Arizona: Housing Trust Fund	Less than 50% median income; less than 80% if homeowner program	Priority: projects that serve designated target group for at least 15 years
Delaware: Housing Development Fund	Less than median income	One among several alternative requirements: units must remain affordable for minimum of 15 years

Table 9-4. Continued

Location	*Income Targeting*	*Continued Affordability Requirements*
Florida: Housing Trust Fund (Partnership Program)	Very low, low, and moderate income; at least 30% to very low and 30% to low	Requirement: rental housing reserved for eligible households for 15 years or term of assistance, whichever greater
Hawaii: Rental Housing Trust Fund	Less than median income; half of assisted units less than 60% median income	Priority: projects committed to serving the target population over a longer period of time
Idaho: Housing Trust Fund	Less than 80% median income Set-asides for less than 50%	Priority: projects that demonstrate a strong possibility of serving original target group or income level for a period of at least 40 years
Illinois: Affordable Housing Trust Fund	Less than 80% median income; majority must serve less than 50%	Requirement: must have a deed restriction, agreement, or other legal document providing for recapture of assistance
Indiana: Low Income Housing Trust Fund	Less than 80% median income; half must serve less than 50%	Requirement: units must remain affordable for minimum of 15 years
Kentucky: Affordable Housing Trust Fund	Less than 50% median income Set-aside for less than 30%	Requirement: rental units must be deed restricted for 30 years, homeowner units for 5 years
Minnesota: Housing Trust Fund	75% of funds must serve less than 30% median income	Review criteria: projected long-term affordability of the units
New Jersey: Neighborhood Preservation Balanced Housing Program	Less than 80% median income; half of funds to serve less than 50%	Requirement: units must remain affordable for 10–20 years, depending on locality
North Carolina: Housing Trust Fund	Less than 80% median income Set-asides for less than 30% and 50%	Requirement: rental projects must ensure that 20% of units are occupied by eligible households for no less than 10 years

Location	*Income Targeting*	*Continued Affordability Requirements*
Ohio: Low and Moderate Income Housing Trust Fund	Less than 80% median income Set-aside to less than 50%, preference to less than 35%	Requirement: recipient must reasonably ensure that rental projects will be affordable for the life of the project or 30 years, whichever is longer
Oregon: Housing Fund	Very low and low income Set-asides for each	Priority: projects that ensure the longest use of the units as low or very low income housing units
Rhode Island: Housing and Conservation Trust Fund	Low and moderate income	Requirement: units must remain affordable for at least 99 years with first right of refusal
South Carolina: Housing Trust Fund	Very low and low income	Requirement: projects must guarantee continued affordability for no less than 30 years
Tennessee: Housing Program Fund	Less than 80% median income	Requirement: local housing programs are to establish compliance periods for each program providing for affordability for a minimum of 15 years
Texas: Housing Trust Fund	Very low and low income	Requirement: multifamily housing must remain affordable for a minimum of 20 years
Utah: Housing Development Restricted Account	Less than 80% median income; half to less than 50%	Priority: projects that demonstrate strong probability of serving original target group or income level for at least 15 years
Vermont: Housing and Conservation Trust Fund	Less than median income; encourage less than 80%	Review criteria: long-term effect of proposed activity and likelihood that activity will prevent the loss of subsidized housing units and will be perpetual
Washington: Housing Trust Fund	Less than 50% median income	Priority: projects that demonstrate a strong probability of serving the target group for at least 15 years

Housing trust funds will not be able to replace the lack of federal support for needed low-income housing; they are not simple or easy to get underway. Nonetheless, the evidence to date strongly suggests that these funds can make a timely contribution in housing the poor; they have established an excellent track record in addressing important, if not tough, housing objectives.

Providing housing for low-income people often depends on taking advantage of unique or unusual circumstances that make a particular project possible. A good land deal, a house that would otherwise be demolished, a special need that must urgently be addressed—any number of unexpected opportunities are the very spice of low-income housing development. Many housing trust funds make just these kinds of projects possible by making available flexible funds that can be used in a variety of ways and adjusted to make the deal work.

In addition, housing trust funds have been supportive of projects that provide housing for special populations, or involve creative homeownership opportunities, or involve tenants in construction or management, or preserve threatened existing housing, among many nontraditional housing programs.

Housing trust funds may help set the trend that every program designed to provide housing for low-income citizens should provide some guarantee to present and future occupants that government support means continuous affordability.

10

Zigzagging toward Long-term Affordability in the Sunbelt: The San Diego Housing Trust Fund

NICO CALAVITA, KENNETH GRIMES, AND SUSAN REYNOLDS

Except for a few cities with progressive council majorities or progressive mayors, U.S. communities that adopt third sector housing policies do so incrementally and unevenly. In 1990, when San Diego began that incremental process, the city council voted to create a housing trust fund (HTF) to finance housing that would be "forever affordable," requiring assisted rental housing to remain affordable for the life of the building. The HTF, funded by a linkage fee on commercial development and by a portion of the local hotel room tax, devotes most of its revenue to households with very low incomes and provides funding for nonprofits' training and operating needs, a first step toward building a nonprofit development capacity.

Like many cities, especially in the sunbelt, San Diego has long been governed by a noninterventionist and politically conservative council that has alternated between hostility and indifference toward the housing problems of poor and working people. Before the adoption of the HTF, San Diego had primarily financed and supported affordable housing in the for-profit sector, and there had been little commitment to long-term affordability or to alternative, social forms of housing ownership.

The HTF represented a local policy change of near seismic proportions. How was such a radical ordinance adopted in a conservative town that deeply believes in citizens' God-given right to reap the double-digit annual inflation of property values? The San Diego experience has a number of lessons for other cities that lack progressive political traditions.

THE SAN DIEGO CONTEXT

San Diego is a U.S. Navy town and a tourist town—two of the defining characteristics of an economy heavily dependent upon government (military and local) and upon the low-wage service sector supported by the "visitor industry." San Diego is also a border city adjacent to Tijuana, one of the fastest growing cities in Mexico, where two million residents live and through which thousands of undocumented workers pass every day en route to the United States. There are also streams of immigrants from Southeast Asia and the Philippines, spouses of military personnel, and jobless new residents from other parts of the United States who moved to San Diego "for the weather" and for work. New residents are endemic, and today they are as likely to be from Phnom Penh or a Mixtec village as from Iowa.

San Diego's population increased from 334,000 in 1940 to 1,118,000 in 1990. Much of this growth occurred from 1970 to 1990; the population increased by 421,000 in those twenty years. This surge has led to periods of intense housing speculation and wild housing cost increases. In the 1960s, San Diego was considered a relatively low-cost housing area, but by the late 1970s, its owner-occupied housing was regarded as some of the most expensive in the nation (Leasure, 1988).

The sharp increases in the cost of shelter since 1970 have contributed to higher cost of living increases in San Diego than in the average U.S. city. Since 1970, prices have risen 260 percent in the San Diego region, compared to about 210 percent nationally. At the same time, next to Miami, San Diego has experienced the slowest growth in per capita income. "The region's real average wage has declined some 20.5 percent or 1.3 percent per year since 1970" (Drew, 1990: 2). The above-average rise in the cost of shelter, coupled with a decrease in average wages, has created a housing crisis of unprecedented proportions in San Diego.

The crisis became especially acute during the late 1980s when high growth led to a rapid worsening of public facility problems (see Table 10-1), prompting an interim growth limitation in 1987 and the placement of two slow-growth initiatives on the ballot in 1988. The initiatives were defeated at the polls, but they contributed to an expectation of continuous conflicts

Table 10-1. Residential Units Completed in San Diego, 1986–1990

Fiscal Year	*Multifamily*	*Single Family*	*Total*
1986	8,935	4,658	13,594
1987	11,311	4,124	15,435
1988	8,240	3,802	12,042
1989	7,157	3,002	10,159
1990	4,811	2,171	6,982

over growth and to a quick spiral in housing prices, with the average and median price of a San Diego house increasing nearly 27 percent in two years (Babilot, 1990).

By any measure, by the end of the 1980s San Diego faced a very severe housing crisis. It was constantly reported in the press that the city was one of the least affordable in the nation for renters and home buyers alike (San Diego Housing Commission, 1989a). At the root of the problem was the collision between the incomes of the city's lower-income households—fully 42 percent of the population—and the high land and development costs in a high-growth city. In 1989 a family earning a gross income of $18,250, or more than double the minimum wage, faced typical two-bedroom rents of $670, or nearly two-thirds of their after-tax income (San Diego Housing Commission, 1989a).

The resulting city housing situation was truly alarming:

- 50,000 very low income households paying up to 70 percent of their household incomes for housing
- At least 19,000 overcrowded units where families were forced to double up to pay the rent
- A minimum of 26,000 substandard units
- 5,000 to 10,000 homeless men, women, and children

As in other high-cost cities, affordability problems in San Diego extended up the economic ladder to potential home buyers. By 1990, only 18 percent of San Diegans could afford to buy a median-priced single-family home, which cost more than $180,000, and the rate of homeownership was declining (San Diego Planning Department, 1990).

San Diego, a traditionally conservative Republican city, has little history of government intervention in social problems. The city prided itself on its independence, refusing federal and statewide money in several instances in order to preserve local autonomy.[1]

San Diego city government played virtually no role in low-income housing until the 1980s. For years, it had even resisted federal pressure to create a local housing authority. Finally, in 1979, under threat of losing Community Development Block Grant (CDBG) funding, the city council created a housing authority and combined it with other local housing activities in a quasi-autonomous housing commission. With an endowment of City land to sell or develop and access to a portion of annual CDBG funds for homeowner rehabilitation loans, the Housing Commission was born at a time of federal housing cutbacks and a worsening housing crisis.

The San Diego Housing Commission acts as both the public housing authority and the administrator of all the housing loan programs traditionally domiciled in municipal housing agencies. Housing Commission staff do not report to the city manager. Instead, the commission's executive director answers to the Housing Commission itself, which meets publicly to approve all significant actions, from housing authority janitorial contracts to apartment project loans. The mayor and city council control appointments to the Housing Commission, and city council also retains certain review and decision powers.

OBSTACLES TO LONG-TERM AFFORDABILITY

Clearly, San Diego in 1989 was not a hospitable climate for any sort of affordable housing, much less housing with long-term affordability restrictions. The City's disregard for housing must be viewed as consistent with the conservative view of government's role in society that is characteristic of southwestern cities.

In San Diego, the conservative climate presented political, ideological, and organizational obstacles to municipal activism in general and to municipal intervention in the housing market in particular. Any sort of solution that might seek to decommodify housing by imposing long-term controls over affordability appeared to be beyond the pale.

Ideological Obstacles

A conservative political climate fosters deep-seated ideological objections to public programs that assist the economically disadvantaged. Ideological obstacles to housing affordability restrictions are based on perceived self-interest—developers see affordability restrictions as depressing the value of their investment—or on mutual interests—business interests interpret regulation more broadly as adversely impacting the business climate (Molotch, 1976). Furthermore, the poor are typically seen as "undeserving," and public assistance is interpreted as weakening the incentive they need to get ahead (Waxman, 1983). In San Diego, with its dependence on a cheap, plentiful supply of Mexican labor, the situation is compounded by an institutionalized racism and by European-American fears that any assistance provided to brown-skinned and yellow-skinned people only increases the undocumented work force.

All these reactions, from self-interest, to labeling, to fear and racism, are likely to engender certain attitudes to the housing problem: (1) There is no housing problem in San Diego. (2) But if there is a problem, it only affects "them" and not "us"; "they" are to blame for their problems. (3) If a solution is needed for this temporary and overblown "problem," there is no role for the public sector to play; the private market will take care of everything. (4) But if a public solution is called for, it must not burden the private market with undue regulations or private property with long-term social controls. The consequence of these "common sense" attitudes was that affordable housing was essentially a nonissue in San Diego throughout the 1980s.

Political Obstacles

Local governments in the United States, in their search for continuous growth and development, have generally favored business elites to the detriment of the working class and inner-city neighborhoods. There is disagreement among scholars as to whether local governments' progrowth policies are the result of the personal influence and private power of businessmen and landowners (Cummings, 1988; Squires, 1989; Molotch, 1976) or of the economic need of cities to attract mobile wealth (Peterson, 1981). Regardless of the reason, "these special concessions subsidize private profit and promote the class interests of the business elite over those pursued by the working and lower class" (Cummings, 1988).

Under certain circumstances, however, the working class can affect the local decision-making process (Sawers, 1978; Logan and Swanstrom, 1990). This can happen because of local circumstances or because of the evolution of larger societal forces affecting growth and development at the local level. During the 1960s and early 1970s, for example, citizen groups successfully challenged progrowth coalitions in northeastern and midwestern cities. At that time, community preservation activists defeated the urban renewal strategy of progrowth coalitions to refurbish the central business district in many of the older and larger cities in the United States (Mollenkopf, 1983).[2] These conflicts helped to solidify a tradition of community activism in those cities, while southwestern cities were generally bypassed by both urban renewal and the conflicts and community activism it generated.

In San Diego, the influence of prodevelopment leaders has remained largely unchallenged by progressive coalitions and was strengthened by the citywide system of electing city council members, which remained in place until late 1988. Of the ten largest cities in the country in 1988, only San Diego and Detroit still had citywide elections, which made it difficult to challenge the power establishment through the electoral process.

In addition, the delegation of the city's low-income housing activities to the Housing Commission, a separately accountable governmental agency, shielded elected officials from an issue perceived to be politically unpopular. The legitimacy of municipal intervention in housing was further undermined by a major corruption scandal that centered on the Housing Commission's founding director and virtually immobilized the agency from 1986 through 1988.

Organizational Obstacles

The organizational obstacles lay in the past policies of the Housing Commission as well as in the weakness of a nonprofit housing advocacy or production sector.

The Housing Commission had a history of relying heavily upon private developers to produce low-income housing. Most of the units (other than public housing) assisted through the commission in its first ten years were privately developed bond projects or private, federally subsidized projects on commission-held land.

The commission's formal policy on long-term affordability, adopted as part of a broader policy in 1988, required affordability for a minimum of ten years or until the commission's loan was repaid. Long-term affordability was simply not the dominant concern. For instance, the policy favored leases of land over direct sale not because of the opportunity to extend affordability but "in order to preserve Commission assets and recycle

Commission funds" (Financial Participation Policy, San Diego Housing Commission, adopted 2 May 1988, revised 16 October 1989).

The lack of community-based housing advocacy and production organizations in San Diego was perhaps the most debilitating obstacle of all. Weak neighborhood identities produced by high levels of in-migration, the lack of local foundation funding, and an absence of government leadership all contributed to this gap. As a result, between 1970 and 1989, a handful of charitable housing development organizations had produced fewer than fifteen hundred units, most of them federally subsidized Section 202 projects for seniors and disabled people (Reynolds, 1990).

LATE 1980S: SETTING THE STAGE FOR A HOUSING TRUST FUND

The high-growth period of the middle and late 1980s brought certain economic, political, and organizational changes to San Diego that created the preconditions necessary for the establishment of a housing trust fund (HTF) in the city. First of all, the economic boom made it economically possible to establish a sizable HTF. As Connerly (1989: 5, 6) has pointed out, "The amount of money that can be generated for many housing trust funds often depends on the general level of real estate development activity in an area. The faster a state or city is growing in population . . . the more revenues will be collected for housing trust funds that are financed with development related fees and taxes." Secondly, this rapid growth, coupled with inadequate infrastructure and public facilities at the community, citywide, and regional levels led to a vigorous antigrowth sentiment within the population and to the weakening of the hold the "growth machine"[3] had on the city. Developers especially came under attack; they were blamed for all the growth problems the city was facing, including their own inability to provide affordable housing. Even though the growth machine was able to defeat the 1988 slow-growth measures, the city's problems did not go away, and in 1989 the city council passed several elements of the defeated propositions. The growth machine was still on the defensive in 1989, due in large part to voter adoption of district council elections in November 1988.

The district elections initiative won by a slim margin of 7,000 votes out of 320,000 cast. This was the fifth attempt since 1969 to overturn San Diego's hybrid method of council selection in which a district's only primary was followed by a citywide election. Under that system, the candidate receiving the most votes in the local district primary usually ended up losing in the citywide election to candidates supported by the Republican establishment and big-money developers.

It is likely that those forces would have defeated district elections for a fifth time in San Diego if development interests had not been concentrating their energies on defeating the two slow-growth measures placed on the same November 1988 ballot. Citizens for Voters Rights, the predominantly business-oriented group formed to defeat district elections, spent about $10,000 in the campaign. In contrast, developers spent $2 million to defeat the slow-growth propositions. In doing so, they fended off the most direct threat to growth but lost the mechanism that insured, almost without fail, a probusiness majority on council.

The hopes of district election backers were fulfilled in the 1989 council elections when two incumbents were defeated. A new council majority was formed by a five-person mix of environmentalists, limited growth advocates, and progressives. They were quickly labeled by the opposition the "Gang of Five." But such a term can be misleading. It suggests a group under tight leadership that consistently votes as a block. Instead, the group lacked consistent leadership. In fact, Wes Pratt, one of the "Gang of Five" and the representative of the mostly black southeastern area of the city, often was a swing vote on council, siding on more than one occasion with the more probusiness members of council. This was the same councilman who took a leadership role in bringing about the HTF in San Diego, and his ties to the business community served him well in building consensus around the HTF cause.

The last change of the late 1980s that made the HTF possible was organizational. The Housing Commission changed leadership and direction in 1988. The founding director was fired by the city council, and his replacement seemed interested in developing programs that could make "a significant dent" in the housing problem. Shortly afterwards, Wes Pratt, the councilman representing Southeast San Diego, was appointed chair of the Housing Commission and became more active than his predecessors in attempting to find solutions for the San Diego housing problem.

THE HOUSING TRUST FUND CAMPAIGN

The seed for an HTF in San Diego was sown at a "Balanced Communities" conference organized in May 1988 by the Graduate Program in City Planning at San Diego State University to explore mechanisms to increase the production of low-income housing while avoiding its concentration in lower-income neighborhoods. One of the presenters was Mary Brooks of the Housing Trust Fund Project/Center for Community Change. Her presentation on HTFs as a new approach for the provision of affordable housing sparked the interest of a Housing Commission planner, who was then able to convince the new director to support an HTF program in San Diego. Shortly afterwards, Wes Pratt was appointed chair of the Housing Commission and agreed that the concept of an HTF held much promise for increasing low-income housing production in the city. In February of 1989, the Housing Commission formally voted to establish a task force to make recommendations on an HTF program.[4]

The idea of an HTF, then, was initially generated by the Housing Commission staff, not by advocacy groups pushing from below. As a result, the commission staff recognized the need to build a wide base of community support capable of political mobilization.[5] In addition, the commission realized that it was necessary, especially in a conservative city such as San Diego, to define the housing problem in terms responsive to concerns of business and middle-income people and to accommodate competing interests.

Coalition Building

Although lower-income households could be expected to have a considerable stake in the creation of HTFs and, numerically at least, represented a formidable constituency, they were politically disenfranchised in San Diego, lacking the resources and organization needed to exert effective political pressure. Housing Commission planners identified community-based groups, service providers, and other nonprofit organizations representing the interests of lower-income people as the constituency that could potentially create the political pressure needed to establish the HTF. But these groups were atomized, politically unorganized, and only dimly aware of each other.

The Housing Commission organized a meeting in January 1989 with representatives from more than thirty groups to explain the full extent of the housing crisis and to discuss the HTF as a potential solution. Mary Brooks was invited to attend the meeting as an independent expert. After considerable discussion, the assembled community activists took the view that the HTF was potentially a powerful vehicle to generate low-income housing; they decided, moreover, that the major source of funds for an

HTF should be linkage fees so that further growth might pay for the low-income housing needs that it generates. Four points were stressed by the community advocates at this meeting: (1) the HTF should help house those most in need; (2) the community should have control over the HTF; (3) the HTF should be used to support nonprofit development; and (4) long-term affordability should be ensured. These principles were eventually incorporated into the ordinance establishing the HTF, which was adopted by the city council more than a year later.

The meeting organized by the San Diego planners is significant in that commission staff took the initiative, identified the interested groups, brought them together in a single meeting, and put them in touch with an expert who could assist them in coalition building. They were careful, however, not to propose the formation of an HTF coalition. They played the role of housing planning experts fostering public participation and sharing information about the housing crisis and possible solutions.

The individual member organizations coalesced quickly after the January meeting. It had been suggested at the meeting that the activists meet again independently of the Housing Commission. With Brooks's guidance, the San Diego Housing Trust Fund Coalition was formed.

The coalition, led by a San Diego Catholic Diocese staffer and a local environmental activist, became a broad alliance of more than fifty community groups, religious organizations, service providers, and labor unions.

When the Housing Commission met in February to endorse the HTF concept and the establishment of an HTF Task Force, the coalition was ready to outline its conditions for support: a full investigation of the feasibility "of using 100 percent of HTF revenues for the benefit of households earning 50 percent or less of median adjusted income, . . . of ensuring that housing produced remain available to low income residents in perpetuity, [and] . . . of giving Trust Fund priority to projects proposed by community based housing developers" (HTF Coalition statement, Housing Commission meeting, 6 February 1989).

Commission planners continued to play an active role in building agency support by maintaining the contacts they had established with community organizations prior to the initial meeting throughout the effort to establish the HTF. Staff quietly continued to seek the advice of coalition leaders, shared information, and cooperated with them to build support for the HTF. In organizing the January meeting and in working with the coalition, the commission undoubtedly risked the wrath of politicians who had taken a position in opposition to the HTF.[6] However, these support-building activities also undoubtedly increased the capacity of the agency to achieve a successful outcome.

Framing the Issue

To blunt the expected opposition, a process of negotiation and consensus building was necessary. For that process to have any chance of success, it was essential to transform the public perception of the housing crisis from a special interest problem affecting only low-income people to a community-wide problem affecting all social groups and—most important—the city's economy. The resulting information campaign focused on these two themes rather than on principles such as long-term affordability, which motivated and united the HTF Coalition. The goal was to repudiate the argument that San Diego should not spend local money on this problem and to transform the issue into a discussion of how housing problems should be addressed.

Housing Affordability as a Middle-Class Problem. In their reports and documents on the housing crisis, as well as in conferences and letters to the editor, housing advocates and commission planners emphasized the housing problems of the middle class (see San Diego Housing Commission, 1989a; San Diego Housing Trust Fund Coalition, 1989b). An exhibition mounted in the lobby of City Hall highlighted the almost impossible odds facing school teachers, policemen, and nurses in their search for home-ownership. The HTF Coalition, concerned with the difficulty of "selling" low-income housing to the public, developed the theme, "Housing for *Your* Children," in order to bring the issue home to middle-class citizens (San Diego Housing Trust Fund Coalition, 1989b).

Housing Affordability as an Economic Problem. Four arguments were developed to frame the HTF as a response to the local economic problems resulting from an inadequate supply of affordable housing.

1. In high-growth areas, high housing costs slow business expansions, business relocations, and employee recruitment. In San Diego the business community was finding it increasingly difficult to recruit staff from other parts of the country, and business executives and civic leaders were reacting with alarm (Minch, 1991; see also Schwartz et al., 1988; Kruer, 1989).

2. The lack of affordable housing located near low-wage jobs—also called the lack of jobs-housing balance—increases traffic congestion and automobile air pollution. This argument was particularly powerful in San

Diego, a far-flung and car-dependent city in the shadow of congested and polluted Los Angeles. Nationally, planners have documented the impact of geographic separation between jobs and housing on traffic congestion, the emission of tailpipe pollutants (Cervero, 1989), and the effect of long commutes on tardiness, absenteeism, low productivity, and job turnover (Novaco et al., 1990). HTF campaign articles were able to quote the Construction Industry Federation and major employers such as Hewlett Packard on the problems created by separation between the jobs in the developing northern parts of the city and affordable housing in the southern portions (Construction Industry Federation, 1986: 24). The HTF was put forward as a mechanism that could be used not only to increase the supply of affordable housing but also to improve its distribution.

3. The lack of affordable housing increases homelessness in the downtown business district. Homelessness, a burgeoning problem in San Diego throughout the 1980s, became a problem for downtown redevelopment by the end of the decade. Local media spotlighted the argument that the presence of panhandlers and street people intimidates shoppers, interferes with business, and discourages people from living downtown, a primary objective of city government (Flynn, 1990). Housing advocates turned these concerns into a trust fund rationale by relating homelessness to housing rather than to drugs or mental illness, and by citing the growing incidence and visibility of the homeless as having had "an ever expanding impact on everyday life and increased public sensitivity" (San Diego Housing Commission, 1989a). The task force emphasized that increasing the supply of affordable housing would help to reduce homelessness.

4. Affordable housing helps to revitalize older, declining neighborhoods. HTFs can regenerate older neighborhoods by injecting more money into the local neighborhood economy (San Diego Housing Trust Fund Coalition, 1989a; San Diego Housing Commission, 1989b). Advocates argued that high housing costs play an important role in the depressed economies of many older neighborhoods by diverting spending from locally provided goods and services. Commission planners also pointed out that lenders, realtors, construction companies, and apartment owners and managers would directly benefit from the increased construction, lending, and commissions that would result from the HTF (San Diego Housing Commission, 1989b).

The successful transformation of San Diego's housing crisis from a problem affecting mainly the lower classes to a problem affecting the city as a whole helped to legitimize the HTF as a rational approach to the solution of that crisis. This strategy ensured that the economic benefits of the HTF were recognized, blunting charges that the HTF was a purely redistributive program and was detrimental to the city's business interests.

Consensus Building

Promotion of the HTF as a program beneficial to the city's economy and to certain sectors of the real estate industry was a necessary but not sufficient strategy. Even though some benefits might accrue to the city from the HTF, it was probable that the housing industry as a whole would oppose the HTF if it were to derive revenues solely from development. Even if the HTF could be shown to benefit some sectors of the industry, those same sectors would still oppose it if they felt that fees and taxes levied on them were too high. Linkage fees, especially, were feared by the development industry in general and by commercial developers in particular.

Nonresidential developers had enjoyed a privileged position with respect to residential developers in San Diego. The "pay-as-you-grow" growth management approach to suburban development of the city was "explicitly a residential growth management program" in which residential, not commercial, development paid the great majority of the costs of growth (San Diego Planning Department, 1986). Developers and bankers directly involved in commercial development would obviously fight any change in the status quo. In addition, all forces benefiting from growth in the city might be expected to oppose linkage fees as detrimental to economic growth.

It was necessary to develop a consensus-building strategy to meet the concerns of the real estate industry. The strategy developed by the chair and the staff of the Housing Commission was to develop "a communitywide solution to solve a communitywide problem" by ensuring that the burden of meeting the housing need was broadly and fairly distributed. Consensus building was pursued through the creation of a broad-based task force, where the concerns of the development industry could be publicly aired and resolved and, outside the task force, through intensive meetings with influential citizens.

Meetings with Influential Citizens. Meeting with, or making presentations to, individuals or groups representing interested parties or stakeholders is an important consensus-building vehicle (Bryson et al., 1986). Discussions with prominent citizens, or "influentials" (Checkoway, 1986), in particular, pay dividends not only in building support but in gathering information regarding potential weak points in the proposal or the form the opposition might take.

In San Diego, the chair and the executive director of the Housing Commission had at least thirty meetings with representatives of the building and real estate industry and other civic leaders. The purpose of the meetings was "to educate, to get support and, when that was not possible, to at least neutralize the opposition."[7] In these private meetings, the Housing Commission chair and director stressed the enormity of the housing problem, the necessity for an HTF to help mitigate that problem, and how the sources of revenue would be equitably derived, making it possible to keep the linkage fee levels low. The chair of the Housing Commission, Councilman Pratt, would also let it be known at these meetings that "we have five votes" in favor of an HTF. As a result of those meetings, qualified support was obtained from representatives of the real estate industry and other civic leaders. The meetings also helped to blunt the opposition and to prevent it from becoming organized. In addition, Pratt met with the editorial boards of all the major newspapers in town, garnering the support of two of the three, *The San Diego Tribune* and *The Los Angeles Times*, San Diego edition.

Housing Trust Fund Task Force. The HTF Task Force, appointed by Pratt and chaired by a prominent liberal developer, was made up of seventeen members representing the development industry and advocacy groups (see Table 10-2).

Although the task force was evenly balanced between representatives of the development industry and housing advocates, two factors contributed toward creating an atmosphere during the proceedings that favored a sizable and progressive HTF. First, the chair of the HTF Task Force became a strong advocate of an HTF that would have a significant impact on the housing problem in San Diego. The appointment of a developer to chair the task force was controversial, especially among coalition members, but it proved to be an astute appointment. He was well respected in the development community and contributed to the development of a consensus based on the principle that revenue sources should have a broad base and minimal impact on any single sector.

Second, the meetings were open to the public, and participants were almost exclusively HTF Coalition members, including the two co-chairs. Coalition representatives functioned as the home crowd, cheering their team, intimidating the opposition, and possibly influencing the officials.

Table 10-2. Housing Trust Fund Task Force Membership List

Pat Kruer
Patrick Development, Chair

Rinus Baak
Regional Task Force on the Homeless
P&D Technology

Barbara Barsky
San Diego Apartment Association

Art Deutsch
Gray Panthers

Paul Devermann
VP, San Diego Economic Development Corporation

Steve Doyle
VP, Pardee Construction

Joe Francis
San Diego and Imperial Counties Central Labor Council AFL-CIO

Jose De La Garza
Reinvestment Task Force
Dai-Ichi Kangyo Bank of California

Sue Haskin
League of Women Voters

Rich Juarez

Laurie McKinley
McKinley Group

Sammy Moon
United Way

Curtis Moring, Sr.
NAACP
Moring Insurance

Jean Porter
Executive Assistant, Neighborhood House Association

Joe Ramsey
San Diego Interfaith Housing Foundation

Bernie Rhinerson
Director of Government Relations/VP, Home Capital Development Group

Richard Stiener
Legal Aid Society of San Diego

The chairman allowed the "public" to participate in the discussions at any time, and coalition members made good use of that opportunity. In their interventions, they sought to provide the task force members

> with information that would keep them conscious of the impact of the housing crisis on poor people's lives; educate them on the important role of non-profit, community-based organizations in the development of appropriate low-income housing; make them aware of the positive influence a Housing Trust Fund can have in the development of low-income neighborhoods and of the creative housing proposals which could be funded by the Trust Fund; and increase their understanding of the importance of community participation if the Trust Fund is to fulfill its goals. (Ertle, 1989)

The coalition linked the extent of the housing crisis to the need for radical solutions, and in so doing they widened the spectrum of legitimate alternatives. Much of the explanation for the progressive features of the San Diego HTF is to be found in the dedication and strategies of the HTF Coalition, especially its co-chairs.

Also playing an important role in shaping the final task force recommendations were the Housing Commission staff and the consultant, who were committed to a significant HTF. Housing Commission staff had initiated the entire process and had a stake in a positive outcome. They were responsible for bringing forward recommendations based on consultation with the chair, the consultant, and task force members. While the staff was united on most recommendations, there was some disagreement, as is discussed later, on the targeting of resources and long-term affordability restrictions for first-time homebuyers.

The consultant hired to provide the task force with recommendations on a revenue package and beneficiaries of the HTF was David Rosen, principal and founder of David Paul Rosen and Associates. He had assisted more than twenty states and numerous localities in the development of HTFs. Besides an obvious technical expertise in establishing HTFs, the consultant brought to the process a strong commitment to a progressive and significant HTF and a keen political awareness that in creating an HTF, "the single most critical element . . . is the process whereby public consensus is secured in support of the Housing Trust Fund proposal" (Rosen, 1987: 22).

Generally, the HTF Task Force chair, the HTF Coalition, the Housing Commission staff, and the consultant were united in their commitment to an HTF that could make a difference in San Diego, and they all realized that a compromise had to be reached that met the development industry's objections without weakening the needed progressive features.

The Consensus-Building Process on the Task Force. In March 1989, the task force began its deliberations. The first few meetings involved briefings on the extent of the housing crisis in the city, and a discussion about the characteristics of HTFs elsewhere. In May and June the task force selected an administrative model for the HTF and designated the target population.

The task force chose without much controversy a board of trustees as a compromise between a nonprofit organization and an existing city department to administer the HTF. After much discussion about the composition of the board, the task force finally agreed to six trustees appointed from business, industry, and labor and five from nonprofit and community-based organizations.

There was considerable agreement among Housing Commission staff, task force members, and the coalition that the need was greatest among very low income households and that this was the primary population the HTF should serve. But there were differences concerning relative allotment of funds, with housing advocates arguing on behalf of very low income households and industry representatives favoring moderate income households. Staff maintained a centrist position on this issue and interjected the argument that some money should be targeted for a homeownership and rehabilitation program. Housing Commission staff determined that, it was strategically advantageous to target first-time homebuyers, although they did not have the greatest need, in order to broaden the appeal of the fund and make it more palatable politically. The coalition and its representatives on the task force vehemently disagreed at first but eventually accepted a small portion of funds for this purpose.[8] With only one member voting against, the task force adopted staff recommendations that targeted 70 percent of HTF revenue to very low income households, 20 percent to low-income households, and 10 percent to first-time homebuyers earning up to 100 percent of median income.

In June the consultant began to present his findings on possible sources of revenue to the task force. At least twenty-five sources were presented and analyzed. On the basis of those discussions and the charge to develop a revenue package that was sensitive to the needs of the real estate industry, the consultant "applied a series of principles aimed at keeping all assessments modest, reasonably linked to the demand for affordable housing, and equitably shared across the entire city by business and residents alike" (Rosen and Associates, 1989: 17). Five revenue sources were recommended: a citywide linkage fee; a portion of the annual increment of the hotel room tax; a gross receipts business tax; a landscape, lighting, and park maintenance fee; and a 2 percent utility users' fee. Three alternative fee levels were recommended that would generate totals of $36.5, $45.25, and $52 million. Such a wide variety of revenue sources was unusual for an HTF, but it was a natural outgrowth of the strategy that framed the HTF as a communitywide response to a communitywide problem, requiring "sacrifices" from broad segments of the population and businesses in the city, and not from the development industry alone.

As expected, much of the discussion was centered around the impact the proposed fees might have on business in general and on development in particular. Linkage fees were especially challenged by the representative of the Economic Development Corporation, an organization financed both by the city and the private sector and dedicated to fostering a good business climate and encouraging companies to move to or expand in the city. Eventually, however, even development representatives agreed that the linkage fees as proposed "would not adversely affect development decisions" (Task Force Minutes of 26 July: 1).

Objections to the business tax were blunted by the consultant's findings that San Diego's business tax, "when compared to that of other metropolitan California communities, is low by factors ranging from 353 percent to 2,713 percent" (Rosen and Associates, 1989: 188). The consultant proposed a tax based on gross receipts or gross payroll to make the business tax more progressive than a flat business license fee, eliminating possible objections from the coalition or small business representatives.

In its final report (San Diego Housing Commission, 1989a), the task force recommended an HTF of $54 million, the sum estimated to be necessary to meet one-third of the housing need by the year 2000. It stipulated that the HTF should be supported by six broad-based revenue sources, reflecting the strategy to develop a "communitywide response to a communitywide problem." The task force recommended that these revenue sources be considered as a package, and urged the city council to "preserve the principles of a fund based on a broad range of contributions from various segments of the community and to limit the individual revenue sources to the amount recommended to preserve equity among segments of the community" (San Diego Housing Commission, 1989a).

The task force report stated that the HTF should address a broad variety of housing needs in the community, including home ownership, housing rehabilitation, and other preventative measure that can be applied in declining neighborhoods to preserve existing low-income housing but stressed the need to devote most revenue to very low income households (San Diego Housing Commission, 1989a). As a result, it was recommended that fully 70 percent of the revenue should be set aside for very low income households, that is, for households earning less than half the median income. A further 20 percent would be set aside for projects providing affordable housing for low-income households, and 10 percent for first-time home buyer assistance for households earning up to median income.

The City Council Battle

When the HTF ordinance reached the city council, conditions did not seem favorable to its passage. The city was facing a budget deficit of $60 million, and council members opposed to the HTF attempted to postpone its approval until it could be "considered along with the other pressing needs of the city during the budget process" because the HTF "as proposed will drain many of the same funds that could be used to provide police protection, programs to fight drug abuse, and street sweeping and tree trimming."[9] Fearing that to consider the HTF as part of the budgetary process might kill it, Councilman Pratt, the HTF Coalition, and other HTF supporters successfully pushed for its approval as a separate item.

An additional problem was the possible loss of support of a councilman who, under pressure from elements in the business community still opposed to linkage fees and hotel room tax increases, seemed to be wavering. The alarm was sounded, and all the community organizations, activists, and others who had supported his election under the district election format, including many HTF Coalition members, "pounced heavily on him" and the five-vote majority was ensured (personal communication, Daniel Morales, 14 April 1992).

The last threat was not to the entire HTF but to certain components of the revenue package, namely the lighting and landscaping fee and the utility users tax, that were rejected in private meetings by some members of the "Gang of Five." It also became clear that the business tax increase would be seized to help meet the budget shortfall. Councilman Pratt fought to preserve a portion of the business tax increase for the HTF and to find other sources of revenue, but to no avail.

As a result, the council trimmed the size of the fund to $13 million to be derived from the linkage fee and a portion of the hotel room tax. Nevertheless today the HTF remains one of the largest in the country for a locality, and the largest in the sunbelt.

LONG-TERM AFFORDABILITY AND THE SAN DIEGO HOUSING TRUST FUND

What is impressive about the San Diego HTF is not so much its size as its success in establishing a program that supports "accommodative" over "accumulative" uses of domestic property (Davis, 1991), a program that places the residential interests of the low-income resident above the investment interest of the private property owner. This is most evident in the successful effort to ensure that HTF revenue is used in the production of long-term affordable housing where the primacy of accommodative interests is preserved by statute.

Rental Housing Restrictions

Long-term affordability was not a highly visible part of the overall HTF campaign, and the Housing Trust Fund Task Force took no explicit position on the issue. However, it was actively discussed among advocates, commission staff, and consultants as the proposal and the legislation were developed. HTF advocates were highly effective in the effort to establish long-term affordability for rental housing. Rental housing financed by the HTF will remain affordable for fifty-five years or the life of the building, whichever is longer. Affordability requirements run with the land and, most important, cannot be removed by prepayment of the HTF loan.

The rental housing affordability requirements proved relatively noncontroversial, primarily because of the level of community and commission staff support. The Housing Trust Fund Coalition was ideologically and practically committed to preserving the use value of this assisted housing over and above its speculative exchange value. The coalition consistently maintained that anything less than perpetual affordability restrictions was irresponsible, given the enormity of the crisis, and simply unacceptable. Coalition members also argued in support of forms of ownership that "take the speculative value out of the land" (San Diego Housing Trust Fund Coalition, 1989a).

Secondly, in designing the HTF, commission staff were determined not to repeat past mistakes. The housing crisis was exacerbated by the expiration of affordability restrictions on approximately four thousand units of federally subsidized rental housing and the imminent loss of another five thousand mobile home park spaces where rapid increases in the cost of land meant that the "highest and best use" was no longer a mobile home park (San Diego Housing Commission, 1989a).

In the past the commission had come to rely on short-term solutions, but these sources of affordable housing had become increasingly untenable as market forces shifted. Commission staff developed the HTF as a mechanism to respond to the shortcomings of earlier programs and explicitly created a source of revenue that could be used to purchase, and thus preserve the affordability of, federally subsidized units with expiring affordability restrictions and mobile home parks. Anything less than long-term affordability would only repeat past mistakes and actually contribute to the crisis in the long run.

A third, less obvious issue in the success of rental housing restrictions was near silence on the part of developers and realtors. As difficult as it might be for veterans of similar struggles in more politically sophisticated environments to imagine, developers never once seriously contested the long-term affordability provisions in the HTF. Only the board of realtors mentioned this issue in public, in testimony before the city council. HTF proponents initially defined the problem in terms of the need for permanent affordability and successfully focused the debate on terms well beyond the developer's typically short-term, five- to seven-year horizon, making the issue unimportant to them. The lack of long-term affordability restrictions on the homeowner set-aside may also have muted the realtors' protest.

A partial explanation may be found in the very small number of low-income housing developers in the city. The HTF as proposed was to target a majority of its funds to low and very low income households, a market that developers in San Diego were uninterested in and unfamiliar with. Without a politically sophisticated coterie of for-profit, low-income housing developers dependent on local housing funds, whose interests are threatened by long-term affordability restrictions, there was little opposition to restrictions on rental housing.

Homeownership Restrictions

HTF proponents were less successful in applying long-term affordability restrictions to homeownership programs financed by the HTF. The ordinance states: "The Commission shall impose enforceable resale restrictions on the owner toward the end of keeping the housing unit affordable for the longest feasible time, while maintaining an equitable balance between the interests of the owner and the interests of the Commission" (Housing Trust Fund Ordinance, Sec. 98.0505[b]).

The battle for homeownership provisions was lost early on in negotiations between the coalition and the Housing Commission staff who finalized the legislation. Antirestrictions forces on the Commission staff raised two arguments. The primary and most influential one was that homeowners have an innate right to property appreciation, so long as the government loan is repaid. Housing Commission staff also argued that future affordability restrictions would prevent subsidized homeowners from reinvesting their appreciation in moving out (and up) in the private housing market. These arguments were effective, in part, because most of the decision makers were themselves homeowners and felt a personal investment in these "rights." Since the HTF Coalition had originally opposed the inclusion of first-time homebuyers in the program, housing advocates felt less inclined to fight for long-term affordability in this arena.

Social Forms of Housing Ownership

The HTF ordinance specifies that five of the eleven governing board members must be representatives from nonprofit and community-based organizations supporting the needs of lower-income households. Unlike the trustees appointed from the housing industry, trustees from these community-based organizations have explicitly favored funding projects ensuring not only long-term affordability but alternative, social forms of housing ownership. Several trustees have publicly stated that they wish to fund land banking and projects like community land trusts and limited equity coops, which take property out of the speculative market altogether and preserve affordability forever. The ordinance specifically lists these as permissible uses of HTF revenue.

CONCLUSION: SPREADING INCREMENTAL CHANGES

Like many political campaigns, the San Diego HTF owed its success to a combination of well-placed timing, outstanding leadership, artful strategy, in-depth organizing, good publicity, and luck. The political, ideological, and organizational obstacles facing the campaign were formidable. Long-term affordability within the trust fund programs seemed especially unlikely. How did it happen? What are the lessons for other cities?

The political obstacles to long-term affordability in San Diego included the historic lack of constituency for low-income affordable housing in the short or long term. The HTF campaign attacked this problem by creating the conditions for the formation of the HTF Coalition and by broadening the actual and perceived constituency for the HTF program. This was accomplished by setting aside funds for first-time homebuyers with median incomes and through a public information campaign that reframed the housing problem of low-income people as a problem that directly affected the whole city.

This allowed the HTF to win a measure of support from the local realtor association and to be perceived as providing something more than "low-income housing." The decision was part of an overall strategy to promote the HTF as providing much broader benefits to the city: programs that met the full range of affordable housing needs of San Diegans, from homeless people to renters to first-time homebuyers; a tool for the rehabilitation and revitalization of center-city neighborhoods; a strategy to prevent the lack of affordable housing from choking the local economy. Expanding the dialogue beyond the moral imperative to house needy families was a critical factor in expanding support for the HTF and in neutralizing the potential opposition of industry groups and business organizations.

There are also some clear political and strategic advantages to attaching extended affordability restrictions to new funding mechanisms and new programs at the very outset. When a proposal for a new tax or fee for affordable housing is combined with a particular approach to spending that fee, hostile interest groups may focus largely upon the revenue-raising mechanisms and not upon spending approaches or long-term affordability. Thus opposition to the San Diego HTF tended to involve questions concerning the "fairness" of the revenue sources, the percentage of revenue for homeownership programs, governance of the fund, and the extent of community participation in funding decisions—not on the long-term aspect of the program.

HTF advocates expected the primary ideological obstacle to long-term affordability to be the general resistance to removing the profit motive from housing. In a politically conservative climate, a frontal focus on removing property from the speculative market may not be a very useful way to achieve a commitment to permanent affordability. The HTF Coalition advocates often spoke to potential supporters who were sympathetic to the housing needs of very low income people or to the housing impact on the city economy but who were ideologically opposed to long-term restrictions on appreciation. When the issue arose in San Diego, HTF proponents responded in a way designed to appeal to the city's fiscal conservatism. A basic tenet of the commission-appointed task force was that the HTF should use local resources as judiciously and productively as possible. Consequently, it was argued that providing windfalls to developers—or even lower-income homeowners—after the short-term affordability restrictions expired would be an irresponsible use of scarce public funds and would fail to derive the highest public benefit.

These ideological concerns also guided the way in which long-term affordability was actually guaranteed within the ordinance. In San Diego, largely because the nonprofit sector was very small, housing advocates pressed for permanent affordability requirements rather than for preferences for nonprofit or resident-controlled forms of ownership. The affordability language that was later incorporated in the ordinance is widely expected to discourage private developers and to create the same permanent affordability outcomes as a nonprofit preference. Although the affordability language raised no opposition from the construction industry, language that specifically excluded for-profit participation might well have stirred active protest.

The last category of obstacles faced by the San Diego HTF campaign were its organizational obstacles—historically weak support within the Housing Commission and an unorganized constituency. The HTF Coalition overcame these obstacles the old-fashioned way: consistent outreach and organizing, careful use of public information and the media, and repetition of the basic campaign themes. The San Diego HTF also overcame these obstacles through the steadfast and passionate advocacy of two highly visible public figures, the council member who chaired the commission and the commission's executive director. Campaigns for long-term affordability are no different in this regard: prominent leadership and effective organizing increase the chances of political success.

Housing advocates in San Diego expect the HTF to have a positive effect on affordability provision in other locally funded programs. Along with trends in affordability requirements in California and federal housing programs, HTF policies have contributed toward normalizing the expectation of permanent affordability among government program administrators and locally elected officials. The effect of these policies on the attitudes of industry groups to long-term affordability is unclear; they could serve to stimulate or mollify future industry opposition. However, a more important effect of the struggle to establish an HTF has been to strengthen the hand of housing advocates and nonprofits in San Diego. Opportunities for third sector housing have been irrevocably expanded as a result.

NOTES

Acknowledgment: Some of the materials contained in this chapter appeared in a shorter, earlier article, with a very different focus, by Calavita and Grimes (1992).

1. In 1965, for example, the citizens of San Diego defeated a general plan at the polls because it recommended use of federal urban renewal funds, "earning the city the singular distinction of being the only major city to vote upon and reject its general plan" (Corso, 1983).

2. That success contributed to the displacement of private investment from northeastern toward southwestern cities, where "conservative pro-growth political patterns reign unchallenged" (Mollenkopf, 1983: 217).

3. Growth machine theory maintains that growth is the essence of local politics and that a land-based elite is generally able to legitimate the ideology of growth and to manipulate the planning process to foster growth and increase land use intensities. See, for example, Molotch (1976) and Logan and Molotch (1987).

4. The Housing Commission leadership may have been partly motivated to explore the idea of new local funds for housing because two of the commission's other major sources were decreasing or under threat. The federal Community Development Block Grant allocations had been shrinking, and local competition for those funds was heating up. The commission's other flexible resource for housing loans and staff costs was a small set-aside of local funds generated through the sale and lease of City-owned land and through bond issuance fees. These funds were also not increasing. If these trends were not reversed, cutbacks in staff and in multifamily new construction loans were a real possibility.

5. The political weakness of the Housing Commission during this period offered a direct motivation for building a coalition with community organizations. In 1989, at the beginning of the HTF campaign, the new executive director was still struggling to build credibility and recognition for the agency. At the commission itself, the Housing Commission chair was a first-term member of city council. Neither the new director nor the new chair could mount a campaign on a controversial subject without outside political support.

6. During the height of the political debate surrounding the HTF, a reporter from the *San Diego Business Journal* questioned the unusually close links between the coalition and the housing coalition: "City Hall sources have complained that the Housing Trust Fund Coalition is working too closely with the San Diego Housing Commission" (Lassa, 1990b: 4).

7. Personal communication from Daniel Morales to Nico Calavita, 14 April 1992. Mr. Morales was Councilman Pratt's staff person in charge of the HTF. He was the authors' principal source for their description of the meetings with "influential citizens."

8. Coalition Co-Chair Linda Martin stated at the June 21 task force meeting that

"one reason for looking at a broader target population is a political one, to make an attractive appeal to the City Council" (Task Force Minutes, 21 June 1989).

9. Letter from Councilman R. Roberts to Nico Calavita, 22 January 1990.

REFERENCES

Babilot, George. *San Diego Economic Outlook*. San Diego: Center for Public Economics, San Diego State University, 1990.

Bryson, J., et al. "Strategic Planning in the Public Sector: Approaches and Directions." In Barry Checkoway (ed.), *Strategic Perspectives on Planning Practice*. Lexington, Mass.: Lexington Books, 1986.

Calavita, Nico, and Kenneth Grimes. "The Establishment of the San Diego Housing Trust Fund: Lessons for Theory and Practice." *Journal of Planning Education and Research* 11, no. 3 (1992): 170–184.

Cervero, Robert. "Job-Housing Balancing and Regional Mobility." *Journal of the American Planning Association* 55, no. 2 (1989): 136–150.

Checkoway, Barry. (ed.), *Strategic Perspectives on Planning Practice*. Lexington, Mass.: Lexington Books, 1986.

Connerly, Charles. *A Guide to Housing Trust Funds*. Washington, D.C.: Neighborhood Reinvestment Corporation, 1989.

Construction Industry Federation. *White Paper: An Analysis of Land Use Planning Issues*. San Diego, September 1986.

Corso, Anthony. "San Diego: The Anti-City." In R. M. Bernard and R. B. Rice (eds.), *Sunbelt Cities: Politics and Growth since World War II*, pp. 328–344. Albany: State University of New York Press, 1983.

Cummings, Scott (ed.). *Business Elites and Urban Development*. Albany: State University of New York Press, 1988.

Davis, John Emmeus. *Contested Ground: Collective Action and the Urban Neighborhood*. Ithaca, N.Y.: Cornell University Press, 1991.

Drew, Joseph. *Income Trends in the San Diego Region: Regional Economic Perspective*. San Diego: Center for Public Economics, San Diego State University, 1990.

Ertle, Jeanne. "Letter: Dear Coalition Member or Friend." San Diego: San Diego Housing Trust Fund Coalition, 24 July 1989.

Flynn, G. "Downtown Confronts Homeless Problem." *San Diego Union*, 19 August 1990, pp. B-1, 6.

Kruer, Patrick. "Fair, Equitable Housing Trust Fund." *San Diego Daily Transcript*, 8 December 1989, p. A-8.

Lassa, T. "Homeless Group Lobbies to Keep Housing Trust Fund." *San Diego Business Journal*, 4 February 1990, pp. 2–4.

Leasure, J. William. *Population Growth in San Diego County*. San Diego: Center for Public Economics, San Diego State University, 1988.

Logan, John, and Harvey Molotch. *Urban Fortunes*. Berkeley: University of California Press, 1987.

Logan, John, and Todd Swanstrom (eds.). *Beyond the City Limits*. Philadelphia: Temple University Press, 1990.

Minch, H. "Execs Blast City Politicians' Lack of Affordable Housing." *San Diego Business Journal*, 7–15 January 1991.

Mollenkopf, John. *The Contested City*. Princeton: Princeton University Press, 1983.

Molotch, Harvey. "The City As a Growth Machine." *American Journal of Sociology* 75, no. 2 (1976): 309–330.

Novaco, R., D. Stakols, and L. Milanesi. "Objective and Subjective Dimensions of Travel Impedance as Determinants of Community Stress." *American Journal of Community Psychology* 18, no. 2 (1990): 231–257.

Peterson, Paul. *City Limits*. Chicago: University of Chicago Press, 1981.

Reynolds, Susan. "Nonprofit Housing and Community Development in San Diego." Memorandum, San Diego Housing Commission, October 1990.

Rosen, David. *Housing Trust Funds*. Report 406, Planning Advisory Service. Chicago: American Planning Association, 1987.

Rosen and Associates. *Consultant Recommendations for Core San Diego Housing Trust Fund Revenues*. Oakland, Cal.: Rosen and Associates, 1989.

San Diego Housing Commission. *Creating Affordable Housing for San Diegans: Final Report and Recommendations of the San Diego Housing Trust Fund*. San Diego, 1989a.

———. *The San Diego Housing Trust Fund*. Report 89-030, Planning Department. San Diego, 1989b.

San Diego Housing Trust Fund Coalition. "Income, Housing, and the Local Economy: How the Trust Fund Can Avert a Local Recession." Informal paper. 1989a.

———. "Short Term Strategy." Pamphlet. 11 July 1989b.

San Diego Planning Department. "Background Summary: City of San Diego Growth Management Program." San Diego, 1986.

———. "Draft Housing Element." San Diego, 1990.

Sawers, Larry. "New Perspectives on the Urban Political Economy." In William Tabb and Larry Sawers (eds.), *Marxism and the Metropolis*. New York: Oxford University Press, 1978.

Schwartz, David C., Richard C. Ferlauto, and Daniel N. Hoffman. *A New Housing Policy for America: Recapturing the American Dream*. Philadelphia: Temple University Press, 1988.

Squires, Gregory D. (ed.). *Unequal Partnerships*. New Brunswick, N.J.: Rutgers University Press, 1989.

Waxman, C. *The Stigma of Poverty*. New York: Pergamon Press, 1983.

About the Contributors and Index

About the Contributors

RACHEL G. BRATT has been on the faculty of Tufts University since 1976. She is an associate professor in the Department of Urban and Environmental Policy. Among her published works on housing policy and community-based housing development are *Critical Perspectives on Housing* (1986), which she coedited, and *Rebuilding a Low-Income Housing Policy* (1989), which she wrote; both are published by Temple University Press.

MARY E. BROOKS directs the Housing Trust Fund Project, a special project of the Center for Community Change. Brooks has produced several publications on housing trust funds and publishes a quarterly newsletter providing current information about housing trust fund organizing around the country. All of these materials are available through the Project (570 Shepard Street, San Pedro, Calif. 90731).

NICO CALAVITA is an associate professor at San Diego State University and coordinator of the Graduate Program in City Planning in the School of Public Administration and Urban Studies. Calavita's teaching and writing are focused on the politics of growth, the history of urban planning, and community development. He is a member of the San Diego Housing Trust Fund Coalition and vice chair of the San Diego Housing Trust Fund's Board of Trustees.

HELEN S. COHEN has worked in the fields of community economic development and community investment for the past eight years. She is currently a consultant with Women's Educational Media in San Francisco, producing film and video resources for community development organizations and other public interest groups. She was the founding organizer of the Northern California Community Loan Fund and was formerly a consultant to the Institute for Community Economics, providing technical assistance to West Coast groups developing community land trusts.

CHUCK COLLINS is coordinator of the HOME Coalition in Massachusetts, a coalition of grassroots organizations working on income, homelessness, and housing issues. He served on the staff of the Institute for Community Economics from 1983 to 1992. Collins is co-author of *A Legal Manual for Community Land Trusts* (Institute for Community Economics, 1991).

JOHN EMMEUS DAVIS has spent the last twelve years helping to develop third sector housing models, organizations, and policies, first as a field organizer for the Institute for Community Economics and then as housing director for the City of Burlington, Vermont. He has taught at Tufts University's Institute for Management and Community Development, New Hampshire College's Graduate Program in Community Economic Development, and MIT's Department of Urban Studies and Planning. Davis is co-author of the *Community Land Trust Handbook* (Rodale Press, 1982) and author of *Contested Ground: Collective Action and the Urban Neighborhood* (Cornell University Press, 1991).

PETER DREIER was Mayor Ray Flynn's assistant for housing from 1984 to 1986 and director of housing for the Boston Redevelopment Authority from 1986 to 1992. He is currently the E. P. Clapp Distinguished Professor of Politics at Occidental College. Dreier is the author of numerous articles on tenants' rights, affordable housing, and urban policy.

KENNETH GRIMES is a senior planning analyst for the San Diego Housing Commission, where he has worked since 1988. Grimes helped to establish the San Diego Housing Trust Fund. He worked previously as a union organizer and administrator.

J. DAVID HULCHANSKI is a professor of housing policy and community development at the University of Toronto's Facility of Social Work. He was formerly the director of the University of British Columbia's Centre for Human Settlements (1986 to 1991) and a professor of community planning and housing policy at the University of British Columbia (1983 to 1991).

ALAN MALLACH is a city planner and housing advocate who has played key roles in framing and implementing New Jersey's *Mount Laurel* decision. The author of *Inclusionary Housing Programs: Policies and Practices* (New Brunswick, N.J.: Rutgers Center for Urban Policy Research, 1984) and numerous articles on housing and planning issues, he currently serves as director of Housing and Development for the City of Trenton, New Jersey. Mallach is also a composer of chamber music and vocal music who has written extensively on Italian opera.

SUSAN REYNOLDS is a housing advocate and housing finance consultant with the California Housing Partnership Corporation. She has worked previously for the San Diego Housing Commission, the Pratt Institute Center for Community and Environmental Development, and the Association for Neighborhood and Housing Development in New York City.

KIRBY WHITE has worked for the Institute for Community Economics (ICE) since 1981. He is the editor of ICE's quarterly publication, *Community Economics*. White is general editor and co-author of *The Community Land Trust Handbook* (Rodale Press, 1982) and *A Legal Manual for Community Land Trusts* (Institute for Community Economics, 1991).

WOODY WIDROW was the editor of *Shelterforce* from 1985 to 1990. He is currently deputy director of the National Community Reinvestment Coalition in Washington, D.C. Widrow has recently begun a research project in Cleveland, Ohio, seeking further answers to the question, "What do tenants want?"

Index